LEARN TO PLAY
Guitar

Publisher and Creative Director: Nick Wells
Commissioning Editor: Polly Willis
Editorial Consultants: Rusty Cutchin, Michael Leonard
Editor: Paul Robson
Picture Researcher: Melinda Revesz
Design: Mike Spender
Production: Chris Herbert, Claire Walker
Notation by Alan Brown of Take Note

Special thanks to: Geoffrey Meadon, Sonya Newland, Ross Plotkin, Sara Robson, Julia Rolf

STAR FIRE BOOKS
Crabtree Hall, Crabtree Lane
Fulham, London, SW6 6TY
United Kingdom
www.flametreepublishing.com

Music information site: www.musicfirebox.com

First Published 2005

05 07 09 10 08 06

1 3 5 7 9 10 8 6 4 2

Star Fire is part of the Foundry Creative Media Company Limited

© 2005 The Foundry

The CIP record for this book is available from the British Library.

ISBN 184451 330 0

Every effort has been made to contact copyright holders. We apologize in advance for any omissions and would
be pleased to insert the appropriate acknowledgment in subsequent editions of this publication.

LEARN TO PLAY
Guitar

General Editor: Michael Leonard

Authors: Cliff Douse, Richard Riley, Michael Ross, Tony Skinner

STAR
FIRE

CONTENTS

If music is a universal language, there is no instrument more global than the guitar and it is easy to see why. It's a great do-it-yourself invention; like the piano, on a guitar it's relatively easy to play a melody and rhythm simultaneously but, unlike a piano, a guitar is portable. There is no other instrument that's musically as versatile either: 'guitar player' can mean African bushman, preening metal axe-god, classical virtuoso, rural bluesman and much more.

This book will help you to become a better guitar player, and with the rich heritage and history of the guitar – acoustic and electric – we've got plenty to cover. There is plenty on techniques – from basic tuning and simple chord sequences to string-bending, tapping and bottleneck tricks. We dissect guitar styles and show you how to play different types of music, as well as how to improve your lead and rhythm guitar techniques. There is detailed information on the wide range of effects available and how to use them in your playing, and valuable information on guitar maintenance, including how the various guitars are constructed and the best ways for you to perform your own repairs. Finally, there is an extensive chord dictionary – an essential resource for every guitar player, whatever your preferred musical style!

The Basics

Tuning 8

Hand Positions 10

First Chords 12

Simple Chord Sequences 14

Strumming 16

Fingerpicking 18

More Chords 20

Keys 22

Playing Rhythm Guitar

Introduction 24

Timing 26

Time Signatures 28

Rhythm Notation 30

Chord Charts 32

Following Chord Charts 34

Rhythm Charts 36

Strumming Patterns 38

Playing Lead Guitar

Introduction 40

Basics of Notation 42

Major Scales 44

Minor Scales 46

Further Scales 48

Modes. 50

Further Modes 52

Pitch 54

Chords and Tunings

Introduction 56

Intervals 58

Major Triads 60

Minor Triads 62

Chord Construction 64

Extended Chords 66

Chord Substitution 68

Altered Tunings. 70

Essential Techniques

Introduction 72

Changing Chords 74

Power Chords 76

Barre Chords 78

Chord Riffs. 80

String Damping 82

Slurs 84

Slides 86

Vibrato. 88

String Bends 90

Plectrum Technique 92

Basic Arpeggios 94

More Arpeggios 96

Octaves 98

Harmonics 100

Bottleneck 102

Tremolo Arm. 104

Tapping 106

Constructing Solos 108

Stagecraft. 110

Rhythmic Delays & Looping. . . . 128

Reverb 130

Volume and
Wah-wah Pedals. . . . 132

Combining
Effects 134

Maintenance

Introduction & the Electric Guitar 136

Anatomy of an Acoustic Guitar 138

Anatomy of an Electric Guitar 140

Guitar Care 142

Fret Care 144

Choosing Strings 146

Fitting Strings: Acoustic 148

Using Effects

Introduction 112

Compression 114

Fuzz 'n' distortion. 116

Chorus. 118

Flanging and Phasing 120

Ambient Effects: Delay and Reverb 122

Delays 124

Using Delay 126

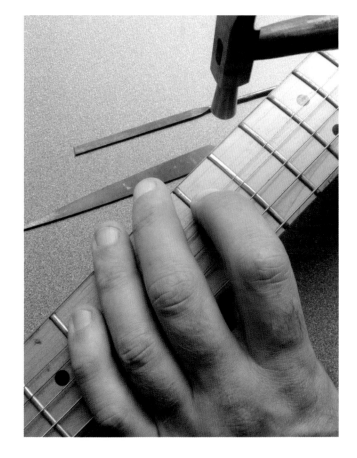

Fitting Strings: Electric 150

Setting the Action. 152

Setting the Bridge for Intonation 154

Adjusting the Neck Relief 156

How the Electrics Work 158

Tools 160

Pickups 162

Troubleshooting 164

Musical Styles

Blues. 166

Classical 172

Country 176

Flamenco. 180

Folk 184

Jazz 188

Metal 192

Rock 196

Chord Dictionary

Introduction 202

A Main Chords. 204

A Advanced Chords 206

B♭/A♯ Main Chords 208

B♭/A♯ Advanced Chords 210

B Main Chords. 212

B Advanced Chords. 214

C Main Chords. 216

C Advanced Chords. 218

C♯/D♭ Main Chords 220

C♯/D♭ Advanced Chords 222

D Main Chords 224

D Advanced Chords 226

E♭/D♯ Main Chords. 228

E♭/D♯ Advanced Chords. 230

E Main Chords 232

E Advanced Chords 234

F Main Chords 236

F Advanced Chords 238

F♯/G♭ Main Chords. 240

F♯/G♭ Advanced Chords. 242

G Main Chords 244

G Advanced Chords. 246

A♭/G♯ Main Chords 248

A♭/G♯ Advanced Chords 250

Glossary 252

Contributor Biographies and Picture Credits . . 253

Index. 254

Tuning

Tuning is the most essential skill any guitarist has to master: it doesn't matter how many hours you spend learning chords, scales or riffs – they won't sound any good if the guitar is out of tune! Although you can use an electronic tuner, the ability to tune by ear will always prove useful.

Pitch

A guitar can be tuned so that all the strings are 'in tune' with one another, and this can sound fine if you are just playing chords on your own. However, if you intend to play with other instruments or a CD then you'll need to make sure that your guitar is tuned to the correct pitch. Traditionally, guitarists use a 'tuning fork' so that they can hear the exact pitch that either the E or A string should be tuned to. If you have access to a keyboard, or a well-tuned piano, this could be used instead. The open strings of the guitar, from the lowest note (thickest string) to the highest (thinnest string) should be tuned to the following notes.

Tuning at the fifth fret

Once you have tuned the low string to the pitch of E you can use this as the starting point from which to tune all the other strings.

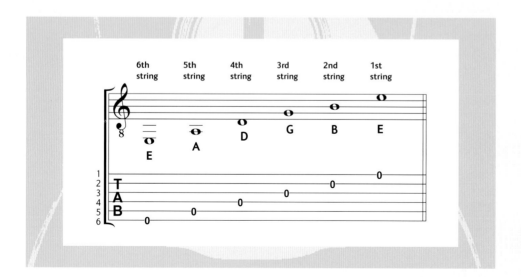

1. Begin by playing a note on the fifth fret of the low E string; this will produce the note A. You should then turn the fifth string machine head (tuning peg) until the pitch of this open string matches the fretted note on the lower string.

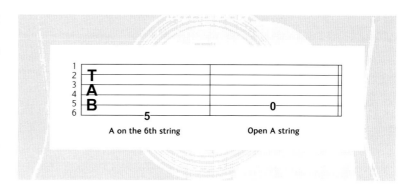

A on the 6th string   Open A string

If the open fifth string sounds higher than the fretted A note then you should rotate the machine head to slacken the string; if the open fifth string sounds too low then you should tighten the string.

2. Once you have tuned the A string, you can produce the note of D by playing at the fifth fret; this will provide you with the pitch to tune the open D string accurately. You can then use the same method for tuning the open G string,

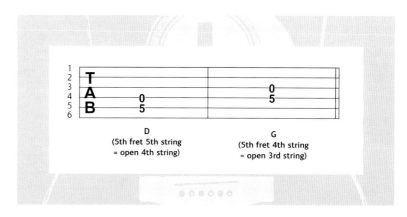

D
(5th fret 5th string
= open 4th string)

G
(5th fret 4th string
= open 3rd string)

i.e. by adjusting it to match the note on the fifth fret of the D string.

3. The system alters slightly when you come to tune the B string. You need to tune this to the pitch of the note on the fourth fret of the G string. Once the B string is in tune, fretting it at the fifth fret will produce the note E; you should adjust the open first string to match this pitch.

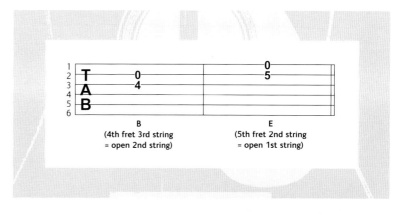

B
(4th fret 3rd string
= open 2nd string)

E
(5th fret 2nd string
= open 1st string)

Once this process is complete you should pick slowly through the notes of a chord that you are very familiar with and make any final tuning adjustments that may be needed.

▲ You should now be able to have a go at tuning your guitar.

Hand Positions

If you don't position your hands in the optimum way, learning to play guitar might prove to be an uphill struggle; playing with a good technique from the start, by positioning your hands correctly, will make learning new things relatively easy.

Fretting Hand

▲ The optimum position for your hand when you are fretting a note: fingers are close to the frets which minimizes any fret buzz.

1. Regardless of whether you are playing chords or single notes, you should always press the fretting-hand fingers as close to the fretwire as possible. This technique minimizes the unpleasant 'fretbuzz' sounds that can otherwise occur. Pressing at the edge of the fret also greatly reduces the amount of pressure that is required, enabling you to play with a lighter and hence more fluent touch.

2. Try to keep all the fretting-hand fingers close to the fingerboard so that they are hovering just above the strings ready to jump into action when needed. This minimizes the amount of movement required when moving from one chord or note to another.

3. Unless you are playing more than one note with the same finger, you should always use the tips of your fingers to fret notes; this will produce the sound more directly and cleanly than using the fleshier pads of the fingers.

Picking hand

1. If using a plectrum (pick), grip it between the index (first) finger and the thumb. Position the plectrum so that its tip extends only just beyond the fingertip, by about 1/10 in (25 mm). Whilst this measurement doesn't have to be exact, make sure that the amount of plectrum that extends beyond the index finger is not excessive: this

▶ Avoid holding the plectrum at right angles to your index finger, otherwise your wrist may lock.

would result in a lack of pick control, making the plectrum liable to flap around when striking the strings – reducing both fluency and accuracy. Alternatively, if you find that when you try to pick a string you often miss it completely, the cause is most likely to be not enough plectrum extending beyond the fingertip.

2. Although you need to hold the plectrum with a small amount of pressure so that it doesn't get knocked out of your hand when you strike the strings, be very careful not to grip the plectrum too tightly. Excessive gripping pressure can lead to muscular tension in the hand and arm, with a subsequent loss of flexibility and movement.

3. The most efficient way to pick single notes is to alternate between downstrokes and upstrokes. Unless you want to achieve a particular staccato sound, this 'alternate picking' technique should be used for all melodies or lead guitar playing. (For information on fingerpicking, see pages 18–19.)

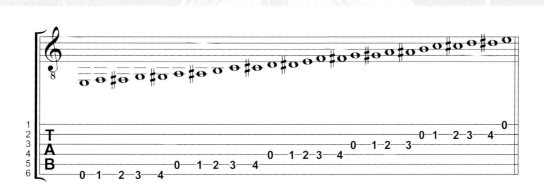

▲ The E chromatic scale consists of a continual series of half steps, which means that every note in 'open position' is played. This makes the scale ideal for building technique as it uses all four fingers to fret notes. It should be played using alternate down and up plectrum strokes.

First Chords

Chords form the backbone of all music. As soon as you've mastered a few chord shapes you'll be well on the road to music-making. The really great thing about chords is that once you've learnt them they'll last you a lifetime: you'll still be using any chord you learn today 20 years from now.

Chord symbols

There are two main types of chords that form the core of most popular music: 'major chords' and 'minor chords'.

1. The chord symbol that tells you when to play a major chord is simply the letter name of the chord written as a capital. For example, the chord symbol for the G major chord is 'G' and the chord symbol for the D major chord is 'D'. Major chords have a bright, strong sound.

Fretboxes

Guitar chord fingerings are written in diagrams known as 'fretboxes'. These indicate which strings and frets to play on, and which fingers should be used for fretting the notes.

1. In this book, fretboxes are written with vertical lines representing the strings: the low E string is represented by the line on the far left and the high E string by the line on the far right.

2. The thick line at the top of the fretbox represents the nut of the guitar, and the remaining horizontal lines represent the frets.

3. The recommended fret-hand fingering is shown in numbers: 1 = the index finger and 4 = the little finger.

4. An 0 above a string line means this string should be played open (unfretted).

5. An X above a string line means this string should not be played.

2. Minor　　　ibols consist of the capital letter of the

ed by a lowercase 'm'. For example, the

ıe E minor chord is 'Em' and the chord

ıor chord is 'Am'. Minor chords have a

ı.

Chord Name	Chord Symbol
G major	G
D major	D
E minor	Em
A minor	Am

ılves only two fretted notes and uses plenty of open strings. Place your fingers on the

ʾely with the fingertips, and then strum across all six strings. Once you're familiar with

ʒ fingers from E minor on to the adjacent higher strings, and add the first finger on

A minor. Notice that the low E string should be omitted when you strum A minor.

ıajor seems like too much of a stretch between the second and third fingers,

ə centre of the back of the guitar neck until the chord feels comfortable. Notice

ə strummed when playing D major.

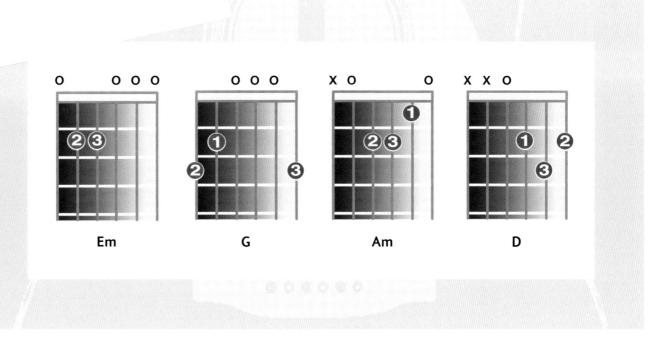

Em　　　　　G　　　　　Am　　　　　D

Simple Chord Sequences

Many songs consist of a short chord sequence that is repeated throughout. Once you have learnt a couple of basic chord shapes you can start playing a chord sequence by changing from one chord to another. It's then only a short step before you can play the chords to a complete song.

Minor chords

Begin by strumming downwards four times on an E minor chord, then without stopping change to A minor and play another four strums, keeping the same tempo. Without stopping or hesitating, move your fingers back to E minor and continuing strumming so that the whole sequence begins again.

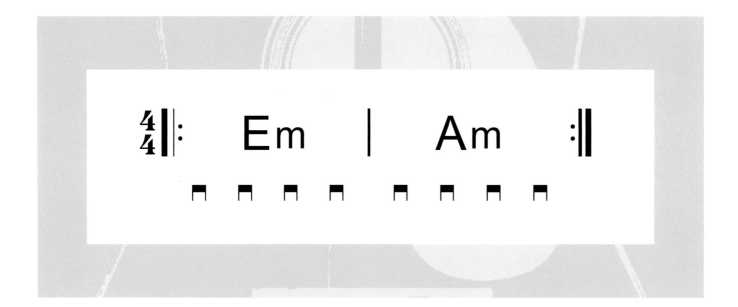

Notice the similarity of the E minor and A minor chord shapes: the second and third fingers are used at the second fret in both chords, the only difference being that they move from the A and D strings in E minor to the adjacent D and G strings in A minor. Try to keep this in mind when you change between these chords, so that you can minimize the amount of finger movement you make – this will make changing between the chords easier and quicker.

Major chords

Begin by playing four downstrums on a G major chord then, without stopping, move your fingers to D major and play another four strums. Repeat the sequence from the beginning by changing back to G major. Try to keep an even tempo throughout and practise slowly until you are able to change between the chords without pausing or hesitating.

Notice how the third finger stays at the third fret for both G and D major. Use this as a pivot point to lead the chord change. Try to move all three fretting fingers as one shape when changing chord, rather than placing the fingers on one at a time; this will make the chord changes smoother.

Combined chords

Once you feel fully familiar with the four chord shapes, try and combine them in this four-chord sequence, playing four downstrums for each chord.

1. Look for any links between the different chord fingerings so that you can minimize the amount of finger movement you need to make.

2. Remember to place the fingers for each complete chord shape on the fretboard together, rather than finger by finger.

3. Practise very slowly so that you don't develop a habit of slowing down or stopping between chord changes.

Strumming

Strumming chords forms the foundation of any guitar player's range of techniques. Strumming can be used to accompany your own or some else's singing; it can also be used to provide a backing for lead-guitar playing. Being able to strum in a variety of styles will enable you to play rhythm guitar in a wide range of musical genres.

▲ Strumming is an essential technique to master.

Strum technique

For the music to flow smoothly it's essential to develop a relaxed strumming action. It will aid the fluency of rhythm playing if the strumming action comes from the wrist: a fluid and easy strumming action is best achieved this way, with the wrist loose and relaxed. If the wrist is stiff and not allowed to move freely then excessive arm movement will occur, as the strumming action will be forced to come from the elbow instead. As this can never move as fluently as the wrist, there will be a loss of smoothness and rhythmic potential.

Strumming exercises

1. Begin by strumming an E minor chord using four downstrums per measure, and then experiment by inserting a quick upstrum between the second and third beats. The upstrum

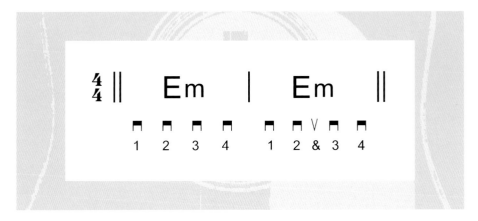

should be played by an upwards movement generated from the wrist, as though the strumming hand is almost effortlessly bouncing back into position ready for the next downstrum. Keep practising this technique until it feels natural, always making sure that the arm itself isn't moving up and down when you're strumming.

2. Progress to adding two upstrums per bar: one between beats two and three, and one after the fourth beat. After the first two bars, try changing chord to A minor and see if you can keep the strumming pattern going. If you can't change chord quickly enough then start again from the beginning, playing at a much slower tempo.

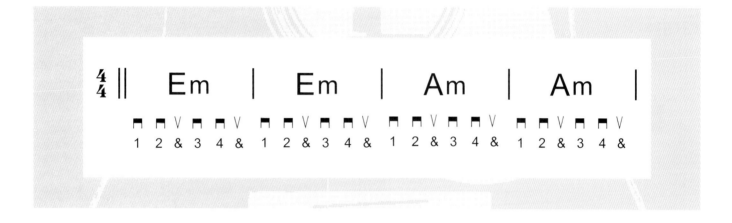

3. To really get the strumming hand moving try adding an upstrum after every downstrum. Although this strumming style would be too busy for most songs, this exercise does provide practise in building a fluent strumming technique. Make sure that you have the plectrum positioned correctly, with its tip extending only just beyond the index fingertip, so that it does not drag on the strings as you strum.

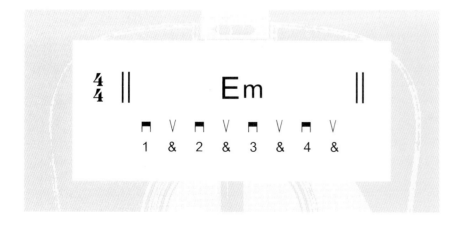

▶ Different strumming techniques can alter the sound of your recordings.

Fingerpicking

Fingerpicking can provide a really interesting alternative to strumming. The technique is not just confined to classical or folk guitarists – many rock and pop players also use fingerpicking as a method of bringing melodic interest to a chord progression and as a way of introducing musical subtleties to a song.

Fingering

In music notation, each picking finger is identified by a letter: 'p' represents the thumb, 'i' the index finger, 'm' the middle finger and 'a' the third finger. (As it is much shorter than the others, the little finger is rarely used in fingerpicking.)

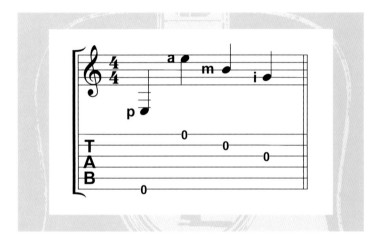

The thumb is mostly used for playing the bass strings (the lowest three strings), while the fingers are used for playing the treble strings. There are many different ways of fingerpicking, but one of the easiest is to use the a finger for picking the first string, the m finger for the second string and the i finger for the third string.

Picking patterns

Many songs use a repetitive fingerpicking pattern throughout to create a continuity of sound. Picking patterns nearly always begin by playing the root note of the chord (i.e. the note that gives the letter name to the chord) on the bass string using the thumb. For example, the low E string would be the first note of a pattern when fingerpicking on a chord of E minor, and the open A string would be the first note when fingerpicking on a chord of A minor. If the picking pattern on a chord is repeated then sometimes a different bass is used the second time. This will normally be another note from the chord, usually the adjacent bass string. This technique can completely transform a simple chord progression, making it sound quite complex because of the moving bass line. This style of fingerpicking is known as 'alternating bass'.

In some musical styles, more complex picking patterns might be used on the treble strings. It is best to practise these types of patterns on one chord until the picking pattern feels totally comfortable. Once you are familiar with a pattern it's relatively easy to apply it to a chord progression. You just need to take care about which bass note to pick on each chord, ensuring you use the root note as your starting point.

More Chords

The more chords you learn, the more songs you'll be able to play. Developing knowledge of only the 10 most common chords will enable you to play literally thousands of songs, providing you practise them enough so that you can change fluently from chord to chord.

Main chord types

Although there are dozens of different chord types, all of these can be considered as just variations of the two core types of chords: major chords and minor chords. For example, if you come across a chord chart that includes Am7, playing a simple A minor chord will work almost as well. Consequently, developing a good knowledge of the most popular major and minor chords will provide a firm foundation for all future chord playing.

Major chords

In addition to the G and D major chords that were covered on pages 12–13, some other important major chords to start with are A, C, E and F.

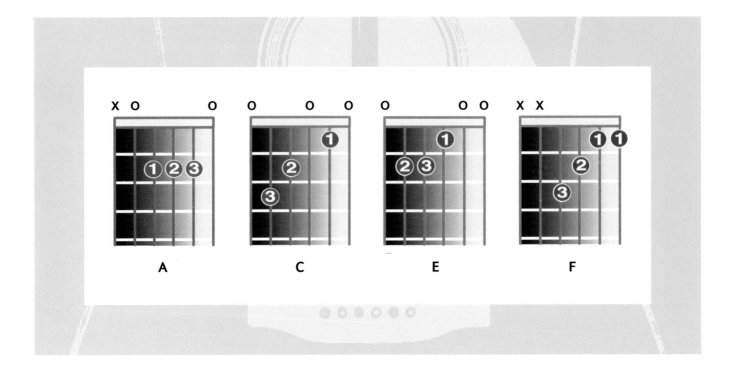

Notice that all the strings can be strummed on the E major chord, whereas the sixth string should be omitted when the A or C chords are strummed. The F major chord is different from the other chord fingerings in that the first finger needs to lie flat across both the first and second strings. You will find this easier if you ensure that your thumb is positioned quite low at the back of the guitar neck; this will help you keep your first finger flat while the second and third fingers press with the fingertips. Make sure that you only strum the top four strings when playing the F major chord.

Minor chords

In addition to the Am and Em chords that were covered on pages 12–13, the other most important minor chords to learn at first are Dm and F#m.

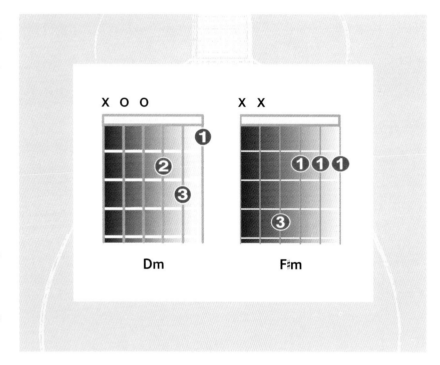

Both Dm and F#m are four-string chords (i.e. the fifth and sixth strings should be omitted when playing these chords). The F#m chord is a development of the technique that you gained when learning to play the F major chord, but this time the first finger needs to fret all the top three strings. If you find this tricky, you might like to try resting the second finger on top of the first finger; this will add extra weight and strength to help the first finger hold down all three strings. Positioning the fretting finger as close as possible to the fretwire will reduce the amount of finger pressure required.

▶ Jazz guitarist Barney Kessel added variety to his music by experimenting with many different chords.

Keys

The 'key' of a song refers to its overall tonality, and dictates which scale will be used as the basis of the melody and which chords will occur. Understanding which chords go together in a key will help you work out the chord structure of songs, and will provide a framework to begin writing your own songs.

Major keys

In each major key, three major chords occur – as shown below:

A song or chord progression will normally begin with the tonic (keynote) chord. This is the chord that has the same name as the key. For example, in the key of C major, C is the tonic (keynote) chord.

Key	Major Chords in the Key
C major	C F G
G major	G C D
D major	D G A
A major	A D E

Key	Minor Chords in the Key
C major	Dm Em Am
G major	Am Bm Em

Minor chords also occur in major keys. Some of the most commonly used minor chords in the keys of C and G major are shown below.

Although there are no fixed rules about which chords can be combined when you are composing a song or chord progression, if you select chords from the same key they will always fit together well. Below is an example of a chord progression using chords in the key of C major.

‖ C | Dm | Em | F | Am | G | F | C ‖

Minor keys

In each minor key, three minor chords are closely related, and most commonly occur in popular songs. For example, in the key of A minor the chords of Am, Dm and Em are the most important. Three major chords also occur in each minor key. For example, in the key of A minor, C, F and G major chords occur. As all these chords are within the same key they can be combined in any order (after starting with the tonic/keynote chord) to make a pleasant-sounding chord sequence. An example is shown below, but you can experiment with rearranging the chords in a different order and then playing them through to hear the musical result.

Here are a few chord progressions demonstrating some of the most common chord sequences used in a few of the most popular major and minor keys.

‖ Am | F | G | C | Am | Dm | Em | Am ‖

▲ Chord progression in the key of A minor.

‖ G | D | C | G | Em | Am | D | G ‖

▲ Chord progression in the key of G major.

‖ D | Em | F♯m | Em | G | A | G | D ‖

▲ Chord progression in the key of D major.

‖ A | E | F♯m | E | D | E | A | A ‖

▲ Chord progression in the key of A major.

‖ Em | D | C | D | Am | G | D | Em ‖

▲ Chord progression in the key of E minor.

Introduction

Knowing a number of chord shapes is useful, but it's only when you can put some of these chords together with an interesting strumming pattern, and change fluently between them, that you'll really start making music by playing rhythm guitar.

Importance of rhythm

Rhythm guitar playing is rarely given as much attention as lead playing, but it's important to remember that it's rhythm playing that forms the backbone of most songs. If you join a band, regardless of the musical style, you'll almost certainly spend more time playing rhythm guitar than lead guitar.

Notable rhythm guitar specialists are Bo Diddley (b. 1928), John Lennon (1940–80), Pete Townshend (b. 1945), Noel Gallagher (b. 1967), Paul Weller (b. 1958), Peter Buck (b. 1956) of REM, Fran Healy (b. 1973) of Travis and Badly Drawn Boy (b. Damon Gough, 1970).

Good rhythm

1. The first essential of becoming a good rhythm guitar player is the ability to keep in time: practising with a metronome, drum machine or backing tracks will provide the ideal preparation; always listen out for the drums and bass and try to stay in time with them. Remember that as a rhythm guitar player you are part of the 'rhythm section' of any band, and you should try to interact closely with the other rhythm section musicians. (See pages 26–27.)

◄ One of the features of Damon Gough's unique sound is his rhythm guitar playing that underpins the majority of his tracks.

2. Another core skill is the ability to change fluently from one chord to another: always look for links, or common notes, between consecutive chords – so that you can minimize the amount of finger movement needed when changing chords; you may be able to keep some fingers on, or at least slide them along a string to the next chord. Leaving gaps between chords when

▲ Pioneering guitarist Pete Townshend was a master of rhythm guitar.

strumming through a song or chord progression is a recipe for musical disaster – the performance will sound fragmented and if you're playing with a singer or other musicians it will prove impossible to keep in time. (See pages 74–75.)

3. Developing a reliable strumming technique is an essential part of becoming a good guitar player. Once you have mastered these basic rhythm-playing skills, then it's time to become inventive with your strumming patterns. It's the uniqueness and inventiveness of strumming that distinguishes great rhythm players from the rest. (See pages 38–39.)

4. Being able to understand and follow chord charts is another required skill for any rhythm guitar player. Depending on the style of music and who has prepared the chord chart, these could appear in a variety of formats, from a simple handwritten list of chords to a fully typeset chart with time signatures, notated rhythms and interpretation markings included. (See pages 32–33.)

Timing

The most important skill any rhythm guitar player needs is the ability to maintain an even tempo and keep in time with other band members. It's essential that your rhythm playing sits in the same groove as the other members of the rhythm section.

Developing timing skills

Some people have a natural sense of rhythm and timing that just needs nurturing, while others have to concentrate on developing a secure sense of timing. A simple test to discover how well-developed your sense of timing is would be to try and clap along to a recording by one of your favourite bands. While listening to the recording, focus your attention on the drums and try to clap a regular beat that matches the main rhythmic pulses within the song. Listen carefully to your clapping and see if you can stay in time throughout the whole song – stamina is an important aspect of rhythm playing. Before you try to play through a song make sure that you have mastered any technical challenges, such as awkward chord changes, in advance. Otherwise, the temptation will be to slow down when approaching the difficult bits and perhaps speed up on the easy bits. You should try to avoid developing such poor timing habits from the start by always choosing a slow practice tempo at which you can master the whole song – difficult bits and all! Once you can play the song without any mistakes or hesitations, it's relatively easy to gradually increase the tempo each time you practise.

◀ Nile Rodgers is known for the crisp timing of his rhythm chops.

Timing aids

Ideally you should always try to practise your rhythm playing with a device that keeps regular time. The simplest method is to practise with a metronome. This is a small mechanical or electronic device that sounds a click on each beat. You can set it to click in increments from a very slow to a super-fast tempo. It's always best to practise anything new at a slow tempo, increasing the metronome setting by a couple of notches each time you've successfully played it the whole way through.

If you have access to a drum machine this can be used in a similar way to a metronome. The advantage of the drum machine is that you can set it to play back interesting drum patterns to help inspire your strumming style. You can program the machine, or use preset patterns, so that it emulates different musical genres.

▲ A metronome – a tried and tested way to keep in good time.

Playing along to records is also a good method of developing a secure sense of timing: the band on the recording won't wait around if you lose time or hesitate over a chord change. Because there will be a longer space between beats, playing along with songs at a slow tempo emphasizes any timing inconsistencies – so don't forget to practise a few ballads alongside the thrash metal!

◄ A drum machine can help you play in time.

Time Signatures

The time signature is the most important element in setting the musical feel and mood of a piece of music. It provides the framework for the rhythmic structure of a song and plays a large part in establishing the character of the music.

Recognizing time signatures

The symbol indicating the time signature is always written at the start of the music or chord chart. The time signature is normally written as two numbers, one above the other. The top number represents the number of beats per measure (bar), while the bottom number refers to the type of beats.

The most common time signature used in all styles of popular music is $\frac{4}{4}$ time. This indicates that there are four beats in a measure, and that these are quarter notes (crotchets). Sometimes the $\frac{4}{4}$ symbol is replaced with **C**, meaning 'common time'.

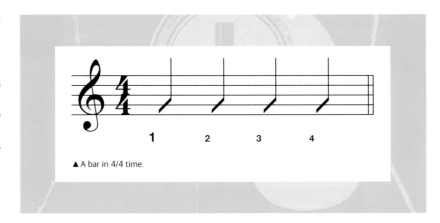

▲ A bar in 4/4 time.

Note that the time signature only tells you the number and type of 'beats' that will occur in a measure; this is not the same as the number of 'notes' you can play in the measure. For example, a measure of music in $\frac{4}{4}$ time will last for the equivalent duration of four quarter beats, but in this space you might play less longer-lasting notes or more shorter notes. In fact, you can play any combination of long, medium or short notes providing the duration per measure is equivalent to four quarter-note beats. (See pages 30–31 for more information on understanding notation.)

Other commonly used time signatures:

$\frac{2}{4}$: this has two quarter-note beats per measure. This time signature tends to give a march-like feel to the music.

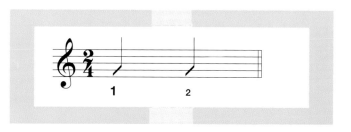

$\frac{3}{4}$: this has three quarter-note beats per measure. This time signature gives a waltz-like character to the music and is often used in country and folk ballads.

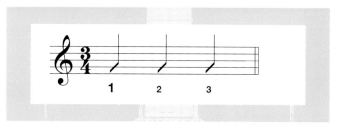

$\frac{2}{2}$: this has two half-note beats per measure. This is equivalent in length to $\frac{4}{4}$ time, but with two long beats per measure instead of four quarter-note beats.

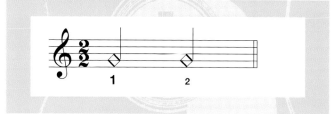

$\frac{6}{8}$: this has six eighth-note beats per measure. However, these are normally played as two groups of three.

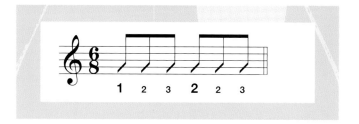

$\frac{12}{8}$: this has 12 eighth-note beats per measure. These are normally played as four groups of three. $\frac{12}{8}$ is commonly used in blues and jazz.

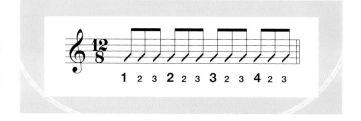

Establishing the time signature

If you were just to play a long series of chords all of equal strength it would be hard for the listener to recognize any rhythmic structure in the music – in other words, they wouldn't be able to 'feel the groove'. So normally the first beat of each measure is slightly accented, as this helps the sense of rhythm in a piece of music. In $\frac{6}{8}$ and $\frac{12}{8}$ time, an accent is normally played on the first of each group of three notes. (If you're playing in a band it might be the drums or other instruments that emphasize these accents.)

Rhythm Notation

Understanding how rhythms are written down will help you play through notated chord charts. The ability to notate your own rhythms is useful for passing the information to other players and as a memory aid. Even if you intend to rely mainly on tablature, a knowledge of rhythm notation will help you get the most out of the many song transcriptions that provide the full notation with the tab.

Note values

Rhythm notation consists of pitchless notes and rests. The type of note used tells you how many beats a chord lasts; the type of rest used tells you how many beats a silence lasts. The diagram below shows the names of the most common types of notes, their symbols and how many of each type of note can occur in a single measure in $\frac{4}{4}$ time.

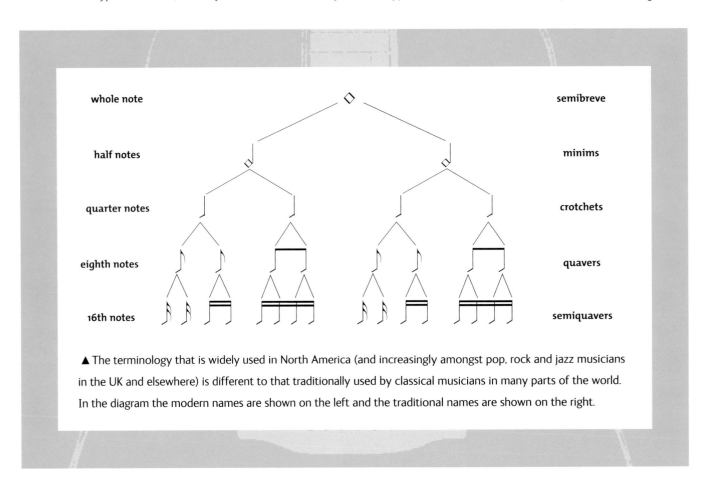

▲ The terminology that is widely used in North America (and increasingly amongst pop, rock and jazz musicians in the UK and elsewhere) is different to that traditionally used by classical musicians in many parts of the world. In the diagram the modern names are shown on the left and the traditional names are shown on the right.

Rests

The table on the right shows the names of the most common types of rests, their symbols, their note equivalents, and the duration of each type of rest in $\frac{4}{4}$ time.

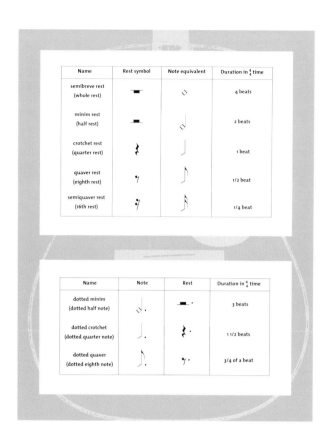

Name	Rest symbol	Note equivalent	Duration in $\frac{4}{4}$ time
semibreve rest (whole rest)			4 beats
minim rest (half rest)			2 beats
crotchet rest (quarter rest)			1 beat
quaver rest (eighth rest)			1/2 beat
semiquaver rest (16th rest)			1/4 beat

Dotted notes

A dot after a note or rest means that the note or rest lasts for half as long again. This chart shows the values of dotted notes and dotted rests in $\frac{4}{4}$ time.

Name	Note	Rest	Duration in $\frac{4}{4}$ time
dotted minim (dotted half note)			3 beats
dotted crotchet (dotted quarter note)			1 1/2 beats
dotted quaver (dotted eighth note)			3/4 of a beat

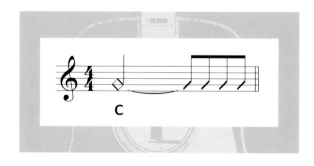

Ties

A curved line known as a 'tie' is used to join together two notes of the same pitch in order to increase the duration of the note.

◀ In this example, the first chord would be allowed to sustain for the equivalent of five eighth notes. It is not possible to use a dot after the initial chord as this would have increased the duration of the note to the equivalent of six eighth notes.

Another common instance where ties are used is across bar lines as a method of sustaining a note beyond the end of a measure.

◀ In this example, a tie is used so that the chord at the end of measure one can sustain into measure two.

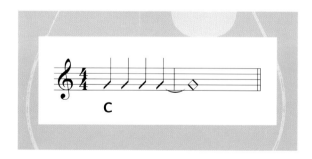

Triplets

A triplet sign indicates where three notes should be played in the space of two notes of the same value.

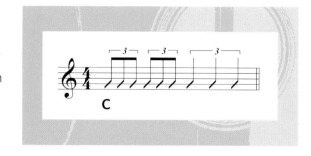

Chord Charts

Simple chord charts are the most commonly used way of notating the chord structure of a song or progression. If you audition for a pop or rock band, the music you'll be asked to play with will most likely be presented as a simple chord chart.

Reading chord charts

A chord chart normally has the time signature written at the very beginning. If there is no time signature then it's usually safe to assume that the music is in $\frac{4}{4}$ time.

Each measure is separated by a vertical line, with two vertical lines indicating the end of the piece. Chord symbols are used to show which chords should be played.

$$\| \, \frac{4}{4} \quad C \mid Am \mid Dm \mid G \mid F \mid Em \mid G \mid C \, \|$$

Split measures

When more than one chord appears in a single measure it can be assumed that the measure is to be evenly divided between the chords that appear within it. In a song in $\frac{3}{4}$ time, if three chords all appear in the same measure then you can assume that the measure is to be divided equally – with one beat per chord.

$$\| \, \frac{3}{4} \quad C \mid Am \mid Em \; F \; G \mid C \, \|$$

▲ In the penultimate measure, each chord lasts for one beat.

In many chord charts, in order to make the intention very clear and avoid any possible confusion, any division within a measure is shown by either a dot or a diagonal line after each chord: each dot or diagonal line indicates another beat.

‖ $\frac{4}{4}$ C ╱ Am ╱ |Dm╱ G ╱ |F ╱ Em ╱ |G ╱ C ╱ ‖

▲ Each chord lasts for two beats: one beat indicated by the chord symbol and an additional beat indicated by the diagonal line.

‖ $\frac{4}{4}$ C Em ╱ ╱ | F G ╱ ╱ |Am Em ╱ ╱ |G C ╱ ╱ ‖

▲ In this example, the first chord in each measure lasts for just one beat and the second chord lasts for three beats.

‖ $\frac{4}{4}$ C . . Dm |Em . . F |Dm . . G |F . . C ‖

▲ In this example, instead of diagonal lines, dots are used to show the rhythmic divisions within each measure. The first chord in each measure lasts for three beats and the second chord lasts for one beat.

Interpreting chord charts

In standard chord charts, while the duration of each chord is clearly shown, the rhythm style that should be played is left to the discretion of the performer. In theory this means that you could interpret the chart in any way you wish in terms of the number of strums per beat, however you should make sure that your rhythm playing relates to the musical style and mood of the song.

◄ Noel Gallagher's rhythm-guitar playing is based on a good understanding of chord progression.

Following Chord Charts

If every bar of a whole song was written out in a chord chart it would take up several pages and become cumbersome to read. Instead chord charts are normally abbreviated by using a number of 'repeat symbols'. In order to follow a chord chart accurately it is essential to understand what each repeat symbol means.

Repeat symbols

╱. This symbol is used when one bar is to be repeated exactly.

╱╱. This symbol is used when more than one bar is to be repeated. The number of bars to be repeated is written above the symbol.

Here is an example of these symbols in use.

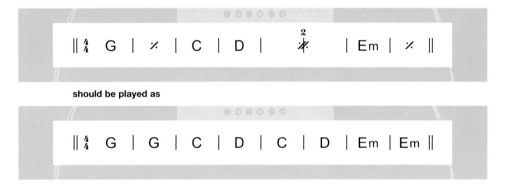

should be played as

‖ ⁴₄ G | G | C | D | C | D | Em | Em ‖

Section repeats

A double bar-line followed by two dots indicates the start of a section, and two dots followed by a double bar-line indicates the end of the section to be repeated. If there are no dots at the start of the section, then repeat from the beginning of the piece. If the section is to be repeated more than once, the number of times it is to be played is written above the last repeat dots.

If two sections of music are identical, except for the last measure or measures, repeat dots are used in conjunction with first-time and second-time ending directions, as shown here.

should be played as

As well as repeat dots there are several other commonly used repeat signs:

• D.C. (an abbreviation of Da Capo) means play 'from the beginning'. For example, if the entire piece of music is to be repeated, D.C. can be written at the end to instruct you to play it again from the beginning.

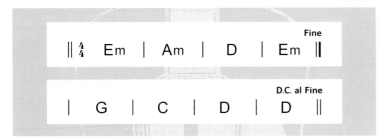

▲ In this example, after eight measures repeat from the beginning and then end after measure four where the sign 'Fine' appears.

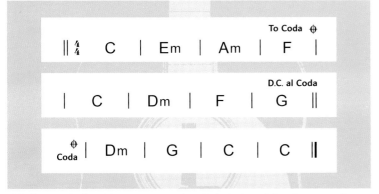

▲ In this example, after eight measures repeat from the beginning and then after measure four jump to the coda section.

• D.S. (an abbreviation of Dal Segno) means play 'from the sign': ✵. For example, if the verse and chorus of a song are to be repeated, but not the introduction, D.S. can be written at the end of the music with the D.S. sign written at the start of the verse. This instructs the performer to start again from the sign.

• Coda is the musical term for the end section of a piece of music. The start of the coda is marked by the sign ⊕.

• Fine is the musical term for the end of a piece of music.

Some of the above repeat signs might be combined together in a chord chart.

▲ In this example, after eight measures repeat from the start of measure three to the end of measure six, then jump to the coda section.

Rhythm Charts

While standard chord charts are commonly used by pop and rock bands, more detailed and complex charts known as 'rhythm charts' are often presented to guitarists involved in recording sessions and those who play in theatre and function band settings. Learning to read rhythm charts will help expand your employability as a guitarist.

Chart styles

Some rhythm charts can be quite elaborate and may include a fully notated rhythm part, as well as detailed instructions about dynamics and tempo. Others may contain notated rhythms only at the beginning, in order to establish the feel of the song, with further rhythm notation only being used where specific rhythmic accents or features occur. The type of rhythm charts you might come across will depend on the context and the transcriber's personal preferences.

Dynamic markings

Symbols are often used in rhythm charts to indicate changes in volume – e.g. when you should play softly and when you should strum strongly. The symbols do not refer to any precise decibel volume level, instead their main function is to highlight changes in overall volume. The most common dynamic markings are shown to the right. Accents, where certain individual beats are played stronger than others, are marked by this sign: >. The letters 'sfz' sforzando) may be also used to indicate an accent.

Symbol	Name	Meaning
pp	pianissimo	very soft
p	piano	soft
mp	mezzo-piano	medium soft
mf	mezzo-forte	medium loud
f	forte	loud
ff	fortissimo	very loud
◁	crescendo	getting louder
◁	diminuendo	getting softer

Tempo

Most rhythm charts will contain an indication of the speed at which the music should be played, and this will usually be written at the start of the music. The tempo indication may appear in either traditional Italian musical terms or their

Italian Term	Meaning	Approximate speed
Largo	very slow	40–60 b.p.m.
Adagio	slow	50–75 b.p.m.
Andante	walking pace	75–100 b.p.m.
Moderato	moderate tempo	100–120 b.p.m.
Allegro	fast	120–160 b.p.m.
Presto	very quick	160–200 b.p.m.

English equivalents. Alternatively, a metronome marking may be shown to indicate the exact number of beats per minute (b.p.m.). The most common tempos are shown in the table above.

Some music may contain changes in tempo. These are usually indicated through the use of Italian terms.

The most widely used are:

- *Accel.* (an abbreviation of *accelerando*) means play gradually faster.

- *A tempo* indicates that you should resume the normal tempo after a derivation.

- *Meno mosso* (less movement) means that you should slow down at once.

- *Rall.* (an abbreviation of *rallentando*) means play gradually slower.

- *Rit.* (an abbreviation of *ritenuto*) means to hold back the tempo.

Playing rhythm charts

Below you'll see a sample rhythm chart, incorporating some of the terms and symbols described above.

Refer to pages 30–31 if you need to be reminded of the note values.

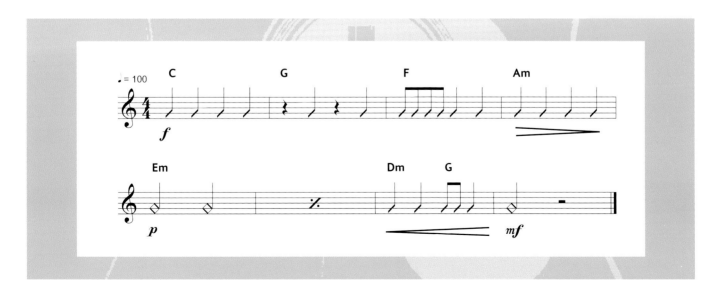

Strumming Patterns

Building up a repertoire of useful strumming patterns is a good way of developing your rhythm guitar playing. Once you've mastered the core patterns used in rock and pop you can easily expand these by adding variations.

Strum technique

Playing with a loose wrist action is an essential ingredient of developing a good strumming technique. Keeping the wrist tight and strumming by using the whole forearm will severely restrict the potential speed and fluency of your rhythm playing – so make sure that the strumming action comes from your wrist. It's a good idea to practise in front of a mirror, or film yourself playing guitar, so that you can see if you're using the right technique.

Chord technique

Be careful not to over-grip with the fretting-hand thumb on the back of the neck as this will cause muscle fatigue and tend to limit freedom of the thumb to move. It is essential that the fretting-hand thumb is allowed to move freely when changing chords. If the thumb remains static this restricts the optimum positioning of the fingers for the next chord, which may result in unnecessary stretching and the involuntary dampening of certain strings (as the fingers are not positioned upright on their tips). Be aware that for the fingers to move freely the wrist, elbow and shoulder must be flexible and relaxed: try to ensure that this is not inhibited by your standing or sitting position.

Strum patterns

Opposite you'll find several examples of popular strumming patterns. It's a good idea to start by playing all the progressions using just four downstrums per measure – this way you'll become familiar with the chord changes before tackling the strum patterns.

In nearly all styles of music, there is no need to strum all the strings on every beat – feel free to add variety, particularly by omitting some bass strings on upstrokes and some treble strings on downstrokes.

▲ The second beat of the measure is accented to create dynamic variety. An upstroke is used after the third beat of the measure.

▲ This pattern uses a mixture of down and upstrokes, but notice how the fourth strum and the last strum are held longer than the others. This variety creates an effective rhythm.

▲ A simple down–up strum pattern, but the use of rests creates a very distinctive rhythmic effect.

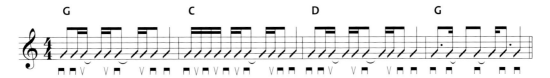

▲ This 'Bo Diddley' type pattern is a good example of how to use rhythmic variations: notice that measure 1 and 3 are the same, while measures 2 and 4 are each variations on the first measure.

▲ This typical rock strumming pattern is essentially just one strum per measure. What makes it distinctive is the rapid down–up 'pre-strum' before the main beat. These 'pre-strums' do not need to be played across all the strings, and open strings can be used on the second of them to help get to the main chord quickly.

Introduction

Whether letting rip in an aggressive rock solo or playing a subtle blues, lead guitar playing is a great way to express your emotions through your instrument. However, underlying every great guitar solo is a foundation of scales and fingerboard knowledge that enables players to turn their musical ideas into reality.

▲ The opening to 'Stairway to Heaven', as first played by Jimmy Page of Led Zeppelin, is one of the most-copied intro riffs of all time.

Influential players

Some of the early pioneers of modern lead guitar styles are B. B. King (b. 1925), Buddy Guy (b. 1936), Eric Clapton

(b. 1945), Jimmy Page (b. 1944), Jeff Beck (b. 1945), Ritchie Blackmore (b. 1945) and Carlos Santana (b. 1947). If

you've never heard these players, try to check out some of their recordings.

Six Stages to Improvising

1. When you first start playing lead guitar you could begin by simply playing the correct scale up and down over the chord progression. This way you can begin to hear the overall sound and tonality of the key, but always bear in mind that just playing scales up and down isn't enough to make a good solo.

2. As the first stage in learning to improvise, rather than playing the scale in straight time, experiment by playing some notes quickly while allowing others to ring on; you'll notice that this sounds more musical and inventive, even though you're still playing the same notes in the same order.

3. Next, try repeating series of notes, so that you begin to establish licks or phrases that will stick in the listener's ear. Once you have a phrase that you like, try to vary it slightly when you repeat it – that way it will sound fresh, while still giving the listener something recognizable to latch on to.

4. Leave some gaps between your phrases so that the music has space to breath. There's no need to fill every second with notes.

5. Try to make your lead playing fit with the musical style and mood of the song, so that it enhances what else is being played or sung.

6. The most important thing is to let your ears, rather than your fingers, guide you. Listen carefully to the musical effect of every note you play.

▲ Buddy Guy has inspired thousands over the years with his strong and inventive lead–guitar playing.

Improvisation

Later in this chapter all the essential scales that underpin lead guitar playing will be illustrated, but it's important to remember that playing scales up and down doesn't make a solo in itself.

Scales simply set the range of notes that will be in tune in any key. It's how well you improvise with a scale that dictates how good your solo will be. To get a feel for the song, it's always a good idea to play through the chord sequence before you play any lead guitar.

Basics of Notation

There are three ways in which scales, licks and solos are written down: traditional notation, tablature and fretboxes. While you don't need to be a great sight-reader to play lead guitar, having a good understanding of each of the notation systems will help you learn lead guitar relatively easily.

Tablature

Tablature (TAB) uses six lines to represent the six strings of the guitar, with the top line representing the high E string and the bottom line representing the low E string. Numbers are written on the lines to indicate which fret to play at. A zero indicates that the string is played open. TAB is great for notating scales or chords and, although it doesn't usually include any rhythm notation, its simplicity means it's ideal for learning music that you have heard before.

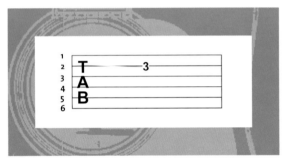

▲ This means play at the third fret on the second string.

Music notation

Traditional music notation is written on a staff of five lines. Each line, and each space between them, represents a different note. For guitar music, a treble clef is written at the start of each line of music. Temporary extra lines (ledger lines) are used for any notes that are either too high or too low to fit on the staff.

▲ Notes on the lines and spaces in the treble clef.

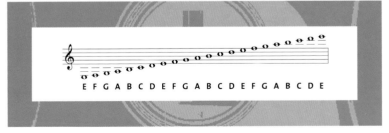

▲ Using ledger lines, this diagram shows the notes from the open low E string to the E at the 12th fret on the first string.

A sharp sign (♯) is written in front of a note, on the same line or space, to raise its pitch by a half step (semitone) i. e. equivalent to one fret higher.

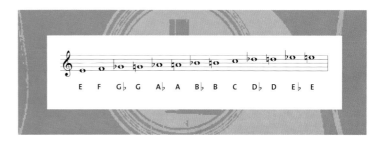

A flat sign (♭) is written in front of a note, on the same line or space, to lower its pitch by a half step (semitone). Any sharps or flats affect all the notes of the same pitch within the bar. A natural sign (♮) on the same line or space is used to cancel the previous sharp or flat.

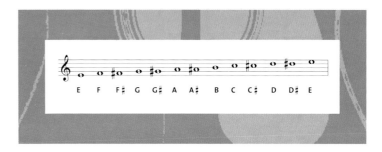

Key signatures

The key of a piece of music determines the main notes that will be included in it. In music notation a key signature is written at the beginning of every line of music to indicate the key. Key signatures make music easier to read because any sharps or flats in the key need only be written at the start of each line and will then apply to all those notes throughout the piece, rather than needing to write a sharp or flat sign every time such a note occurs. Each major key has a unique key signature, consisting of a collection of sharps or flats written in a set order; these sharps and flats match those that occur in the major scale for that key. The key of C major is unusual in that no sharps or flats occur in the keyscale, and therefore the key signature is blank.

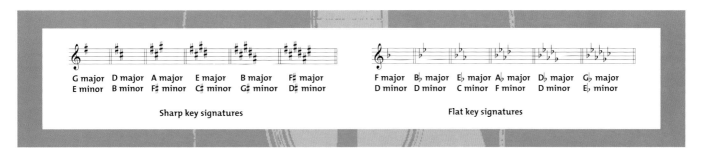

Minor keys share key signatures with their relative major keys (i.e. major keys that have a keynote three half steps higher than the minor key).

Fretboxes   See page 12 for a description of fretboxes.

Major Scales

By far the most important scale in music is the major scale. All other scales, and even all chords, can be considered as stemming from the major scale. The major scale is used as the basis for the majority of popular melodies. When used in lead playing it gives a bright and melodic sound.

Scale construction

The major scale is constructed by using a combination of whole steps/whole tones (W) and half steps/semitones (H). Regardless of the key, the pattern of tones and semitones is as follows: W W H W W W H.

For example, the C major scale, is constructed as follows:

C	plus a **whole** step	=	D
D	plus a **whole** step	=	E
E	plus a **half** step	=	F
F	plus a **whole** step	=	G
G	plus a **whole** step	=	A
A	plus a **whole** step	=	B
B	plus a **half** step	=	C

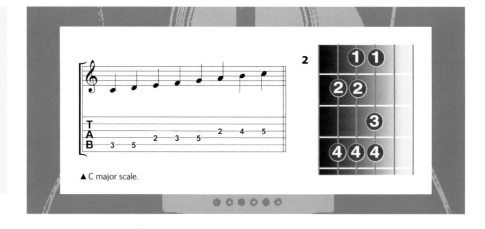

▲ C major scale.

Transposing scales

All the scales illustrated in this chapter are 'transpositional': they can be played in other keys simply by starting the finger pattern at a different fret. For example, to play the D major

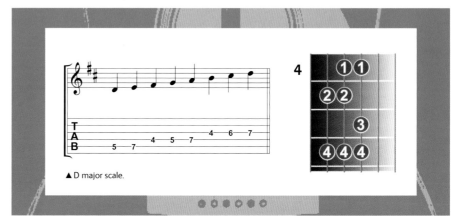

▲ D major scale.

scale, use the exact fingering shown for C major but start two frets higher. For some keys, for example G major, you might prefer to start the scale pattern on the low E string in order to avoid high fingerboard positions.

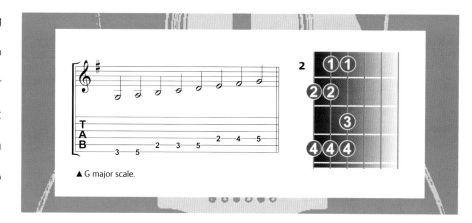

▲ G major scale.

Pentatonic major scale

The term 'pentatonic' means 'five-note'; the pentatonic major scale is a five-note abbreviation of the standard major scale, with the fourth and seventh degrees of the major scale omitted. For example, the notes in the C major scale are C D E F G A B. To convert this into the C pentatonic major scale omit the notes F (the 4th) and B (the 7th), resulting in C D E G A.

The pentatonic major scale has none of the overtly sugary sound often associated with the standard major scale – instead it has a great combination of brightness with a cutting edge. It

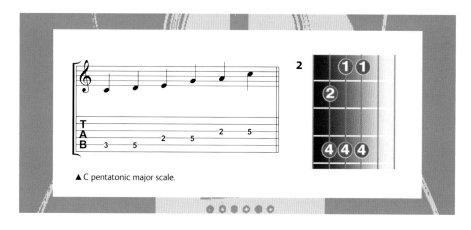

▲ C pentatonic major scale.

is a very useful scale for improvising in major keys; because it contains fewer notes than the standard major scale there is less chance of any of the notes clashing with the accompanying chords.

Traditionally, pentatonic major scales have been used in country music, but many rock bands – from the Rolling Stones and Free to Travis and Supergrass – have used them frequently on their recordings.

Brit Rock bands were great fans of the pentatonic major scale, particularly Noel Gallagher, who relied on them almost exclusively for his solos on the first few Oasis albums. Some of its greatest exponents were country rock players like Danny Gatton (1945–94) and Albert Lee (b. 1943).

Minor Scales

There is a variety of minor scales to suit all musical styles, from the soulful natural minor scale to the exotic harmonic minor scale. But it is the rock–edged pentatonic minor scale that is by far the most widely used scale in lead guitar playing.

Natural minor scale

The natural minor scale is constructed using a combination of whole steps/tones (W) and half steps/semitones (H) in the following pattern: W H W W H W W. For example, C natural minor scale, is constructed as follows:

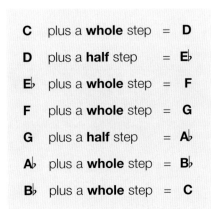

C	plus a **whole** step	=	D
D	plus a **half** step	=	E♭
E♭	plus a **whole** step	=	F
F	plus a **whole** step	=	G
G	plus a **half** step	=	A♭
A♭	plus a **whole** step	=	B♭
B♭	plus a **whole** step	=	C

▲ C natural minor scale.

The interval spelling for the natural minor scale is 1 2 ♭3 4 5 ♭6 ♭7 8, meaning that, in comparison to the major scale with the same keynote, the third, sixth and seventh notes are flattened by a half step. The natural minor scale is widely used in rock and blues based music. The scale has a soulful, yet melodic sound. Carlos Santana and Gary Moore (b. 1952) are two of its best-known exponents.

Pentatonic minor scale

In all forms of rock music, the pentatonic minor scale is the most commonly used scale for lead guitar playing. The interval spelling is 1 ♭3 4 5 ♭7 8. It is a popular scale for improvising in minor keys because it contains fewer notes than the natural minor scale – this makes the scale easy to use and means that there is little chance of any of the notes clashing with the accompanying chords.

Harmonic minor scale

The harmonic minor scale is very similar to the natural minor scale. The only difference is that, in the harmonic minor scale, the note on the seventh degree is raised by a half step. This results in a large interval between the sixth and seventh degrees of the scale, giving the scale its distinctive, exotic sound. The interval spelling is 1 2 ♭3 4 5 ♭6 7 8. Ritchie Blackmore (b. 1945) was one of the first rock guitarists to exploit the melodic potential of this scale.

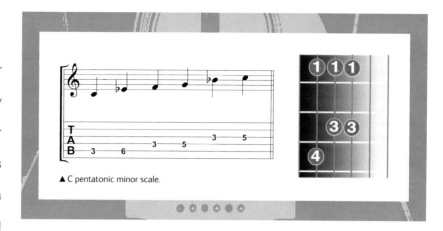

▲ C pentatonic minor scale.

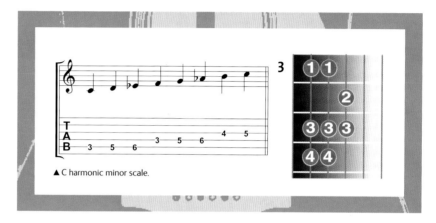

▲ C harmonic minor scale.

Melodic minor scale

The step pattern of this scale alters depending on whether it is being played ascending or descending. When played descending it has the same notes as the natural minor scale; when played ascending the sixth and

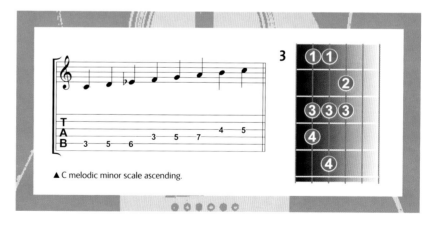

▲ C melodic minor scale ascending.

seventh degrees are each raised by a half step. The interval spelling is 1 2 ♭3 4 5 6 7 8 ascending and 1 2 ♭3 4 5 ♭6 ♭7 8 descending. The scale is mostly used in jazz-rock and fusion.

Jazz melodic minor scale

The jazz melodic minor scale is the same as the ascending version of the standard melodic minor scale. The sixth and seventh degrees of the scale are raised by a half step in comparison to the natural minor scale, giving it a much brighter tonality that is well suited to some forms of jazz music. The interval spelling is 1 2 ♭3 4 5 6 7 8.

Further Scales

Expanding your knowledge of scales beyond the common major and minor scales will broaden your musical vocabulary, enabling you to play lead guitar in a wide range of musical styles. A grasp of a broad collection of scales will also facilitate improvisation over complex chord progressions.

Blues scale

The blues scale contains all the notes of the pentatonic minor scale, but with the addition of a ♭5 note. It is this note that gives the blues scale its distinctive blues flavour. All blues lead guitar

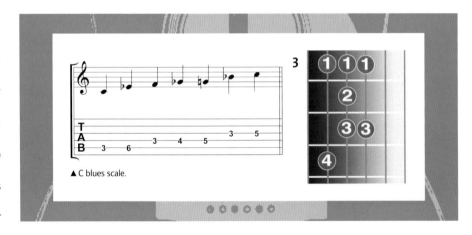

▲ C blues scale.

playing uses the blues scale as its foundation. The interval spelling of the blues scale is 1 ♭3 4 ♭5 5 ♭7. C blues scale contains the notes C E♭ F G♭ G B♭.

Chromatic scale

This scale contains every half step between the starting note and the octave. It is the only 12-note scale in music and does not relate to any particular key. Instead, when improvising, notes from the chromatic scale can be

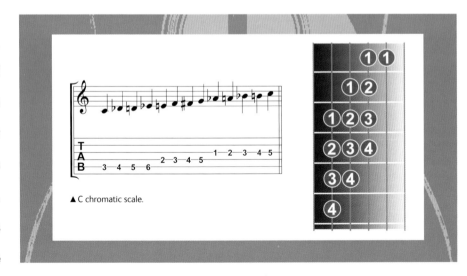

▲ C chromatic scale.

added to introduce notes that are not in the key of the backing. Including these 'outside' notes as chromatic passing notes within a lead guitar solo can help provide moments of harmonic tension.

Country scale

The country scale contains all the notes of the pentatonic major scale, but with the addition of a minor 3rd note. This gives it a slightly bluesy edge that suits 'new country' and 'country rock' guitar styles. The interval spelling is 1 2 ♭3 3 5 6 8.

▲ C country scale.

Diminished scales

These are eight-note scales comprising alternating whole-step and half-step intervals. Diminished scales can start either with a whole step or a half step. Diminished scales that start with a whole step are described as whole/half diminished scales. These are generally used to improvise over diminished seventh chords. The interval spelling is 1 2 ♭3 4 ♭5 ♭6 ♭♭7 7 8. Diminished scales that start with a half step are described as half/whole diminished scales. These are widely used in jazz and fusion to create a sense of musical tension and colour when improvising over dominant seventh chords. The interval spelling is 1 ♭2 ♯2 3 ♯4 5 6 ♭7 8.

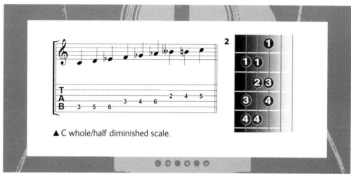
▲ C whole/half diminished scale.

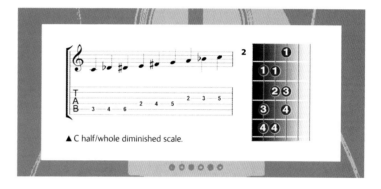
▲ C half/whole diminished scale.

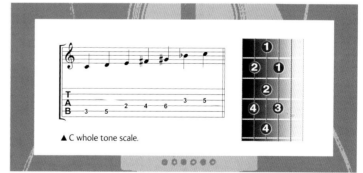
▲ C whole tone scale.

Whole-tone scale

The whole-tone scale is constructed using only whole steps. Between any note and its octave there are six whole steps, therefore the whole-tone scale contains six different notes. Whole-tone scales are rarely used as key scales, but instead tend to be used for improvising over dominant altered chords (such as 7♯5). The interval spelling is 1 2 3 ♯4 ♯5 ♭7 8.

Modes

Modes are scales that are formed by taking the notes of an existing scale but starting from a note other than the original keynote. This results in each mode having a unique tonality. The most common modes played on the guitar are those of the major scale, in particular the Dorian, Lydian and Mixolydian modes.

Dorian modal scale

Taking the notes of the major scale starting from its second degree creates the Dorian modal scale. For example, the notes of the B♭ major scale are B♭ C D E♭ F G A B♭. The second note in the B♭ major scale is C, so the C Dorian modal scale contains the notes C D E♭ F G A B♭ C. The interval spelling is 1 2 ♭3 4 5 6 ♭7 8.

Even though the B♭ major scale and the C Dorian mode derived from it contain the same notes, they have a very different sound and character. For example, the major scale has a major third interval from the first to the third note and a major seventh interval

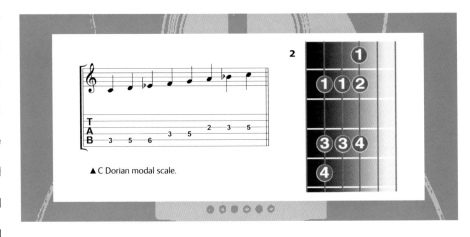

▲ C Dorian modal scale.

from the first to the seventh note. In contrast, the Dorian modal scale contains minor third and minor seventh intervals – making it a type of 'minor' scale. Compared to the natural minor scale, the Dorian modal scale has a brighter, less melancholic, sound and is often used in funk, soul and jazz styles.

Lydian modal scale

The Lydian modal scale has a laid-back sound that is well-suited to jazz, fusion and soul music. The mode is formed by taking the notes of the major scale starting from its fourth degree. For example, the notes of the G major scale are G A B C D E F♯ G. The fourth note in the G major scale is C, so the Lydian modal scale that is generated from the G major scale is the C Lydian modal scale – comprising the notes C D E F♯ G A B C. The interval spelling is 1 2 3 ♯4 5 6 7 8.

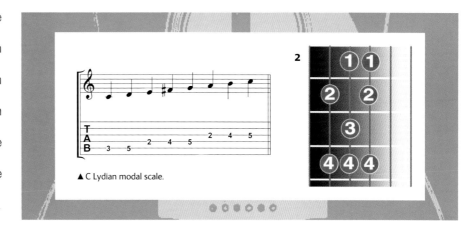

▲ C Lydian modal scale.

You might notice that when compared to the 'tonic major' (the major scale with the same starting note) the only difference is the inclusion of the ♯4 note in the Lydian modal scale.

Mixolydian modal scale

The Mixolydian modal scale is used in blues and rock music. It is formed by taking the notes of the major scale starting from its fifth degree. For example, the notes of the F major scale are F G A B♭ C D E F. The fifth note in the F major scale is C, so the Mixolydian modal scale that is generated from the F major scale is the C Mixolydian modal scale – comprising the notes C D E F G A B♭ C. The interval spelling is 1 2 3 4 5 6 ♭7 8.

When compared to the 'tonic major' (the major scale with the same starting note) the only difference is the inclusion of the ♭7 note in the Mixolydian modal scale. This gives the scale a bluesy, yet melodic, sound.

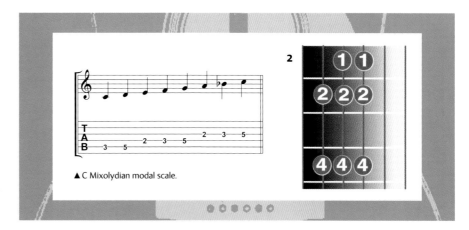

▲ C Mixolydian modal scale.

Further Modes

Learning some of the more esoteric modal scales can be a useful method of making your playing more individual. It can lead you to investigate musical styles and create sounds that you might otherwise leave unexplored; your playing might begin to include elements of Spanish flamenco or avant-garde jazz that you'd never even dreamed of.

Phrygian modal scale

The Phrygian modal scale is quite unusual in that it starts with a half-step interval between the first two degrees. This gives it a typically Spanish flamenco sound. The scale is formed by taking the notes of the major scale starting from the third

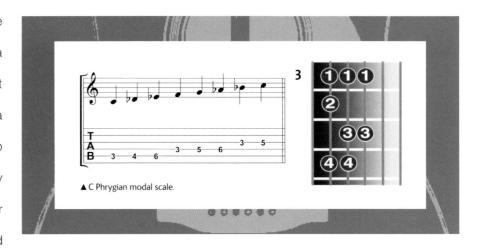

▲ C Phrygian modal scale.

degree. For example, the notes of the A♭ major scale are A♭ B♭ C D♭ E♭ F G. The third note in the A♭ major scale is C, so the Phrygian modal scale that is generated from the A♭ major scale is the C Phrygian modal scale – comprising the notes C D♭ E♭ F G A♭ B♭ C. The interval spelling is 1 ♭2 ♭3 4 5 ♭6 ♭7 8.

Phrygian major modal scale

The Phrygian major modal scale is actually the fifth mode of the harmonic minor scale, but it can be considered as a variation of the Phrygian modal scale: all the

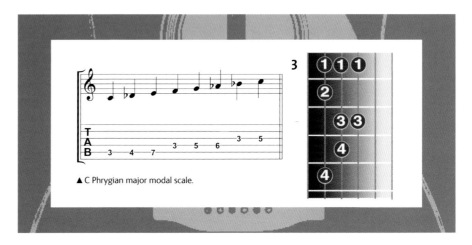

▲ C Phrygian major modal scale.

notes are the same except that the Phrygian major modal scale contains a major (rather than flattened) third. The interval spelling is 1 ♭2 3 4 5 ♭6 ♭7 8. As well as flamenco, it is commonly used in heavy metal guitar styles.

Locrian modal scale

The Locrian modal scale is the mode that starts on the seventh degree of the major scale. For example, C is the 7th note in the scale of D♭ major, so the Locrian modal scale that is generated from the D♭ major scale is the C Locrian modal scale. The C note

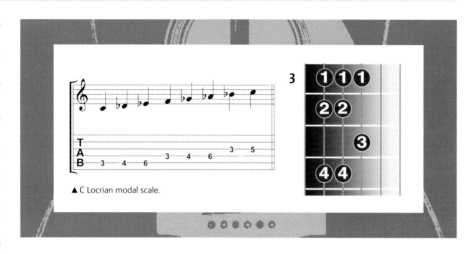

▲ C Locrian modal scale.

becomes the keynote of the Locrian modal scale and the remaining notes in the D♭ major scale make up the rest of the C Locrian modal scale. The interval spelling is 1 ♭2 ♭3 4 ♭5 ♭6 ♭7 8.

The Locrian modal scale is a minor scale with a diminished tonality, making it well suited for improvising over half-diminished chords.

Lydian dominant modal scale

The Lydian dominant modal scale is actually the fourth mode of the jazz melodic minor scale. However, the scale is often referred to as the Lydian ♭7 modal scale. This is because, apart from containing a ♭7 interval, it comprises

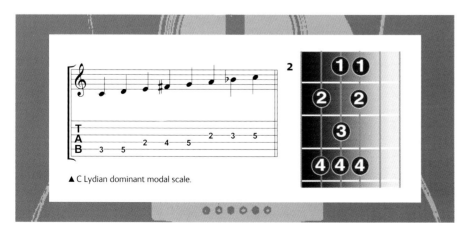

▲ C Lydian dominant modal scale.

the same notes as the Lydian modal scale. The interval spelling is 1 2 3 ♯4 5 6 ♭7 8.

The scale is mostly used in jazz and fusion styles.

Pitch

In this chapter, scales have been shown with a starting note of C. You can alter the pitch of any scale easily by starting the same finger pattern at a different fret. However, you may need to change the fingering for each scale to play it in a higher or lower octave – or simply in a different fingerboard position.

Fingerboard positions

One of the interesting things about the guitar fingerboard is that the same note can be played at exactly the same pitch in several different places on the fingerboard.

If you play through the example to the right, you'll notice that each E note, although at exactly the same pitch, has a slightly different tonal quality. The same applies to scales and riffs – they will have a slightly

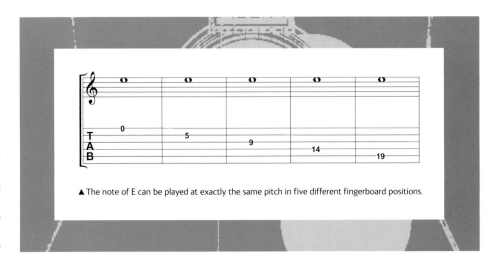

▲ The note of E can be played at exactly the same pitch in five different fingerboard positions.

different tone depending upon the chosen fingerboard position. You will also find that some riffs or licks might be easier to play in one fingerboard position compared to another.

If you're really serious about studying the guitar, you should make it a long-term aim to learn as many different fingerboard positions as possible for all your scales, because this will provide you with the maximum amount of flexibility in your playing.

To start you on your way, here are three positions of the C major scale – all at the same pitch.

Changing octave

As well as learning scales of the same pitch in different fingerboard positions, you also need to be able to play them in different octaves. This will give you a wider sonic range to play across – from deep bassy riffs to high-pitched screaming solos. This fingerboard knowledge will help you play sympathetically with other elements in a song, for example, playing in a range that will merge well with the vocals or other instruments in some sections of the song, while moving to an octave that will make the guitar jump out of the mix in other sections.

Practising scales in a variety of fingerboard positions and octaves will help you develop a good knowledge of the location of notes on the fingerboard; this in turn will enable you to target notes to match with the chord structure when improvising.

Ideally you should aim to develop a practise regime that will enable you, over a period of time, to learn all the scales in this book in all keys and in all possible octaves and fingerboard positions.

As a starting point, the fretboard diagrams below show the same C major scale that is illustrated above, but this time in a higher octave and in five different fingerboard positions.

Introduction

Knowledge of a wide range of chord types will enable you to play songs from almost any musical genre, and will provide a platform for writing your own songs. Understanding the music theory behind chord construction means that you'll be able to explore chord fingerings that suit your playing style, without reliance on a chord book.

Exploring chords

While some players prefer the simplicity of sticking to common major and minor chords, others have made their music unique by exploring the range of chordal variations that can be played on the guitar. Some of the most experimental chord players include Barney Kessel (1923–2004), Pat Metheny (b. 1954), Peter Buck, Johnny Marr (b. 1963), Joe Pass (1929–94) and John McLaughlin (b. 1942).

▲ Peter Buck provides the complex chordal structure that's integral to REM's sound.

Chord fingerings

Because the guitar has a three to four octave range, and some notes can be played at exactly the same pitch in several fingerboard positions, the harmonic possibilities on the instrument are almost endless: even simple major or minor chords can be played in numerous fingerboard positions – each with a multitude of possible fingerings. It's important to remember this, because no instruction books will have space to illustrate all the possible fingering options available for every chord type. Therefore, gaining an understanding of how chords are formed will allow you to devise your own chord fingerings – using shapes that suit your fingers and that work well with the other chord shapes you're playing in the song. Often you'll find that, rather than having to jump around the fingerboard to play the next chord in a song, you can devise an alternative fingering near to the previous chord.

Building chords

Although there are dozens of different chord types that exist in music, all of them stem from the basic major and minor triads (illustrated on pages 60–63). Once you have a good knowledge of the basic triads and an understanding of chord construction you'll realize that all other chords are merely extensions or variations of these foundation chord types.

Tunings

Using alternative tunings opens up a whole new world of harmonic possibilities on the guitar. You'll be able to discover chords that might be difficult or even impossible to play in standard tuning, yet which fall easily under the fingers in a new tuning. Of course, the main disadvantage is that none of the chord or scale shapes you've learnt in standard tuning will produce the same results when played in a different tuning. This means that a lot of effort will have to be put into exploring the possibilities of any new tuning – but, given the tremendous musical potential, you might just decide it's worth it.

▶ Johnny Marr adds texture to his playing by making full use of a huge variety of chords.

Intervals

Intervals are the spaces between notes from the major scale, or other scales. Chords are constructed by combining various intervals. The name of a chord is often based upon the largest interval contained within that chord.

Major second

A major second is the interval from the first to the second note of the major scale (e.g. in the key of C, from C to D).

If you play the major second note an octave higher it forms a major ninth interval. This interval is included in all major, minor and dominant ninth chords.

Major third

A major third is the interval from the first to the third note of the major scale (e.g. in the key of C, from C to E). This interval is important in that it defines the tonality of a chord; a chord that is constructed with a major third interval from its root note will always be a type of major chord.

If you lower the major third interval by a half step it becomes a minor third. Just as the major third interval determines that a chord has a major tonality, the minor third interval determines that a chord is minor.

Perfect fourth

A perfect fourth is the interval from the first to the fourth note of the major scale (e.g. in the key of C, from C to F).

Perfect fifth

A perfect fifth is the interval from the first to the fifth note of the major scale (e.g. in the key of C, from C to G).The perfect fifth occurs in nearly all chords, apart from diminished or augmented chords.

If you lower the perfect fifth interval by a half step it becomes a diminished (flattened) fifth. This interval occurs in diminished chords and any chords labeled with a flattened fifth note.

If you raise the perfect fifth interval by a half step it becomes an augmented (sharpened) fifth. This interval occurs in augmented chords and any chords labeled with a sharpened fifth note.

Major sixth

A major sixth is the interval from the first to the sixth note of the major scale (e.g. in the key of C, from C to A). The major sixth occurs in both major and minor sixth chords.

If you add an octave to a major sixth it becomes a major 13th interval. This interval is used in all 13th chords.

Major seventh

A major seventh is the interval from the first to the seventh note of the major scale (e.g. in the key of C, from C to B). The major seventh interval occurs in major seventh chords.

If you lower the major seventh interval by a half step it becomes a minor seventh. This interval occurs in both minor seventh and dominant seventh chords.

Major Triads

Chords that contain three different notes are known as 'triads'. All standard major chords are triads. All other chords, no matter how elaborate, can be considered simply as variations or extensions of these triads. Therefore, learning all the major triads will provide a firm foundation for learning any other chords.

	C Major Scale	C Major Triad
1	C	C
2	D	
3	E	E
4	F	
5	G	G
6	A	
7	B	
8	C	

The first, third and fifth notes of the major scale make up a major triad. For example, the C major triad is formed by taking the first, third and fifth notes of the C major scale.

You can work out which notes are in any major triad by selecting the first, third and fifth notes from the major scale with the same starting note as the chord, as in the table below:

Major Triads	Notes in Triad	Major Triads	Notes in Triad
C	C E G	F♯	F♯ A♯ C♯
G	G B D	F	F A C
D	D F♯ A	B♭	B♭ D F
A	A C♯ E	E♭	E♭ G B♭
E	E G♯ B	A♭	A♭ C E♭
B	B D♯ F♯	D♭	D♭ F A♭

Although major triads only contain three different notes, strumming three-string chords could result in quite a thin sound, so quite often major chords are played with some of the notes doubled so that five or six strings can be strummed. For example, in this open position G major chord, the G note is played three times (on the sixth, third and first strings), the B note is played twice (on the fifth and second strings) and the D note is played once.

Now that you know the notes contained in each major triad you can devise as many different fingerings for each chord as you wish. To help you get started, there follows one fretbox example for each major triad. Other shapes are shown in the chord dictionary at the back of this book.

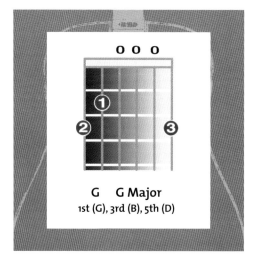

G   **G Major**
1st (G), 3rd (B), 5th (D)

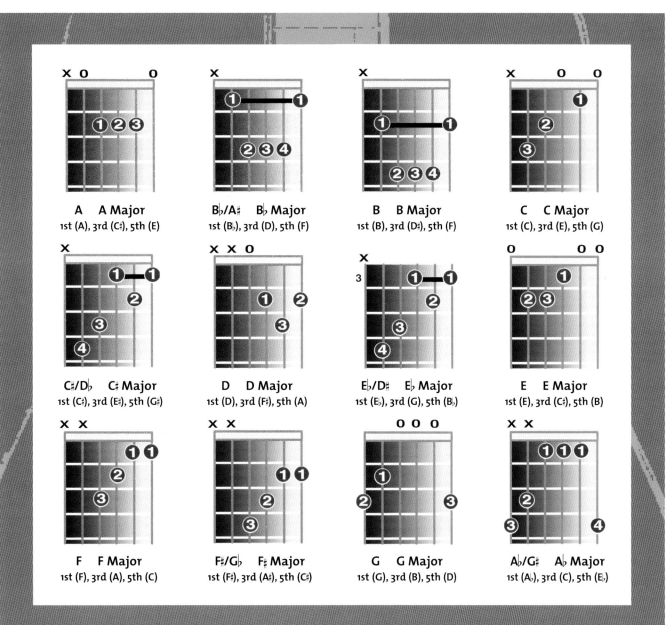

A   **A Major**
1st (A), 3rd (C♯), 5th (E)

B♭/A♯   **B♭ Major**
1st (B♭), 3rd (D), 5th (F)

B   **B Major**
1st (B), 3rd (D♯), 5th (F)

C   **C Major**
1st (C), 3rd (E), 5th (G)

C♯/D♭   **C♯ Major**
1st (C♯), 3rd (E♯), 5th (G♯)

D   **D Major**
1st (D), 3rd (F♯), 5th (A)

E♭/D♯   **E♭ Major**
1st (E♭), 3rd (G), 5th (B♭)

E   **E Major**
1st (E), 3rd (C♯), 5th (B)

F   **F Major**
1st (F), 3rd (A), 5th (C)

F♯/G♭   **F♯ Major**
1st (F♯), 3rd (A♯), 5th (C♯)

G   **G Major**
1st (G), 3rd (B), 5th (D)

A♭/G♯   **A♭ Major**
1st (A♭), 3rd (C), 5th (E♭)

Minor Triads

Minor triads have a more mellow, mournful sound than major triads but, just like major triads, they also contain only three different notes. All other minor chords are built on the foundation of these minor triads, so learning at least the most common minor triads is essential for any rhythm guitar player.

C Natural Minor Scale		C Minor Triad
1	C	C
2	D	
3	E♭	E♭
4	F	
5	G	G
6	A♭	
7	B♭	
8	C	

Minor triads contain the first, flattened third and fifth notes of the major scale. (The flattened third note can be found one fret lower than the major third note.) For example, the C minor triad contains the notes C E♭ and G. Taking the first, third and fifth notes from the natural minor scale will give the same results.

You can work out which notes are in any minor triad by selecting the first, third and fifth notes from the natural minor scale with the same starting note as the chord.

Minor Triads	Notes in Triad
Am	A C E
Em	E G B
Bm	B D F♯
F♯m	F♯ A C♯
C♯m	C♯ E G♯
G♯m	G♯ B D♯

Minor Triads	Notes in Triad
D♯m	D♯ F♯ A♯
Dm	D F A
Gm	G B♭ D
Cm	C E♭ G
Fm	F A♭ C
B♭m	B♭ D♭ F

Remember that although triads consist of only three different notes, you can repeat one of more of the notes when playing them as chords on the guitar.

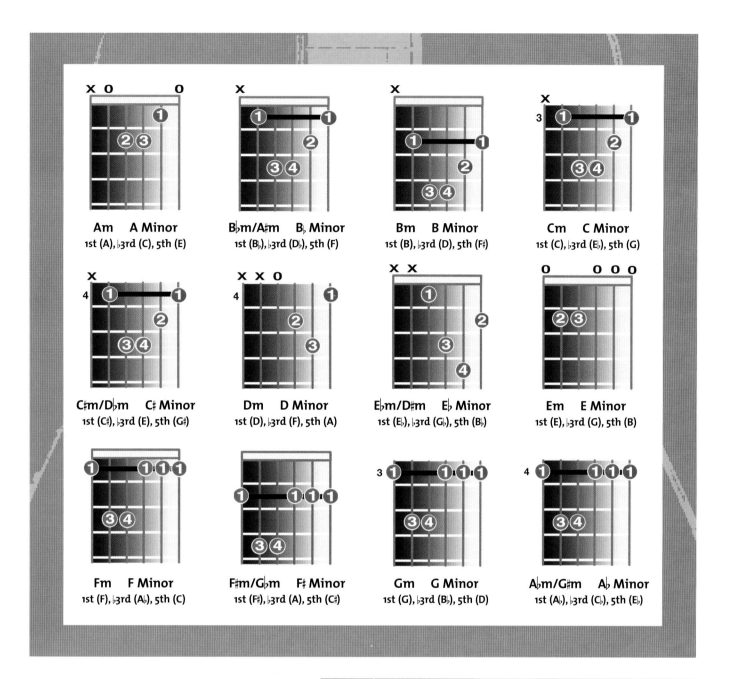

Am   A Minor
1st (A), ♭3rd (C), 5th (E)

B♭m/A♯m   B♭ Minor
1st (B♭), ♭3rd (D♭), 5th (F)

Bm   B Minor
1st (B), ♭3rd (D), 5th (F♯)

Cm   C Minor
1st (C), ♭3rd (E♭), 5th (G)

C♯m/D♭m   C♯ Minor
1st (C♯), ♭3rd (E), 5th (G♯)

Dm   D Minor
1st (D), ♭3rd (F), 5th (A)

E♭m/D♯m   E♭ Minor
1st (E♭), ♭3rd (G♭), 5th (B♭)

Em   E Minor
1st (E), ♭3rd (G), 5th (B)

Fm   F Minor
1st (F), ♭3rd (A♭), 5th (C)

F♯m/G♭m   F♯ Minor
1st (F♯), ♭3rd (A), 5th (C♯)

Gm   G Minor
1st (G), ♭3rd (B♭), 5th (D)

A♭m/G♯m   A♭ Minor
1st (A♭), ♭3rd (C♭), 5th (E♭)

Other triads

As well as major and minor triads, there are other triads: diminished, augmented and suspended (see pages 64–67). There are also some chords, known as 'diads', that contain only two different notes (see 'Fifth Chords' page 65)

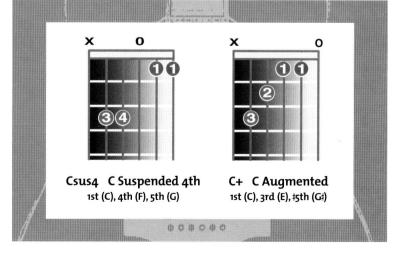

Csus4   C Suspended 4th
1st (C), 4th (F), 5th (G)

C+   C Augmented
1st (C), 3rd (E), ♯5th (G♯)

Chord Construction

Having studied the basic major and minor chords on the previous pages, the good news is that all other chords can be viewed as variations or extensions of these. To convert the basic triads into other chords, all that's normally required is to add to the triad a note from the major scale.

Sixth chords

To work out how to play any major sixth chord you just play through the major scale until you reach the sixth note in the scale. Find out the name of this note by counting up the

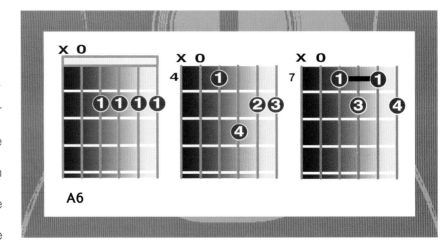

A6

fretboard and then add this note to the basic major triad – thereby converting it into a major sixth chord. For example, to play A major 6 (A6) you should add F♯ (the sixth note of the A major scale) to the A major chord. (You will find an F♯ note on the second fret of the first string.)

Minor sixth chords are formed in the same way, by adding the sixth note of the major scale to the minor triad. Notice that you always use the major scale – even if the chord is minor!

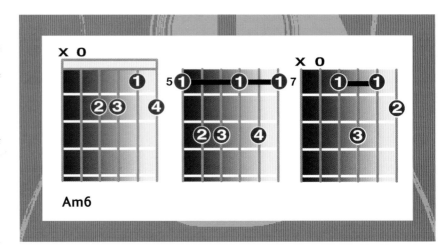

Am6

Seventh chords

There are three main types of seventh chord: major seventh (maj7), dominant seventh (7) and minor seventh (m7). Only the major seventh chord uses the seventh note of the major scale; the other two types use the flattened seventh note of the scale.

The major seventh chord is formed by taking the basic major chord and adding the seventh note of the major scale to it. For example, Amaj7 comprises A C♯ E G♯.

The dominant seventh chord is formed by taking the basic major chord and adding the flattened seventh note of the major scale to it. For example, A7 comprises A C♯ E G.

The minor seventh chord is formed by taking the basic minor chord and adding the flattened seventh note of major scale to it. For example, Am7 comprises A C E G.

Sus chords

Some chords are formed by replacing a note, rather than adding one. Sus chords are a good example of this, as the chord's third is replaced by the fourth note of the major scale in sus4 chords, and by the second note of the scale in sus2 chords. For example, Asus2 comprises A B E, and Asus4 comprises A D E.

Fifth chords

Fifth chords, also known as 'power chords', are unusual in that they do not include a major or minor third. They consist only of the root note and the fifth. For example, A5 comprises A and E.

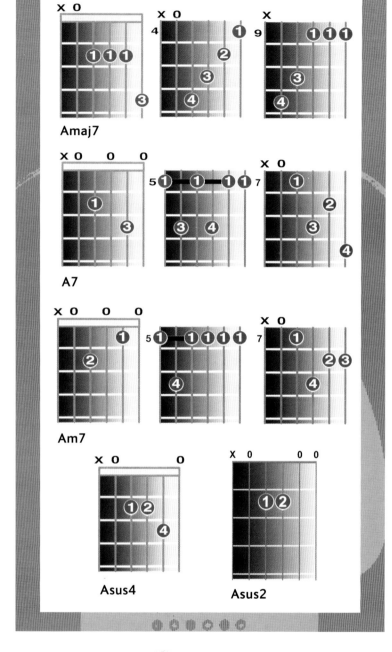

Amaj7

A7

Am7

Asus4　　Asus2

A5

Extended and Altered Chords

Using extended chords, containing five or six notes, helps to create a rich sound and to extend your chordal vocabulary. Altered chords provide an ideal method of creating a sense of tension and adding harmonic dissonance to a chord progression.

Extended chords

Just as seventh chords are built by adding an extra note to a basic triad, extended chords are built by adding one or more extra notes to a seventh chord. The most common types of extended chords are ninths, 11ths and 13ths. Each can be played in either a major, minor or dominant form.

Ninth chords

Major ninth chords are extensions of major seventh chords. They are formed by adding the ninth note of the major scale (with the same starting note) to a major seventh chord. The interval spelling is 1 3 5 7 9. For example, Cmaj9 contains the notes C E G B (the notes of Cmaj7) plus the note of D (the ninth note of the C major scale). Major ninth chords have a delicate sound that makes them highly suitable for use in ballads.

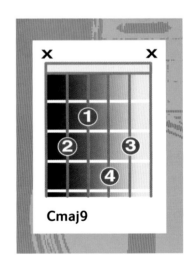

Cmaj9

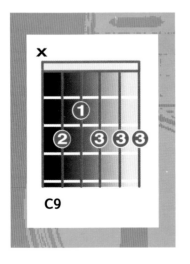

C9

Dominant ninth chords are formed by adding the ninth note of the major scale to a dominant seventh chord. For example, C9 contains the notes C E G B♭ (the notes of C7) plus D (the ninth note of the C major scale). The interval spelling is 1 3 5 ♭7 9. Dominant ninth chords have a rich, bluesy sound.

Minor ninth chords are extensions of minor seventh chords, formed by adding the ninth note of the major scale. For example, Cm9 contains C E♭ G B♭

(the notes of Cm7) plus D (the ninth note of the C major scale). The interval spelling is 1 ♭3 5 ♭7 9. Minor ninth chords have a suave, mellow sound and are often used in soul and funk music.

Eleventh chords

There are three main types of 11th chord as shown here. You'll notice that each incorporates some form of ninth chord, plus the 11th note of the major scale. In practise, the ninth note is normally omitted when playing 11th chords on the guitar.

Dominant 11th:	1 3 5 ♭7 9 11
Minor 11th:	1 ♭3 5 ♭7 9 11
Major 11th:	1 3 5 7 9 11

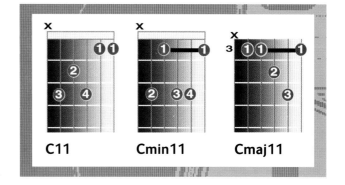

C11   Cmin11   Cmaj11

Thirteenth chords

There are three main types of 13th chord, as shown in the table below. In practice, it is not possible to play all seven notes of a 13th chord on guitar, therefore some notes (normally the 9th, 11th and sometimes the 5th) are omitted.

Dominant 13th:	1 3 5 ♭7 9 11 13
Minor 13th:	1 ♭3 5 ♭7 9 11 13
Major 13th:	1 3 5 7 9 11 13

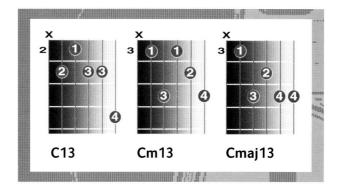

C13   Cm13   Cmaj13

Altered chords

These are chords in which the fifth and/or ninth has been 'altered' – i.e. either raised or lowered by a half step. Altered chords are most commonly used in jazz. These are examples of commonly used altered chords. See the chord dictionary for sample chord fingerings.

Augmented triad:	1 3 ♯5	Dominant 7th ♭5:	1 3 ♭5 ♭7
Diminished triad:	1 ♭3 ♭5	Dominant 7th ♭9:	1 3 5 ♭7 ♭9
Diminished 7th chord:	1 ♭3 ♭5 ♭♭7	Dominant 7♯ 9:	1 3 5 ♭7 ♯9

Chord Substitution

You can make your own interpretations of chords in a songbook by using chord inversions, embellishments and substitutions instead of the original chords. You can also use this approach when songwriting, by starting with a simple chord progression and turning it into something quite elaborate.

Chord embellishment

Chord embellishment consists of varying a chord by substituting a note within it for a new note, or by adding an extra note. Whichever method is used, the new note should be taken from the 'key scale' of the chord: for example, you could add any note from the C major scale to the C major chord without changing the fundamental harmonic nature of the chord. By sticking to notes from the key scale, the new embellished chord can normally be used as a direct replacement for the simpler basic chord without causing any clashes with the melody of the song.

Chord embellishments are often easier to play than the basic major or minor chords. If you lift the finger off the first string when playing an open position D major chord shape, it will become a Dsus2 chord.

Adding an extra note to a chord is also an effective way of creating an embellishment. The ninth note of the major scale is often used, as this brings a certain warmth when added to a basic major chord.

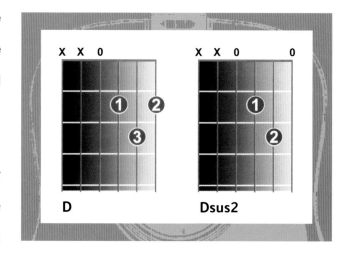

The same approach can be taken with minor and dominant seventh chords. The table opposite gives examples of the most commonly used chord embellishments – none of which will cause problems within an existing chord progression as the basic chord's harmonic nature will not be changed.

Basic Chord	Possible Embellishments
Major	major 6th, major 7th, major 9th, add 9, sus2, sus4, major 6th, add 9
Minor	minor 7th, minor 9th, sus2, sus4
Dominant 7th	dominant 9th, dominant 13th, dominant 7th sus4

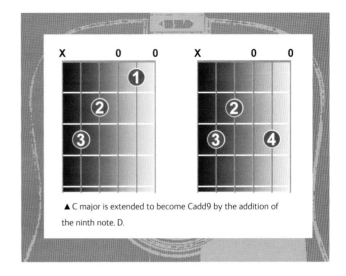

▲ C major is extended to become Cadd9 by the addition of the ninth note, D.

Chord inversions

Rather than play every chord starting from its root note, you can play an 'inversion' by choosing another chord tone as the lowest note. There are three main types of inversion:

• First inversion: the third of the chord is played as the lowest note.

• Second inversion: the fifth of the chord is played as the lowest note.

• Third inversion: the extension of the chord is played as the lowest note.

Inversions are normally notated as 'slash chords': C/E is 'C major first inversion'.

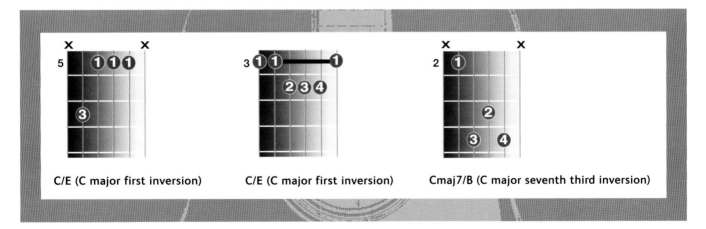

C/E (C major first inversion)   C/E (C major first inversion)   Cmaj7/B (C major seventh third inversion)

Chord substitution

An interesting effect can be achieved by substituting one chord for another. Most commonly, a major chord can be replaced by its 'relative minor' (i.e. the minor chord with a root note three half steps lower). For example, A minor might be substituted in place of C major. Alternatively, a minor chord could be replaced by its 'relative major' (i.e. the major chord with a root note three half steps higher). For example, C major might be substituted in place of A minor.

Altered Tunings

Discover a new range of beautiful chordal harmonies by simply tuning your guitar in a different way. If you sometimes start to feel restricted by sticking to the same chord shapes you've played before, then experimenting with alternative tunings is a great way of generating some fresh sounds and ideas.

Dropped D tuning

There are numerous ways in which a guitar can be retuned, but the simplest and most commonly used is 'dropped D tuning'. All you need to do is lower the pitch of the low E string by a whole step until it reaches the note of D (an octave lower than the open fourth string). You can check that you've retuned correctly by playing on the seventh fret of the sixth string and comparing the note to the open fifth string – they should produce exactly the same pitch.

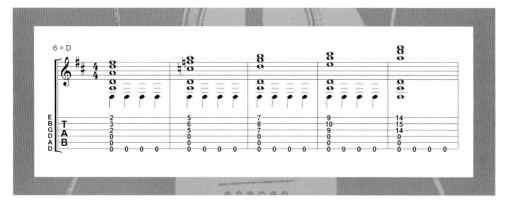

Dropped D tuning is perfect for playing songs in the keys of D major or D minor. Having the low D bass string is almost like having your own built-in bass player – it can add great solidity and power to your sound. To make the most of this bass effect many guitarists use the low D string as a 'drone' – i.e. they repeatedly play this low D note while moving chord shapes up and down the fingerboard. Moving a simple D major shape up the fingerboard while playing a low D drone gives a very effective sound.

D modal tuning

Tuning the sixth, second and first strings down a whole step creates what is known as 'D modal tuning': D A D G A D. When you need to reach this tuning unaided just remember that the A D and G strings are tuned as normal. Playing the open D string will give you the pitch for the lowered sixth string when it is played at the 12th fret. Playing the A string at the 12th fret will give you the pitch to tune the second string down to, and playing the D string at the 12th fret will give you the pitch to tune the first string down to. Once the guitar is correctly tuned it will give you a Dsus4 chord when the open strings are all strummed, thus creating instant ambiguity and a sense of interest. When first using this tuning, playing in the key of D will prove the easiest: by placing the first finger on the second fret of the G string you will make a nice deep-sounding D major (D5) chord. Traditional chord shapes will not work in the same way with any altered tuning, so it's really a case of experimenting to find chord sounds that you like. The secret is to be adventurous and see what ideas you can come up with when freed from the restrictions of conventional chord shapes.

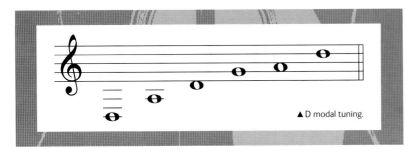
▲ D modal tuning.

Other tunings

If the two altered tunings described above have given you the taste for experimentation, then here are a few other tunings you can try (all shown starting with the low sixth string).

Slack key tuning – D G D G B D (the first, fifth and sixth strings are 'slackened' down a whole step to form a G major chord).

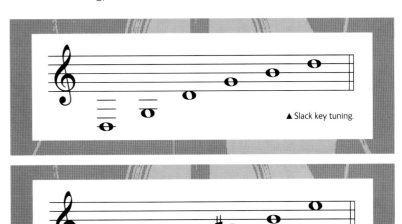
▲ Slack key tuning.

Open E tuning – E B E G♯ B E (the third, fourth and fifth strings are tuned higher than normal to make an E major chord).

▲ Open E tuning.

Open D tuning – D A D F♯ A D (the first, second, third and sixth strings are tuned down so that the open strings form a D major chord).

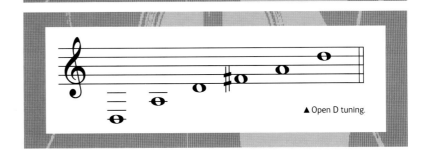
▲ Open D tuning.

Introduction

Once you've learnt the fundamentals of guitar playing, such as scales and chords, it's time to put these into action in a practical music-making setting. Applying specialist guitar techniques, such as string bending and vibrato, will enhance the sound of your performance and enable you to add your own individuality to both lead and rhythm playing.

Lead techniques

Throughout this chapter the most essential lead guitar techniques will be explained in some depth. Some of these techniques, such as hammer-ons and pull-offs, will help you develop fluency and smoothness in your playing. Others, such as vibrato and string bending, will enable you to make your lead playing more expressive and individual. Guitarists who are renowned for their skill in using string bends include David Gilmour (b. 1946), Gary Moore, Eric Clapton and Buddy Guy.

Blues guitarist B. B. King is widely acknowledged as the master of vibrato playing. Other guitarists who excel with this technique include Peter Green (b. 1946), Albert Collins (1932–93) and Paul Kossoff (1950–76).

▶ Blues legend B. B. King uses a
well-practised vibrato technique to
add richness to his playing.

An arpeggio is created by playing the notes contained within a chord individually rather than simultaneously. When playing licks or solos, arpeggios can provide just as important a role as scales, in fact, some players – such as Yngwie Malmsteen (b. 1963), Albert Lee and Mark Knopfler (b. 1941) – rely very heavily on arpeggios in their lead guitar playing.

▲ Dave Davies (centre) used chords in the introductory riff of the Kinks' hit song' 'You Really Got Me'.

Rhythm techniques

Techniques that can make your rhythm guitar playing more creative and exciting are also covered in this chapter. These include topics such as using string damping as a method of extending the dynamic range of your rhythm playing, and playing riffs using chord shapes rather than just single notes. Listen to the guitar playing of Dave Davies of the Kinks (b. 1947), Mick Ronson (1946–93), Angus Young (b. 1953) and Paul Weller for some of the best examples of rhythm guitar techniques in action.

Specialist techniques

Exploring some advanced techniques, such as octave playing and harmonics, can really add range and variety to your playing. If your guitar is fitted with a tremolo arm, experimenting with this can lead to some interesting sonic discoveries. Compare the subtle use Hank Marvin (b. 1941) makes of the tremolo arm with the wild sounds made by Steve Vai (b. 1960) and Jeff Beck.

If you don't already own one, try to get hold of a bottleneck (slide). Using one of these will provide you with musical possibilities unobtainable through normal playing. Although their use originated in blues and country music, many rock players also regularly use slides as an alternative to their usual solo styles. Some great slide players include Duane Allman (1946–71), Ry Cooder (b. 1947), Muddy Waters (1915–83) and George Thorogood (b. 1950).

LEARN TO PLAY
Guitar

Changing Chords

It's one thing to know some chord shapes, but it's a far more difficult skill to change fluently between them without leaving any gaps in between. Luckily, there are a few short cuts you can take to make your chord changes easier and faster.

Minimum movement principle

It's essential that chord changes are crisp and prompt. This might not be too hard when using chords that you're very familiar with, but it can seem daunting with chords that are new to you. However, changing between any chords can be made much easier if you follow the 'minimum movement principle'. This involves making only the smallest finger movement necessary between chords, and avoiding taking fingers off strings or frets only to put them back on again for the next chord. Excess movement between chords is what slows chord changes down; the less your fingers move, the faster your chord changes will be.

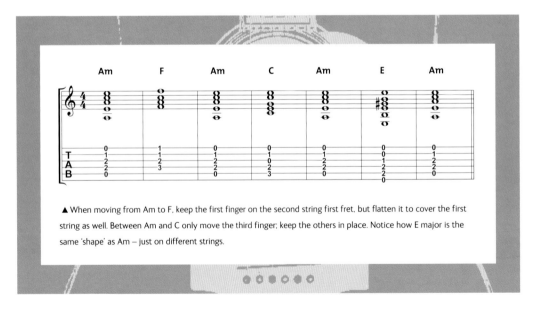

▲ When moving from Am to F, keep the first finger on the second string first fret, but flatten it to cover the first string as well. Between Am and C only move the third finger; keep the others in place. Notice how E major is the same 'shape' as Am – just on different strings.

Some chords have one or more notes in common. For example, the open position A minor and F major chords both include the note C (first fret on the B string). The C major chord also includes this note and, in addition, has another note in common with the A minor chord (E on the second fret of the D string). The chord progression shown above uses the chords Am, F, C and E: notice the common fingering between each chord change; in particular, how the first finger stays on the first fret and how the second finger stays on the second fret throughout.

Even if different chords don't contain too many common notes, changing between them can still be made easier if you look out for any possible links. For example, when changing between the D and A major chords the third finger can be slid along the second string (between frets two and three) rather than being taken off the string only to be put back on a fret higher a moment later.

Following the principle of minimum movement saves time and makes the chord changes smoother. No matter how remote a chord change appears to be, there will always be some kind of link between the

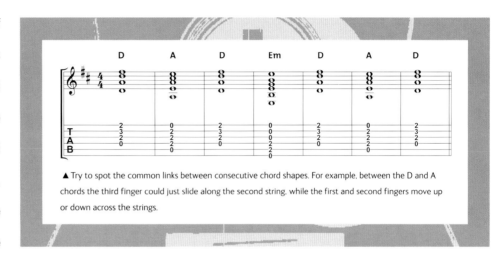

▲ Try to spot the common links between consecutive chord shapes. For example, between the D and A chords the third finger could just slide along the second string, while the first and second fingers move up or down across the strings.

chords; once spotted, this will make changing between them easier.

'Open vamp' strum

If all else fails, there is a 'pro-trick' you can use that will mask any gap between chord changes: using an 'open vamp' strum. This simply involves strumming the open strings while your fingers move between the

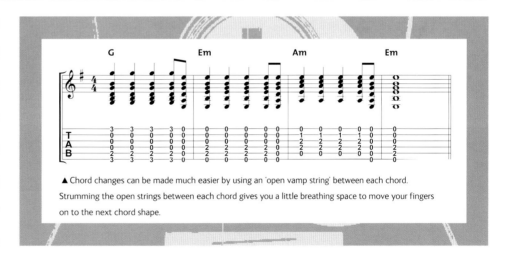

▲ Chord changes can be made much easier by using an 'open vamp string' between each chord. Strumming the open strings between each chord gives you a little breathing space to move your fingers on to the next chord shape.

chord change. While not ideal, it does mean that, crucially, the overall fluency and momentum of the performance is maintained. In fact, some players actually make a feature of this technique to bring out accents within their rhythm playing. Whatever technique you use, the golden rule in rhythm playing when you come across difficult passages is 'never stop – always keep strumming'.

Power Chords

Playing only selected notes from a chord can actually give a stronger sound than playing the whole chord – especially when you add a touch of distortion. You can get a tighter and more easily controlled sound by just using two or three notes from a chord.

Fifths

In rock music, instead of full chords, abbreviated versions just using the root and fifth note are often played. These 'fifth chords' are commonly called 'power chords'. Apart from the tone, one of the main advantages of using fifths is that it's much easier to move quickly from chord to chord because there are only a couple of fingers involved. To play a fifth power chord, simply fret a note on any bass string and add a note two frets up on the adjacent higher string.

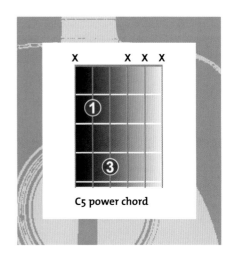

C5 power chord

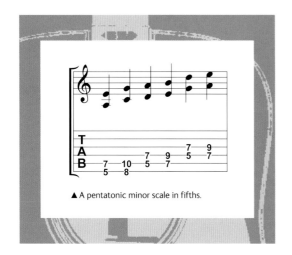

▲ A pentatonic minor scale in fifths.

Songs that use fifths are normally in minor keys, so learn a minor scale in fifths as this will prepare you for the type of progressions commonly used.

To hear the differences in sound between fifths and standard chord shapes, play through the following short chord sequence, first using normal open position chords and then with the chords as fifths. Once you've done this, you could experiment by converting songs that you already play with open chords into a version using fifths.

Seventies rock bands like Judas Priest and Black Sabbath (the heavy metal pioneers) specialized in writing songs based upon riffs played in fifths – often adding an octave note to the chord to get a more powerful sound.

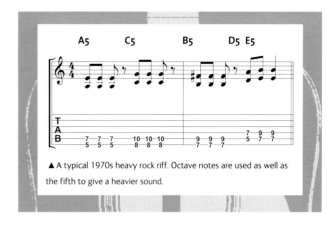

▲ A typical 1970s heavy rock riff. Octave notes are used as well as the fifth to give a heavier sound.

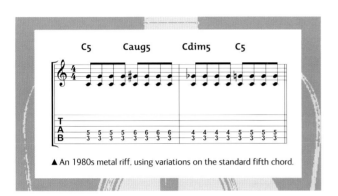

▲ An 1980s metal riff, using variations on the standard fifth chord.

Eighties heavy metal bands like Iron Maiden and Metallica used plenty of fifths in their songs, but often varied the fifth shape a little by using augmented or diminished fifths to create a more foreboding sound.

In the early 1990s, the Seattle grunge sound was based on the use of fifths. Bands like Pearl Jam and Nirvana tended to use a less distorted sound than their metal predecessors and also tended to strum using down and up strokes.

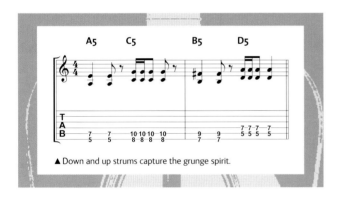

▲ Down and up strums capture the grunge spirit.

More recent rock bands such as Slipknot and Blink-182 base much of their rhythm playing on fifth power chords, often using dropped tunings to create an even stronger sound.

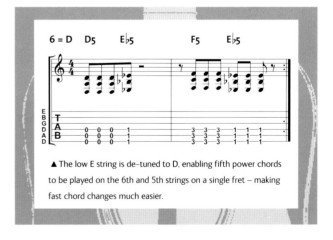

▲ The low E string is de-tuned to D, enabling fifth power chords to be played on the 6th and 5th strings on a single fret – making fast chord changes much easier.

To make sure that power chords are played clearly you need to do the following:
*   Adapt your hand stretch to the size of the fret at which you're playing (fret-spacing gets narrower as you progress up the fingerboard).
*   Move your whole hand (not just reaching with the fingers) when you change fret position.
*   Only strum the strings that you are fretting; beware of hitting unwanted open strings.

Barre Chords

Playing open position chords is a great way to begin learning the guitar, but if you take a careful look at any professional players you'll soon notice that most of their chord positions are further up the fretboard; more often than not they'll be playing shapes known as 'barre chords'.

Advantages of barre chords

Playing a barre chord involves re-fingering an open position chord so as to leave the first finger free to play the barre by fretting all six strings. The whole chord can then be moved up the fingerboard to different pitches. The main advantage of using barre chords is that you can move the same shape up or down the fingerboard to create new chords without the need to memorize a whole host of different fingerings for each chord. Using barre chords will allow you to play more unusual chords (like B♭ minor or F♯ major), which are unobtainable in open position.

Major barre chords

To play major chords in barre form, begin by re-fingering an open position E major chord using the second, third and fourth fingers. Then move this up to different fingerboard positions, with the first finger fretting all the strings on the adjacent lower fret. Most guitars have marker dots on frets three, five and seven, and moving the barre of the E major shape to these positions will give the chords of G, A and B major.

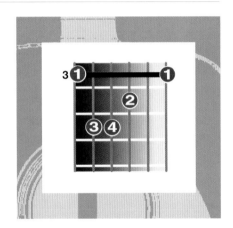

▲ G major barre chord – based upon an E major shape. Move this shape to the fifth fret for A major and to the seventh fret for B major.

In theory, you could play all major chords with just this one barre chord shape. In practise, however, this would involve leaping around the fingerboard too much when changing from one chord to another. Therefore, knowing at least two shapes for each chord type will enable you to play through most songs without ever having to shift more than a couple of frets for each chord change. The second major shape you can convert to a barre chord is the open position A major shape;

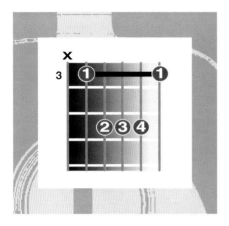

▲ C major barre chord – based upon an A major shape. Move this shape to the fifth fret for D major and the seventh fret for E major.

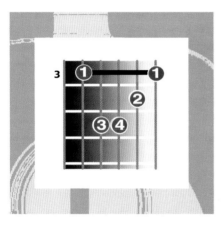

▲ C minor barre chord – based upon an A minor shape. Move this shape to the fifth fret for D minor and to the seventh fret for E minor.

moving this shape with the barre on the marker dots on frets three, five and seven of the A string will give the chords of C, D and E major.

Minor barre chords

Open position minor chords can also be converted to barre chords. The E minor and A minor shapes can be re-fingered to leave the first finger free to make the barre. When the E minor shape is moved up, the pitch of the chord should be taken from the barre position on the E string. When the A minor chord is moved up, the pitch should be taken from the barre position on the A string.

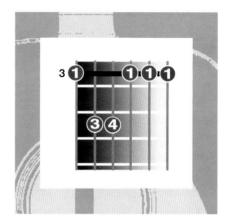

▲ G minor barre chord – based upon an E minor shape. Move this shape to the fifth fret for A minor and to the seventh fret for B minor.

Mixing barre chords

Most songs will combine a mixture of major and minor chords. Whether you decide to use an E or A shape barre chord will depend on the position of the previous and the following chord; the trick is to choose the shape that will avoid any large fingerboard shifts.

Barre Chord Technique

- Keep the first finger straight and in line with the fret.

- The creases between the joints of the barring finger should not coincide with strings.

- Position all the fretting fingers as close to the fretwire as possible.

- Press down firmly, but avoid using excessive pressure.

- When you move between barre chords ensure your thumb also shifts, so that your whole hand position is moving with each chord change.

Chord Riffs

Don't assume that chords are used purely for strumming an accompaniment – in some musical styles chords are quite frequently used to create the main riffs within songs. Some of the strongest and most memorable riffs in the history of rock music have been created using chords rather than single notes.

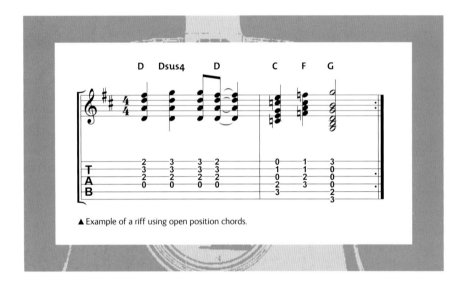

▲ Example of a riff using open position chords.

Creating riffs

A riff is a short musical phrase that is repeated many times throughout a song. Using chords to play riffs will nearly always result in a much more powerful sound than a riff played just using single notes. Listen to anything by the Rolling Stones, AC/DC or the White Stripes to hear some fine examples of chordal riffing. When creating riffs with chords, you'll normally need to use more than one chord per measure in order to give a sense of movement. This might mean changing quickly to a totally different chord, or the riffs may just consist of chordal variations (such as major chords changing to suspended chords).

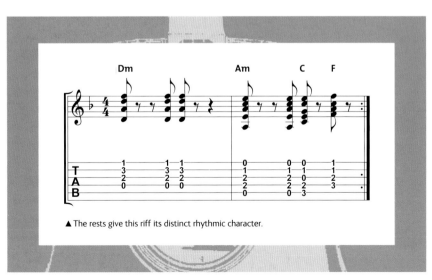

▲ The rests give this riff its distinct rhythmic character.

Using rests

Using rests (silences) between chords will help add a well-defined rhythm to your riff, giving it musical shape and character. Place the strumming hand against the strings when you wish to mute them.

Separating strings

An effective technique for chord riffing is to separate the bass and treble strings when a chord is played. This will allow you to create a piano-like effect, with the bass part clearly separated from the treble.

▲ Begin the E and G major chords by striking only the bass strings, followed by just the treble strings of each chord.

Using power chords

When playing chord riffs it's not always necessary to strum all of the strings – often just strumming the root and fifth notes of a chord (normally the bottom two strings of the chord) will suffice. In fact, for riffing, playing 'power chords' often sounds better than strumming all the strings of the complete chord shape as the sound will be tighter and better defined.

▲ Example of a riff using power chords.

Adding single notes

Chord riffs do not need to consist exclusively of chords: adding an occasional single note, particularly an open bass string, can add variety to a riff and often make it easier to play.

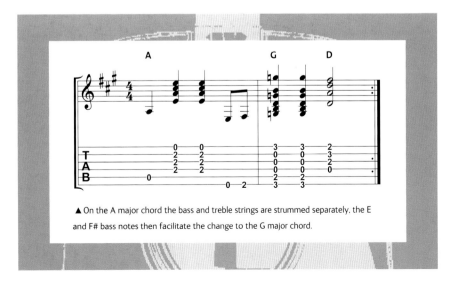

▲ On the A major chord the bass and treble strings are strummed separately, the E and F# bass notes then facilitate the change to the G major chord.

String Damping

Nearly all rock and blues players use string damping as a way of controlling the guitar's volume and tone. By resting the side of the strumming hand lightly on the strings, close to the saddle, a choked or muted sound can be achieved by deadening the sustain of the strings.

Damping technique

String damping is an essential technique for varying the tone and volume of your guitar playing. The technique can be used after a note or chord has been played to achieve a short and detached 'staccato' effect. The technique can also be used to bring out accents in a rhythm, by maintaining the muting effect throughout and releasing only intermittently on the beats to be accented.

Strumming-hand damping

To learn this technique, first strum slowly across all the open strings to hear the natural sound of the guitar. Then, place your strumming hand at a 90-degree angle to the strings, close to the saddle, with the side of the hand (in line with the little finger) pressing lightly against all six strings. Maintain contact with the strings with the edge of your hand, and then rotate the hand towards the strings and strum again. The pressure of the hand against the strings will dampen the volume and sustain – this is known as 'palm muting'. Notice how this is very different from the normal sound of strummed open strings. Now try this again with an E minor chord. When you use string

▶ String damping, using 'palm mute' technique: the edge of the fretting hand rests against the strings next to the bridge; the hand stays in position when you strum, to mute the strings.

damping it's not necessary to always strum all the strings of the chord; often – particularly in rock styles – it's better just to strum the bass string and a couple of others. Vary the amount of pressure with which the side of the hand rests on the strings: if you press too hard the notes will just become dead thuds, but if you press too lightly the strings will start to ring and sustain again. Be aware that it's all too easy at first to pull the damping hand away from the strings as you begin to strum, so losing the muting effect. Although it may take a while to gain control of this technique, and to strike the right balance of pressure and release, it's well worth the effort as string damping is an essential tool in any guitarist's technique.

◄ Palm muting. Measure 1: press firmly against the strings. M. 2: lighten the pressure. M. 3: release damping hand. M. 4: re-apply damping hand, increasing pressure in the final measure.

► Palm muting can also be used in lead playing, resulting in a very staccato sound (with all the notes short and detached). This technique is often used in funk music.

Fretting-hand damping

You can also mute the strings by slightly relaxing the pressure on the strings that you are fretting; the fingers still touch the strings, but do not press them all the way down to the fretboard. This technique can be used after a note has been picked to achieve a staccato effect, or after a chord has been strummed to achieve a chord 'chop'. The technique can also be used to bring out accents, by damping the fretting hand continuously while the strumming hand plays a rhythm – the fretting hand only pressing the chord intermittently, so that it sounds only on the beats to be accented.

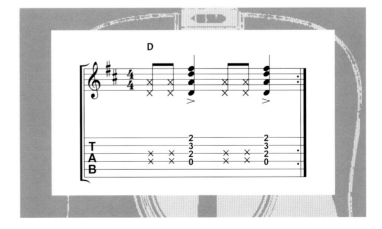

► Fretting-hand damping: the fretting hand begins by touching, rather than pressing, the strings. This causes the notes to be muted. On the accented beats, the notes of the chord are fretted normally so that the chord sounds clearly when strummed strongly.

Slurs

Slurring is a method that not only enables you to play much faster than with normal picking, but also provides a much smoother (legato) sound. There are two slurring techniques: 'hammering-on' and 'pulling-off'.

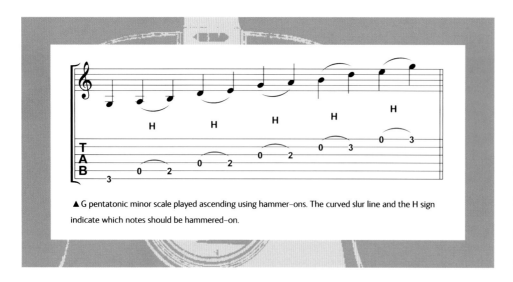

▲ G pentatonic minor scale played ascending using hammer-ons. The curved slur line and the H sign indicate which notes should be hammered-on.

Hammer-ons

To 'hammer-on' a note, don't pick the string; instead, rapidly hammer the tip of your finger right next to the fret of the note that you want. It's important to make sure that you hammer-on as close as possible to the fretwire, otherwise it will be very difficult to get the note to sound clearly. Ideally, the note should come out just as though you had picked it normally. If it doesn't, then you're probably not hammering hard enough – the string should leave a slight imprint on your fingertip if you're doing it right.

Pull-offs

To 'pull-off', first fret a note, then pull your fretting finger lightly downwards until it plucks the string, and the open string or a lower fretted note, is sounded. Avoid just lifting

▲ G pentatonic minor scale played descending using pull-offs. The curved slur line and P sign indicate which notes should be pulled off.

your finger off into the air – you have to make a slight downward movement for the note to sound clearly.

Combining hammer-ons and pull-offs

Once you have mastered the basic techniques described above, try the slurring exercises below, which combine both hammer-ons and pull-offs.

◀ Combination slur. Exercise 1. Two pull-offs lead to an open string, then hammer back on and start again, so that only the very first note is picked.

► Combination slur. Exercise 2. Use a hammer-on, then a pull-off, on each note of the A natural minor scale descending along the fifth string – picking only the first of each three notes.

▲ Trill: alternately hammering-on and pulling-off rapidly between the notes G and A.

Trill

If you repeatedly hammer-on and pull-off between the same two notes it is known as a 'trill'. This is a technique favoured by many rock guitarists, from Jimi Hendrix to Steve Vai.

Slides

Sliding from one note or chord to another is a great way of creating a seamless legato sound that can make your playing sound relaxed and effortless. The technique also provides an easy way of adding passing notes to make your playing more individual and inventive.

Slide technique

To slide a note means to fret it and then, while maintaining the fretting pressure, to move the finger to another fret on the same string without picking the note again. The second note is sounded only because of the continued pressure of the fretting hand; it is not picked again.

In a standard slide you only hear the first and last notes. However, you can also play a 'glissando' type of slide, in which all the intervening notes are also sounded.

Controlling the amount of grip with the fretting hand is the secret to good sliding. You should try to ensure that the thumb at the back of the guitar neck relaxes its grip when you are in the process of sliding a note up or down. This doesn't mean that the thumb needs to be released totally, but simply that it shouldn't be

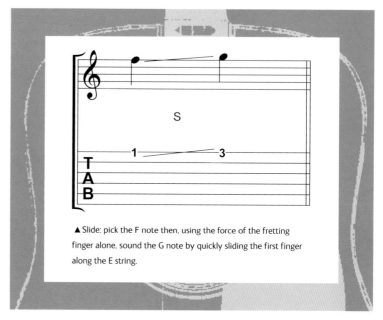

▲ Slide: pick the F note then, using the force of the fretting finger alone, sound the G note by quickly sliding the first finger along the E string.

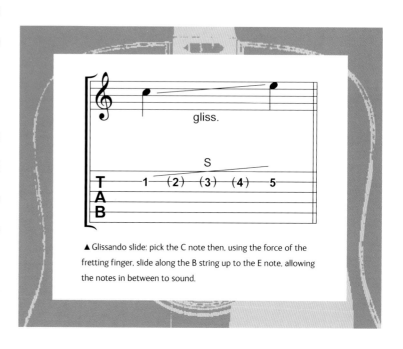

▲ Glissando slide: pick the C note then, using the force of the fretting finger, slide along the B string up to the E note, allowing the notes in between to sound.

squeezing tightly against the back of the guitar neck. However, just as your hand reaches the note that you want to slide into, the thumb should squeeze the neck slightly harder to act as a brake, preventing your fingers sliding beyond the destination fret.

Sliding chords

The guitar is one of the few instruments on which you can slide chords up and down, changing their pitch easily and smoothly; the technique creates a fluidity and smoothness of sound that piano players can only dream of! Because slides

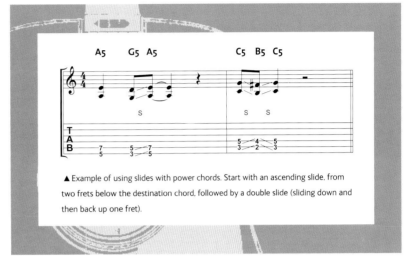

▲ Example of using slides with power chords. Start with an ascending slide, from two frets below the destination chord, followed by a double slide (sliding down and then back up one fret).

are so natural to the guitar they form a core component of any good rhythm guitarist's technique. Slides are used by guitarists in nearly all musical styles, from metal and blues to country and ska.

When sliding chords it is important to ensure that the chord shape is maintained, so that one finger doesn't end up a fret ahead of the rest! The trick is to achieve a neutral balance whereby the chord shape is kept under control, yet at the same time the fingers are relaxed enough to slide up or down the fingerboard.

Playing fifth 'power chords', where only two notes are fretted, is the ideal introduction to sliding chords. Playing power chords with a copious amount of distortion is the easiest way to begin chord sliding, the distortion will provide sustain which will encourage you not to grip too hard when sliding the chords. Using ascending slides (raising the pitch of a chord) is easier at first – the volume tends to disappear quite quickly with descending slides.

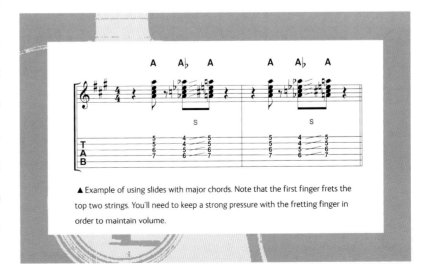

▲ Example of using slides with major chords. Note that the first finger frets the top two strings. You'll need to keep a strong pressure with the fretting finger in order to maintain volume.

Vibrato

By repeatedly varying the pitch of a note very slightly you can achieve an effect known as 'vibrato'. This is used on most string instruments, but it is particularly useful on electric guitar because of the instrument's potentially long sustain – especially if an overdriven sound is used.

▲ Paul Kossoff is well known for his excellent use of vibrato

Using vibrato can turn a plain solo in something that sounds really classy. Vibrato can help you make the most of the guitar's sustain, and make your playing more expressive.

Vibrato is often confused with string bending (see page 90), but in fact they are two completely different techniques (although the two are sometimes played together within a lick). The main difference between the two techniques is that string bending involves substantially changing the pitch of a note (usually by a half step or more), whereas vibrato is more subtle, with the note being only 'wavered' with a very small variation in pitch (always returning to, and alternating with, the original pitch).

Vibrato types

There are three main types of vibrato.

1. Horizontal vibrato: rock the fretting hand from side to side, along the direction of the string. Keep the fretting finger in contact with the string, but release the pressure of the thumb on the back of the neck. This type of vibrato will give you increased sustain with just the tiniest variation in pitch. You can rock the hand either slowly

or quickly, and for as short or long a time as you wish, depending upon the sound you want to achieve. Classic exponents of this type of vibrato include Mike Oldfield (b. 1953), Mark Knopfler, Dominic Miller (b. 1960), Carlos Santana and John Williams (b. 1941).

2. Wrist vibrato: while the first finger frets a note, the pitch can be wavered by rotating the wrist away from the fingerboard and back again repeatedly. This is one of the best-sounding vibratos, and can result in a sweet singing tone. However, it can only be used on notes that are fretted by the first finger. The undisputed master of this technique is blues legend B. B. King. Modestly he states: 'I won't say I invented it, but they weren't doing it before I started.' This style of vibrato has been an everyday tool of blues and rock guitar players. B. B. King tends to keep his thumb pressed on the back of the neck to get a fast but short pitch-range, 'stinger' vibrato. Other players, such as Eric Clapton, prefer to release the thumb in order to achieve a slower, wider-ranging vibrato.

3. Vertical vibrato: while fretting a note, repeatedly waggle the tip of the fretting finger to move the string up and down slightly. You don't need to move it too far and you should always make sure that you return the string to its starting position. This type of vibrato is ideal for adding to a string bend. Once a note is bent you can add vibrato to it to add a subtle enhancement to the bend and add sustain. Peter Green and Paul Kossoff were two of the classic exponents of this technique. Other guitarists employed their own variations on the technique: Buddy Guy and Ritchie Blackmore for example, often prefer to use a very fast 'stinging' vibrato after a bend, while Gary Moore and Yngwie Malmsteen tend to use wider, more extreme vibrato.

Vibrato notation

In music notation, vibrato is indicated by a horizontal wavy line. Sometimes the abbreviation 'vib.' is also written. Occasionally, the word 'wide' might be written to indicate wide vibrato, but generally the type of vibrato used is left to the discretion of the performer.

String Bends

String bending is one of the most essential techniques for any electric guitarist. Nearly every rock or blues guitarist since the 1950s has used string bending as part of their technique, and as a way of expressing emotion through their playing.

String bending is the perfect vehicle for adding emotion, expression and individuality to your lead playing. By carefully pushing a string upwards while fretting it you can alter the pitch of the note that you are playing without needing to move to another fret. Classic exponents include Jimi Hendrix, Eric Clapton, B. B. King, David Gilmour and Ritchie Blackmore, but listen to any guitar-based band today and you'll still hear the technique in regular use in almost every solo.

Bending technique

In theory, you can bend any note in any scale as long as you bend it up to reach another note in that scale. In practise, most bends will be restricted to the next note in the scale – i.e. a half step (the equivalent of one fret) or a whole step (the equivalent of two frets) higher than the fretted note. You can use any finger to bend a note but, so as not to move out of position and lose fluency, it's best to use the finger that you would normally use to fret the note within the scale. If you're executing the bend with the third or fourth finger, it's really important that you use the remaining fingers, on the same string, to give you added strength when bending. Ignoring this advice will mean that your bends won't go high enough to be in tune, or if they do, then you could end up straining your finger.

Bending in tune

In order to get your string bends in tune, it's a good idea to practise fretting the higher note first, and then singing that note aloud, while bending the note into tune with your voice. Another method is to repeatedly pick the string while bending it up very slowly so that you can hear the note gradually bend into tune. The essential thing is to listen as you bend because not much sounds worse than badly out-of-tune string bending! It's important to practise string bends in a range of keys, because the amount of pressure that you need will vary greatly depending upon your

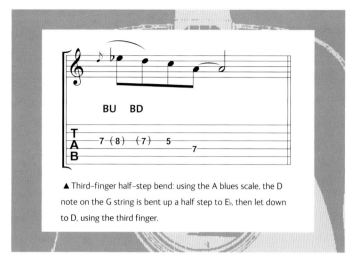

▲ Third–finger half–step bend: using the A blues scale, the D note on the G string is bent up a half step to E♭, then let down to D, using the third finger.

position on the fingerboard. For instance, bending a note on the third fret of the third sting will be much harder than bending on the 12th fret on the same string.

Once you feel confident that you are able to bend a note in tune, try playing through these examples, which start with third-finger half-step bends, before progressing to third- and fourth-finger whole-step bends.

◀ Third– and fourth–finger whole–step bend: using the A pentatonic minor scale, all the bent notes are raised up a whole step. Bend each note slowly until it's in tune, and then hold it there. Use the fourth finger to bend the notes on the second and first string; when doing so, make sure that the second and third fingers are also on the string to give extra strength and support to the fourth finger.

Types of String Bends

- **Choke**: bend the note, and then quickly choke the sound by letting the right hand touch the strings.

- **Hold**: bend the note slowly until it's in tune – then just hold it there.

- **Release**: bend the note up without picking it – then pick it and slowly release it.

- **Up-and-down**: bend the note up and then without re-picking let it down.

- **Double**: bend the note up, let it down, and then bend it up again – but only pick the string the first time.

- **Unison**: while bending a note, fret and play the same note on the next string – or alternate between the two.

- **Vibrato**: bend the note up and then add vibrato by lowering and raising the note repeatedly.

- **Rising**: rapidly pick the string while bending it up very slowly.

- **Harmony**: bend a note while playing or holding a note higher in the scale.

- **Teasing bend**: use several very small bends before fully bending the note into tune. This creates almost a speaking effect – much used by blues players.

Plectrum Technique

Nearly all electric guitarists want to play fast, but this relies upon having great control over your plectrum. If you start by holding the plectrum the wrong way you can slow down your playing for years to come.

Gripping the plectrum

The best method is to grip the plectrum between the thumb and index finger. Position the plectrum so that its point is about half a centimetre beyond the fingertip. Use only the tip of the plectrum to pick the strings or you will create a physical resistance that will slow down your playing. However, bear in mind that if you show too little plectrum you might end up missing the string altogether. Experiment until you get just the right balance. Also, be careful how tight you grip the plectrum. If you use too much pressure your

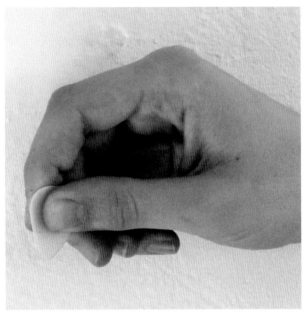

▲ How to hold your plectrum. Notice the angle and amount of plectrum tip showing.

hand muscles will tighten and so reduce your fluency, but if you hold it too loosely you'll keep dropping it.

Hold the plectrum so that it is in line with your fingernail. Avoid holding it at right angles to your index finger, as this will cause your wrist to lock.

Alternate picking

If you want to achieve any degree of speed with the plectrum for lead playing then it's best to use 'alternate picking' as the mainstay of your plectrum technique. This involves alternating downstrokes and upstrokes. Alternate picking is the most logical and economical way of playing, since once you have picked a string downwards, the plectrum will then be ideally positioned to pick upwards, whereas if you try to play two downstrokes in a row you will need to raise the plectrum back up before you can strike the string again.

When alternating down and upstrokes, make sure that the picking action is generated by swivelling the wrist; try to avoid moving the elbow up and down as this will make your picking style much too cumbersome and will hamper your fluency. For fast lead playing, alternate picking and a relaxed wrist action are the fundamental requirements.

Picking exercises

Begin by practising alternate picking on the open sixth string. Once you have a secure plectrum technique you can make your licks sound faster by doubling,

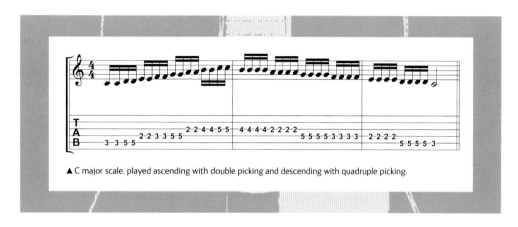

▲ C major scale, played ascending with double picking and descending with quadruple picking.

or even quadrupling, your picking on some notes. The fretting hand may be moving quite slowly, but the lick will sound more mobile because of the activity of the picking hand. Practise this technique at first by playing scales with double and quadruple picking.

A fast rock sound can be achieved by mixing fretted notes with an open string – while the right hand keeps picking with alternate down and up strokes.

Triplet picking

A great way of making your playing sound super-fast is to use triplet picking patterns. Because these patterns cut across the standard 4/4 rhythm, they give the

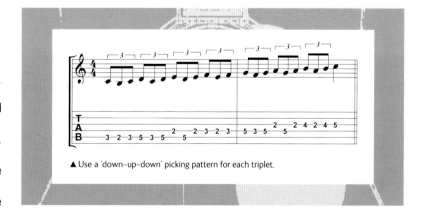

▲ Use a 'down–up–down' picking pattern for each triplet.

impression of being much faster than they really are. This repeated 'down-up-down' picking style can give a rolling or galloping effect to a piece of music. (The term 'triplet' here refers only to the three-part picking action; the rhythm doesn't have to be a triplet in the traditional musical sense.)

Basic Arpeggios

Learning arpeggios is a good way of developing a comprehensive knowledge of the guitar fingerboard. But arpeggios aren't just technical exercises – they're great for soloing and can make your lead playing more melodic by emphasizing the harmonic structure of the underlying chord progression.

Constructing arpeggios

An arpeggio is simply the notes of a chord played individually. Standard major and minor chords, and therefore their arpeggios, contain only three different notes. For example, if you look closely at the open position C major chord you'll notice that although you're playing five strings, there are in

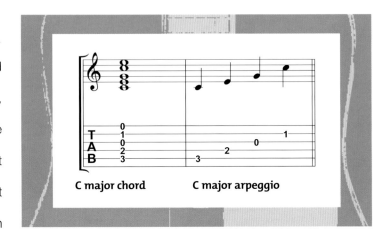

C major chord   C major arpeggio

fact only three different notes (C E G) in the chord. If you play these notes consecutively, rather than strum them simultaneously, this forms the C major arpeggio.

When you're first learning arpeggios it's helpful to practise them in the set order (1st, 3rd, 5th, 8th), but once you know them you can improvise freely by swapping the notes around, or repeating some, to make up an interesting lick or riff, just as you would when improvising with a scale. The really useful thing is that, because the C major arpeggio contains exactly the same notes as the C major chord, whatever notes you play from the C major arpeggio when improvising will always be totally in tune with a C major chordal accompaniment.

Major and minor arpeggios

Each basic major or minor arpeggio will only contain three notes; you can work out which notes these are by analyzing the relevant chord shape. Another method is to take the first, third and fifth notes of the major scale with the same starting note (for example, C E G are the 1st, 3rd and 5th notes of the C major scale and so form the C major arpeggio).

To work out minor arpeggios flatten the third note of the major arpeggio by a half step (e.g. C minor arpeggio contains C Eb G).

Aim to acquire knowledge of all major and minor arpeggios in as many fingerboard positions as possible. Here are some fingerboard positions for C major and C minor arpeggios. They can be transposed to other pitches by moving them up or down the fingerboard.

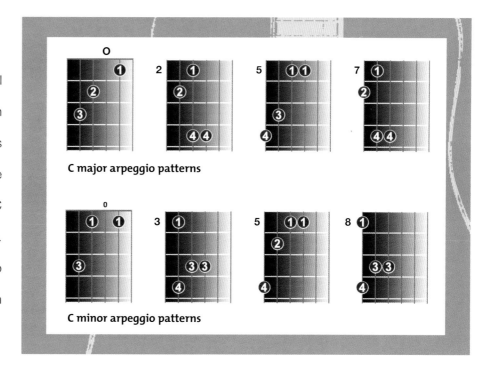

C major arpeggio patterns

C minor arpeggio patterns

Using arpeggios

You can use arpeggios for riffs and lead playing. When you use a scale for a lead solo you'll have noticed that some notes sound more resolved against certain chords than other notes. This problem disappears when you use arpeggios; because the notes of each arpeggio are taken from the chord they will all sound completely 'in tune' – providing you're playing the right arpeggio for each chord. If you've only used scales before, this takes a little getting used to as you'll need to change arpeggio every time there is a chord change.

In a normal playing situation guitarists rarely use arpeggios throughout a whole solo, as

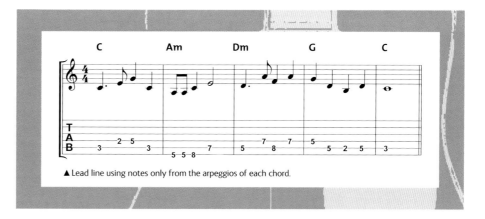

▲ Lead line using notes only from the arpeggios of each chord.

this approach can tend to sound almost too 'in tune'. Instead, arpeggios are used to add colour over just a couple of chords, and the normal key scale is used for the majority of the solo.

More Arpeggios

Once you've learnt the basic major and minor arpeggios it's not too difficult to extend these to learn the arpeggios for other chords, such as sevenths and even extended and altered chords. A secure knowledge of arpeggios will mean that you'll always be able to improvise over any chord progression.

Seventh arpeggios

These are formed by taking the notes of the relevant seventh chord and playing them in a scale-like pattern. There are three main types of seventh chord arpeggios: dominant seventh, minor seventh and major seventh. Although

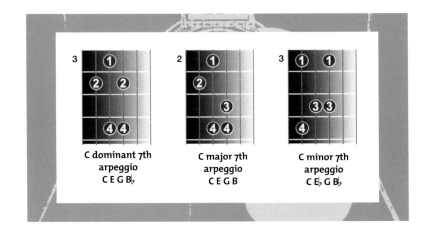

C dominant 7th
arpeggio
C E G B♭

C major 7th
arpeggio
C E G B

C minor 7th
arpeggio
C E♭ G B♭

they have some notes in common, the sound varies considerably between each one: dominant seventh arpeggios are great for blues and R&B, minor sevenths are used a lot in both rock and funk, and major sevenths give a very melodic sound suited to ballads.

Sixth arpeggios

Major and minor sixth arpeggios are commonly used for creating riffs. The typical rock 'n' roll riff on the right is taken directly from the C major sixth arpeggio.

Altered arpeggios

One of the most useful applications of arpeggios is over altered chords, such as diminished or augmented chords. Although you may have difficulty choosing a scale to improvise over such chords, arpeggios will always work –

because they contain exactly the same notes as the chords you cannot fail to play in tune. Therefore, a thorough knowledge of altered arpeggios will prove highly useful if you wish to improvise over advanced chord progressions, such as those used in jazz and fusion. Here are some of the most useful altered arpeggios. They are all illustrated with a root note of C, but can be easily transposed simply by starting at a different fingerboard position.

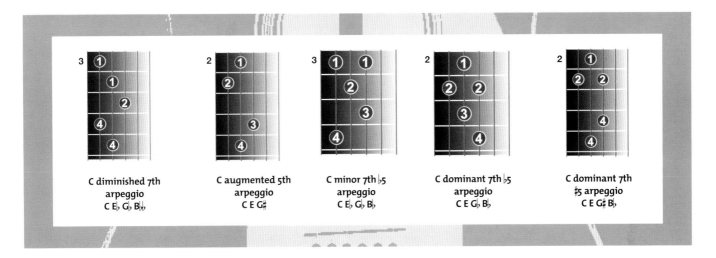

C diminished 7th
arpeggio
C E♭ G♭ B♭♭

C augmented 5th
arpeggio
C E G♯

C minor 7th ♭5
arpeggio
C E♭ G♭ B♭

C dominant 7th ♭5
arpeggio
C E G♭ B♭

C dominant 7th
♯5 arpeggio
C E G♯ B♭

Extended arpeggios

When improvising or creating riffs, using arpeggios over extended chords, such as ninths or 13ths, is an ideal way to explore the full melodic potential of these chords. Scale-based lead playing, unlike arpeggio playing, will rarely be able to exploit the full range of chord tones that these extended chords have available. Below you'll find some of the most frequently used extended arpeggios. Remember to shuffle the notes around and play them in a musical and improvised way when using arpeggios in your lead playing. This way they won't sound like a series of technical exercises.

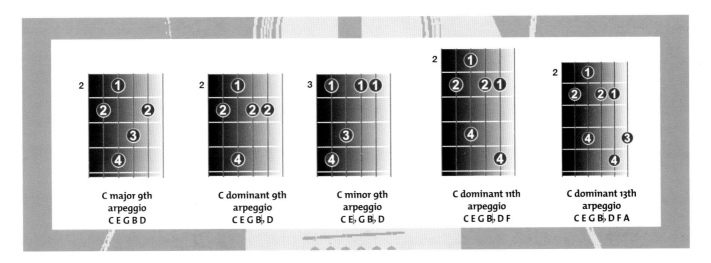

C major 9th
arpeggio
C E G B D

C dominant 9th
arpeggio
C E G B♭ D

C minor 9th
arpeggio
C E♭ G B♭ D

C dominant 11th
arpeggio
C E G B♭ D F

C dominant 13th
arpeggio
C E G B♭ D F A

Octaves

Octave playing is an instant way of giving more power and solidity to your playing, and because of this it is a technique that is often used by jazz and rock musicians alike. Learning octaves is also one of the quickest ways of getting to know all the notes on the fretboard.

Playing octaves involves playing two of the same notes together (e.g. C and C), but with one of those notes at a higher pitch (i.e. an octave above). The fact that the two notes are the same is what gives octave playing its very powerful sound and avoids any of the sweetness that is often associated with other pairings of notes.

Bass octaves

There are various ways in which octaves can be played, but for notes on the bass strings by far the most common way is to add a note two frets and two strings higher. For example, if your original note is A on the fifth fret of the sixth string, then the octave A will be on the seventh fret of the fourth string. Similarly, if your original note is D on the fifth fret of the fifth string, then the octave D will be on the seventh fret of the third string. This system, of finding the octave two frets and two strings higher than the original

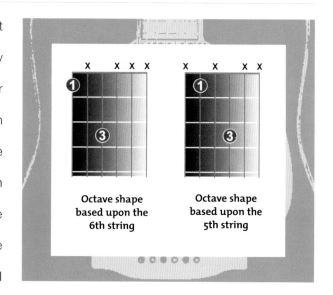

Octave shape based upon the 6th string

Octave shape based upon the 5th string

note, will work for all notes on the sixth and fifth strings. The lower note should be played with the first finger, while the octave can be fretted with either the third or the fourth finger.

The most important technique when playing bass octaves is to ensure that the string between the lower note and the octave is totally muted. This should be done by allowing the first finger to lie across it lightly – not fretting the string but just deadening it. You should also be careful not to strum the strings above the octave note, and as a precaution it's a good idea to mute them by allowing the octave-fretting finger to lightly lie across them.

Treble octaves

The easiest way of playing octaves on the treble strings is to use a similar approach to that described above, but with the octave note requiring a further one fret-stretch. For the fourth and third strings the octave notes can be found by playing three frets and two strings higher. For example, if your original note is G on the fifth fret of the fourth string then the octave G will be on the eighth fret of the second string. This system of finding the octave three frets and two strings higher than the original note will work for all notes on the fourth and third strings.

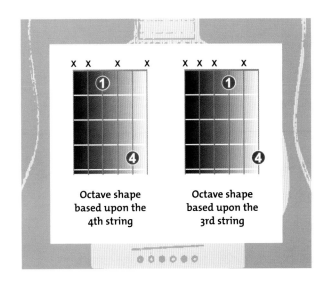

Octave shape based upon the 4th string

Octave shape based upon the 3rd string

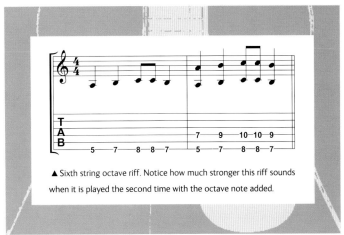

▲ Sixth string octave riff. Notice how much stronger this riff sounds when it is played the second time with the octave note added.

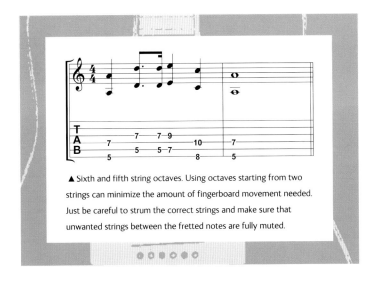

▲ Sixth and fifth string octaves. Using octaves starting from two strings can minimize the amount of fingerboard movement needed. Just be careful to strum the correct strings and make sure that unwanted strings between the fretted notes are fully muted.

Playing octaves

Once you're familiar with the octave shapes shown above, try to play through the examples of octave use given below.

Fingerboard knowledge

Once you're familiar with the octave shapes you can use them to learn the notes all across the fingerboard.

For example, assuming that you can memorize the notes on the sixth string you can then use your octave shape to work out instantly where the same notes will appear on the fourth string.

Harmonics

Harmonics can add interesting bell-like chimes to your guitar playing, and are a useful way of sustaining notes. Harmonics are also a great way of adding an extended pitch range to your playing by enabling you to play notes that are much higher than the pitch you can normally reach on the fingerboard.

Natural harmonics

There are various forms of harmonics that can be played on the guitar, but natural harmonics are the easiest to learn at first. Natural harmonics occur on all strings on frets 12, seven and five (and 12 frets up from these). Natural harmonics also occur on frets nine and four, although making these ring clearly is a bit harder.

The best way to start playing natural harmonics is to pick the low E string and then touch that string right above the 12th fret. Do not fret the note in the normal way by pressing down on to the fingerboard; instead just lightly touch the string directly over the fretwire.

▲ Natural harmonics at the 12th fret.

The harmonics on fret 12 produce the same notes (although with a different tone) as the 12th-fret fretted notes, but harmonics at all other fingerboard positions affect the pitch of the note produced: the harmonic notes on fret seven are an octave higher than the fretted notes; the harmonic notes on fret five

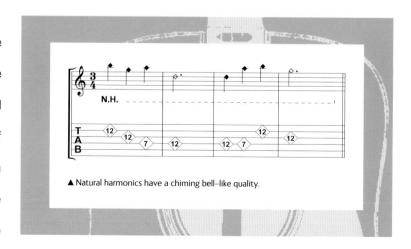

▲ Natural harmonics have a chiming bell-like quality.

are the same as the 12th fret fretted notes but an octave higher; the harmonic notes on fret four are two octaves higher than the fretted notes. Natural harmonics also occur on fret nine, and 12 frets up from the previously mentioned fret numbers (e.g. 17, 19, 24).

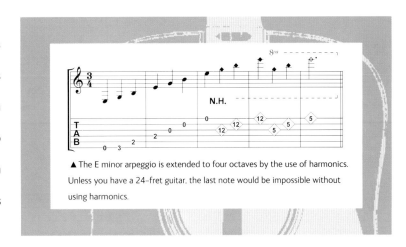

▲ The E minor arpeggio is extended to four octaves by the use of harmonics. Unless you have a 24-fret guitar, the last note would be impossible without using harmonics.

Other harmonics

• 'Tapped harmonics' (also known as 'touch harmonics') are most easily played by fretting and picking a note as normal and then touching the same string 12 or seven frets higher.

▼ Harmonics enable notes higher than those fretted to be played.

• 'Artificial harmonics' are similar to tapped harmonics, in that you touch the string 12 frets higher than the fretted note. However, in this technique, instead of picking the fretted note first, you pick the string with the third finger of the picking hand after you have positioned the first finger over the 'harmonic note'.

• 'Pinched harmonics' are often used in rock for making screeching high notes appear out of nowhere in the middle of a lick. The effect is achieved by fretting a note as normal and then picking the string with the side edge of the plectrum while allowing the side of the thumb to almost immediately touch the string – so creating a harmonic. The quality and pitch of the sound that you achieve depends upon where you pick the string. Start by trying to locate the 'nodal point' – that is the equivalent of 24 frets (i.e. two octaves) higher than the note you are fretting.

Bottleneck

A bottleneck (also known as a 'slide') is a tubular device that can be used instead of the fingers for sounding notes. Using a bottleneck is perfect for musical styles such as blues, country and rock music when you want to slide between notes and achieve smooth glissandos.

Originally, the bottleneck guitar sound was created by running a glass neck from a bottle along the strings. Early blues players sometimes used other objects, such as whiskey glasses, knives and beer cans. Nowadays guitarists can benefit from specially manufactured metal, glass or plastic tubes. The metal

▲ When using a bottleneck, the centre of the tube must rest over the centre of the fret, rather than just behind it.

versions are technically known as 'slides', although in practise the terms 'slide' and 'bottleneck' are often interchanged. Glass bottlenecks give a more rounded tone, but they have less sustain than the metal versions.

Using the bottleneck

Most players tend to place the bottleneck on the third or fourth finger: using the fourth finger enables the third finger to remain free for normal fretting, but this is dependent upon the fourth finger being large enough to support the bottleneck. To reach the correct

► Bottleneck guitar lick in standard tuning. A slide movement is made on the second string from two frets below up to a two-note chord. Be sure to mute unused strings with either the side of the picking hand or with the lower fingers of the bottleneck hand.

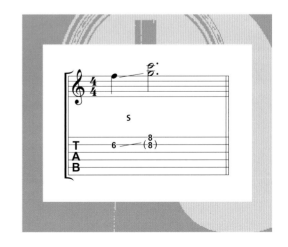

▶ Vibrato is essential for any bottleneck guitarist. It can be achieved by keeping the bottleneck vertical and moving slightly from left to right above the fret, but always returning to the correct pitch.

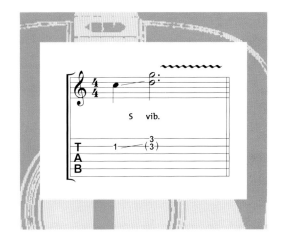

pitch, the middle of the bottleneck should be held directly over the fret, rather than behind it as when fretting a note. The bottleneck only needs to touch the strings; you should not try to press against the frets with the bottleneck as this will cause fretbuzz and result in the notes being out of tune.

Bottleneck is usually played using some vibrato. This is achieved by moving the bottleneck slightly backwards and forwards along the strings above the target fret.

Tuning

So that a full chord can be played with the bottleneck over just one fret, altered tunings are often used when playing bottleneck guitar. The most common bottleneck tunings are D tuning (D A D F# A D) and G tuning (D G D G B D). Using a D tuning and placing the bottleneck across all strings over the 12th fret will produce a D major chord. Doing the same on the seventh and fifth frets will produce the two other major chords in the key: A and G. By picking the strings one at a time as arpeggios you can make interesting melodic licks.

To take advantage of the chordal-based tuning, quite often block chords are used in bottleneck playing – usually sliding into a chord from a fret below, as shown here.

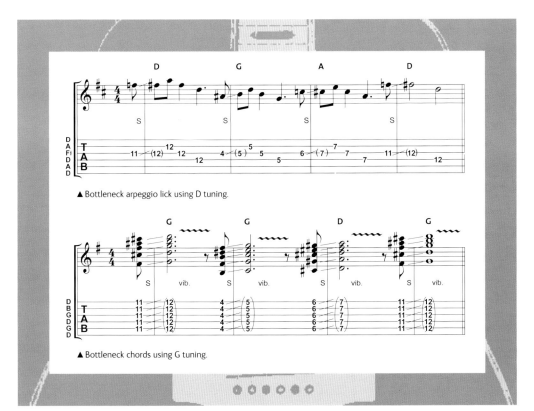

▲ Bottleneck arpeggio lick using D tuning.

▲ Bottleneck chords using G tuning.

Tremolo Arm

The tremolo arm can be one of the most expressive tools available to the electric guitarist. Note that tremolo means a variation in volume, so the arm – which produces a variation in pitch – should really be called a vibrato arm.

To compound the misnomer, the device is often referred to amongst rock guitarists as a 'whammy bar'. The arm or bar can be used in a wide variety of ways, from very subtle vibrato to extreme variations in pitch.

No matter what style of music you might be playing, using the tremolo arm can always add that extra something to give your playing a lift, enabling you to add some extra expression and individuality to your playing. Duane Eddy (b. 1938) and Hank Marvin (of the Shadows) were two of the first guitarists to pioneer the use of the tremolo arm – putting it to good use in their many instrumental hit records of the 1960s. Marvin remains one of the true experts of the technique – called 'the master of the melody' because of his ability to use the tremolo arm to make his guitar lines expressive and vocal-like.

▲ The tremolo arm (or whammy bar) of an American Duluxe Stratocaster HSS

Tremolo arm techniques

1. The tremolo arm can be used simply as a way of adding vibrato (either subtle or wide) to a note, by gently but repeatedly raising the bar up and down. In fact, this was what the bar was first invented for. This technique generally works best on notes either at the start or end of a phrase, or on any individual notes that you might

wish to emphasize – but, just as with a vocal performance, too much vibrato can sound contrived, so use this technique with care and thought.

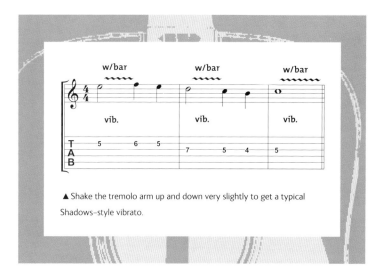

▲ Shake the tremolo arm up and down very slightly to get a typical Shadows–style vibrato.

2. By pushing or pulling the bar a little further you can actually change the pitch of the note, rather like bending a string. You can lower a note by pushing the bar inwards or you can raise a note by pulling the bar upwards. It takes some practise, but you'll soon begin to get a feel for the amount of pressure required in order to reach the exact pitch of the note you require; notice that less tremolo arm movement is required to alter the pitch of notes higher up the fingerboard compared to lower-fretted notes.

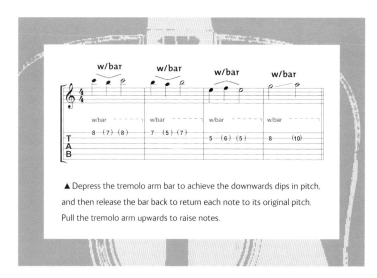

▲ Depress the tremolo arm bar to achieve the downwards dips in pitch, and then release the bar back to return each note to its original pitch. Pull the tremolo arm upwards to raise notes.

3. Use of the tremolo arm need not be restricted to single notes – it also works really well with chords, giving a keyboard-like effect to a single strummed chord.

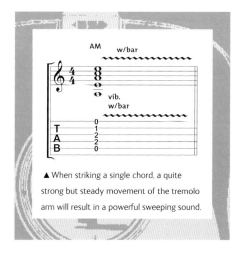

▲ When striking a single chord, a quite strong but steady movement of the tremolo arm will result in a powerful sweeping sound.

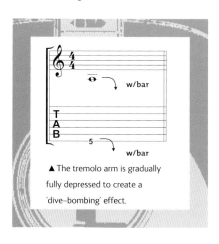

▲ The tremolo arm is gradually fully depressed to create a 'dive–bombing' effect.

4. Rock players from Jeff Beck to Eddie Van Halen (b. 1957) and Steve Vai have extended the range of whammy bar techniques with effects like the 'dive bomb' (depressing the bar to lower the note fully until the strings are completely slack).

Tapping

Rather than using a plectrum to pick a note, you can play it by tapping the string firmly against the fretboard using a picking-hand finger. Rock guitarists, such as Eddie Van Halen, Randy Rhodes (1956–82), Nuno Bettencourt (b. 1966) and Joe Satriani (b. 1956), use tapping as a regular part of their lead playing.

Tapping allows the guitarist to change between low and high notes on the same string, making possible large interval leaps that are unobtainable in normal playing. Eddie Van Halen was one of the pioneers of tapping. His straightforward approach was 'since you've got fingers on both hands why not use both of them to fret notes?' The world of rock guitar has never looked back, and today tapping is a widely used technique in rock circles.

Tapping techniques

If you intend to play an entire solo with nothing but tapping, you could jettison your plectrum and use your first finger

to tap. However, most guitarists prefer to keep the plectrum ready for use between the first finger and thumb, and instead use the second finger to tap notes. Whichever finger you use, make sure that you tap with the bony tip of the finger, rather than the soft fleshy pad to get the clearest sound.

You can angle your tapping finger so that it is in line with the fretboard (horizontal tapping, or position the tapping finger at right angles to the fretboard (vertical tapping) – either method will suffice for basic tapping patterns, but a vertical tapping technique will provide you with more

▶ Eddie Van Halen's tapping technique is showcased on 'Eruption' and 'Spanish Fly'.

possibilities as your playing develops. To get a good tone, tap the fingerboard with a fast, strong action just behind the fretwire.

Although you can perform tapping with a clean sound, it's easier at first to use some distortion because the extra sustain means that you don't need to tap so hard to fret each note.

▲ Tapping enables guitarists to mix high and low notes.

Taps and slurs

Tapping is often combined with pull-offs to create fast legato licks. These are often based upon arpeggio patterns, with the high tapped notes taken from the same arpeggio as the fretted notes.

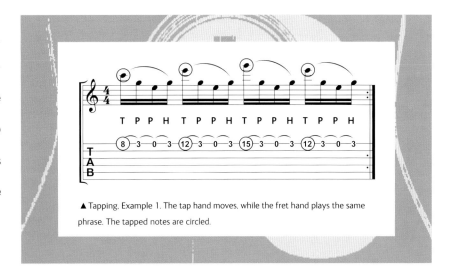

▲ Tapping. Example 1. The tap hand moves, while the fret hand plays the same phrase. The tapped notes are circled.

Guitar set-up

The lower the action on your guitar the easier you'll find it to produce notes clearly when tapping. Make sure that your guitar's intonation is set up accurately, as the large interval leaps that tapping allows will highlight any intonation problems. Many tap specialists use a string damper near

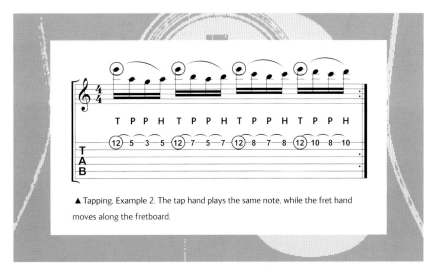

▲ Tapping. Example 2. The tap hand plays the same note, while the fret hand moves along the fretboard.

the nut in order to minimize the unwanted ringing of adjacent strings. Tapping is easiest on an electric guitar with powerful pickups; try adjusting your pickups so that they are close to the strings. Using compression will help disguise any volume imbalances between notes.

Constructing Solos

The real benefit of having studied all the scales and lead playing techniques covered in the earlier pages of this book, can be realized when you begin to put all this knowledge into action by constructing your own lead guitar solos.

Using scales

To solo over any chord sequence you'll need a scale, as this will set the range of notes that will fit with the backing chords. For example, if a song uses chords from the key of C major, all the notes of the C major scale can be used as the basis for your solo. However, you don't need to play all the notes of the scale, or play them in any set order. You should always aim to make your solo sound fresh and inventive, rather than scale-like.

Phrasing

Once you've spent hours practising a scale it's all too easy to keep playing it in a continuous way when soloing. The best method of breaking this habit is to leave spaces between notes so that you start to create short phrases. Within these phrases use notes of different lengths: some long notes that you sustain, balanced by some very quick short notes. This rhythmic variety will add interest and shape to your phrases. To start with, experiment with the C major scale; instead of playing it in strict time, vary the length of some notes and leave some gaps.

Try to incorporate rhythmic variety into your improvisations, remembering that you should also vary the direction in which you play: there's no need to play up the whole range of the scale

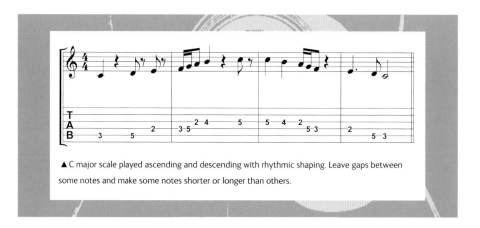

▲ C major scale played ascending and descending with rhythmic shaping. Leave gaps between some notes and make some notes shorter or longer than others.

before you play some descending notes. Adopt a melodic approach in which your improvisation can weave up and down the scale.

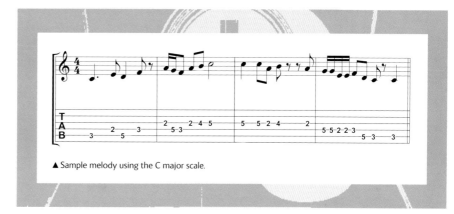

▲ Sample melody using the C major scale.

Using intervals

One thing that always makes a solo sound too scale-like is using notes that are adjacent to each other in a scale. This type of playing gives the game away to the listener – they can hear, almost instantly, that the improvisation is

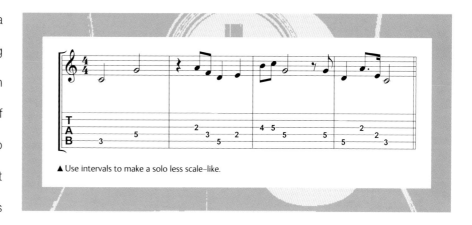

▲ Use intervals to make a solo less scale–like.

derived from a scale. Using interval gaps when playing a scale is a perfect way to break away from this scalic sound.

Repetition

By repeating short series of notes you will begin to establish phrases that will give your solo a sense of structure. By repeating these phrases, or variations on them, you

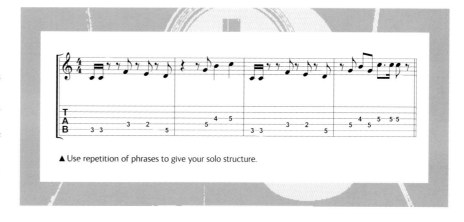

▲ Use repetition of phrases to give your solo structure.

will give the listener something recognizable to latch on to, instead of a seemingly random series of notes with no direction.

Specialist techniques

Don't forget to use some of the specialist guitar techniques that have been covered in this chapter. String bends, vibrato, slides or slurs will all help give your solo an individual character and will turn it from a melody into a true guitar solo.

Stagecraft

Once you feel confident that you can cope with the technical challenges of rhythm and lead guitar playing covered so far in this book, then it's time to think of joining a band and playing your first gig. Spending a little time thinking about stagecraft will mean you are fully prepared.

Cables

Avoid cost cutting when it comes to buying guitar cables. For stage work you need a cable you can rely upon: one in which the connections won't pull loose as you leap across the stage. Choose a cable long enough to allow you freedom of movement around a stage. If you're planning a really boisterous stage act you should consider investing in a radio transmitter – this will eliminate the need for a cable between the guitar and amplifier.

▲ Buy the best cables you can afford to suit your needs, and ensure that they are long enough.

Tuning

Once you set foot on the stage the show begins – so always get your guitar in tune before you come on stage. Obtain an electronic tuner so that you can tune-up easily in noisy environments. You can even set up the tuner in line between the guitar and amplifier so that you can check the tuning between songs.

Noise

Consider buying a compressor, or even a volume pedal, so that you can cut down on unwanted signal noise from distortion pedals or high amp settings, both between songs and during quiet passages.

▶ Using a footswitch will allow you to change sounds without stopping playing.

Feedback

Unless you want to attract feedback (a high-pitched screaming sound) for special effect, try not to stand right next to and facing into the amplifier if the volume is set very high. If your guitar feeds back too easily, ask a guitar technician to check it over.

Balance

Adjust the volume of your amplifier and guitar so that it blends well with the other instruments, but don't be scared of turning it up for solos so that you can be heard when playing single notes.

Listening

It's essential that you listen to what other musicians in the band are playing, so that you can play together as a cohesive unit. Listen to how your guitar tone and volume blends with or stands out from the band, and adjust this to make it musically appropriate for each song.

Foldback

Get to the venue early and conduct a soundcheck so that levels can be set. If possible, use monitors (small wedge-shaped speakers that face towards the musicians) so that you can hear the vocals clearly. At large venues a sound engineer may provide you with a full foldback mix – if so, make sure the sound is adjusted so that you can hear not only your guitar, but also the rest of the band clearly.

Safety

As a gigging musician you could be plugging your amplifier into mains circuits with sometimes dubious wiring. Always use a circuit breaker – it could save your life!

▶ Be prepared and organize all your gear before you go and play.

Introduction

Music starts with sound; the thoughts and emotions you feel when first hearing a live performance or recording are influenced by the sound of the voice or the instruments as much as by the notes they are producing. Part of a guitar sound can be the proper use of effects.

There are few things as stirring as the sound of a great guitar plugged directly into a great amplifier. That said, proper use of effects can add emotional impact for the listener. But improper use can detract as well, so there are a few things to keep in mind when confronting the plethora of sound-altering devices available. Generally the 'less-is-more' principle applies. While lathering on the distortion or delay may sound great when playing alone in your room, it can result in your parts being lost in the mix when competing with bass, drums, keyboards and other guitars. Also, the variety of processors available can be daunting; try to hear the sound that you are seeking in your head or on record first, then look for an effect to create it. This is not to say that just grabbing a pedal and playing with it can't provide musical inspiration of its own sort, but try to avoid using effects just because you can.

► Jimi Hendrix's pioneering electric guitar sound was a result of the 'less-is-more' approach to effects.

The great masters

The rock history books are full of effects masters, some of whom achieved their marvellous tone with surprisingly few effects. Jeff Beck usually uses just a little distortion and delay to wrest an amazing number of tones out of his Stratocaster. Jimi Hendrix used much less distortion than you might think; tunes like 'Little Wing' were built on clean or only mildly distorted tones. A few pedals – Fuzz Face, Octavia, Uni-Vibe and wah-wah – were all he needed to reinvent the electric guitar. At the other end of the spectrum Pink Floyd's David Gilmour and U2's The Edge's (b. 1961) effects and rigs would take books of their own, and Adrian Belew's (b. 1949) style is largely informed by his use of a car-load of effects that allow him to make his guitar sound like an elephant, rhinoceros, cello, trumpet or seagull – anything but a guitar.

In the following sections we will cover individual types of effects: how they work, how to use them and how some of these artists make magic with them. The more fully you understand the principles of each one, the more easily you will recognize their use by your favourite guitarist.

▲ Jeff Beck uses minimum effects for maximum impact.

▶ U2's The Edge favours effects such as delay. compression and pitch–shifting to achieve his band's trademark sound.

Compression

You may have wondered how professional guitarists get their notes to resound so clearly and evenly, or how country guitarists get that 'squeezed-out' sound in their notes. Partly it is the years of practise that have evolved into their technical skill, but another factor is the use of compression.

To understand the use of compressors it helps to understand the difference between distortion and sustain. Distortion is a quality of sound; sustain refers to how long the note, clean or distorted, remains audible. Compression can be used to increase 'apparent' sustain without any distortion.

▲ Adrian Belew's playing with King Crimson and the Bears, as well as his solo material, has made heavy use of compression.

It helps if you think of a compressor as an automatic volume pedal; regardless of how hard or how soft you strike the strings, the compressor brings the signal sent to the amplifier to a pre-set level. As the string vibration slows and the guitar volume drops, an amplifier in the compressor raises it back to the same level as the initial attack.

What does it sound like?

To illustrate how this works, set your amplifier for a clean sound, strike a note and as the volume falls off, turn up your amplifier volume. You will hear the note appearing to sustain longer. To understand why it is 'appearing', as opposed to actually sustaining, try again without turning up the volume. Listen closely. You will hear that the note ends at the same time; it just doesn't remain as loud for as long.

▶ Pedal compressors such as this are used to control volume levels, and reduce dynamic range.

Pedal compressors usually have controls called sustain or threshold, gain or level, and sometimes an attack control. The first knob adjusts the amount of compression. Since adding compression can initially lower the volume, the gain knob helps raise it back up to compensate. The attack control sets how quickly the compression will begin.

Compressor applications

1. For clean rhythms, or country 'chicken picking', you can create a squeezing effect by setting a quick attack.

2. The added sustained volume helps to make chorusing and flanging effects much more dramatic.

3. It can provide controlled feedback with minimal distortion and volume.

You can hear these applications used to great effect by Adrian Belew and Andy Summers (b. 1942).

A compressor will also lower the sound of loud notes and raise the volume of the quieter ones, stabilizing an uneven instrument or player. Compressors are often used on acoustic guitars so that the bass strings do not overpower the treble strings, and in the studio to prevent overloading and to help the guitar stand out in the mix.

▶ Andy Summers' sparse, tasteful rhythm guitar reveals a mastery of effects, including compression, delay and chorus.

Distortion

Distortion is the sound of rock guitar, though even the horn-like tone of Charlie Christian's jazz solos was the product of an amplifier driven to its limits. What is distortion? Without getting into the physics of it, when the ear hears certain overtones surrounding a clean tone it discerns that as distortion.

One way of getting a distorted guitar tone is with a pedal. Discussing these pedals can be confusing because terms like distortion, overdrive and fuzz, are often interchanged; while technically they describe different levels of distorted sound – overdrive being the least amount, distortion next, and fuzz the greatest. For the purposes of this discussion we will use distortion (lower case) as a general term.

▶ Charlie Christian's distorted sound resulted largely from problems with the amplification of the electric guitars that he played.

◄ The sound from an overdrive pedal maintains the character of the original signal.

Fuzztones

Early distortion boxes sounded very little like an overdriven tube amplifier. Dubbed 'fuzztones' due to their buzzsaw-like tone, they have been used creatively by Jeff Beck, Jimi Hendrix, and later by Adrian Belew who showed that you could produce synthesizer, cello and even animal sounds with a fuzz unit. Fuzz has been used for every kind of pop music, from psychedelia to swamp.

Getting the right effect

To emulate the sound of an overdriven amplifier more accurately you might want a distortion or overdrive effect. Some pedals use an actual tube, while others use increasingly sophisticated chips to offer the feel and sound of an overdriven amp. Most distortion devices come with controls marked distortion, drive or gain; level or volume; and tone.

To get the most out of your distorted sound, remember that the level of the input signal will affect the distorted sound – i.e. single-coil pickups will react differently to higher-powered humbuckers plugged into the same pedal. So if your favourite guitarist plays a Les Paul and you play a Strat, you will have to turn the distortion knob up further on the pedal to achieve a similar effect. Also remember the less-is-more theory: too much distortion can make your notes indistinct, especially if you are playing fast. Check out Van Halen or Hendrix and you will find that they are using less distortion than you might think. If your amplifier is already slightly distorted when your guitar volume is fully up, you only need add a little gain on the pedal to make it sing. Fuzz units tend to sound better through a slightly distorted amplifier and/or with the tone rolled back on the instrument.

▶ A distortion pedal produces a grittier, crunchier sound than an overdrive pedal.

Chorus

Think about the rich sound of a 12-string guitar, or the sound of two guitars playing identical parts at the same time. Twelve-strings, and the doubling of guitars, have long been used to fill out recordings. To emulate that sonic girth when you are playing live and alone, with only six strings, is where you'll need chorus.

The fullness of sound and chiming characteristics that you experience in the aforementioned situations are created by notes that are out of sync and out of tune. If you were somehow able to get the strings of the 12-string exactly in tune and pluck them all at the same time, they would not sound nearly as rich. Likewise, if two guitarists play perfectly in tune and in time, the sound won't be much bigger than if only one guitar was playing. It is the delay of the pick hitting one of the doubled strings after the other, and the slight tuning variations, that give a 12-string its distinctive sound, and it is the timing inconsistencies and tuning differences of two guitarists, or an overdubbed

◀ Jimmy Page often used a double-neck guitar when playing 'Stairway to Heaven' to achieve a fuller sound.

part, that expand the sonic field. The chorus pedal was developed in an effort to duplicate this effect in a live situation and uses delay and pitch-shifting to achieve its end.

How does it work?

A chorus device, be it analogue pedal or digital rack-mounted unit, delays the original signal by approximately 20 milliseconds, constantly varying this delay time over a range of up to about five milliseconds (plus or minus). If you take a standard delay pedal, and play a note while turning the delay time control knob back and forth, you will hear the pitch of the note vary. A chorus uses a minimal delay fluctuation and mixes it in with the original signal, thus emulating the effect of twice as many strings being played slightly out of time and tune.

Chorus pedals are provided with at least rate and depth controls. The depth control increases the amount of pitch fluctuation, while the rate knob determines how quickly it fluctuates. Some pedals

▲ A chorus pedal works by mixing a delayed signal with the original sound.

include a blend or level control that allows you to set the amount of effect versus dry signal. This is preferable, especially if you plan to use chorus on solos, where too much can muddy your tone, especially if you are using distortion. Sometimes a feedback control is included to send the delayed signal back to be delayed again for a more intense effect.

▲ A digital chorus unit such as this allows you to control the exact amount of delay time you want.

Flanging and Phasing

The accepted explanation of the origin of the term flanging is that an engineer placed a thumb on a recording tape reel, or 'flange', as they are known in the UK, and liked the whooshing sound that it produced. This whoosh became a favourite sound of the psychedelic era – think 'Itchycoo Park' by the Small Faces.

Our engineer's thumb caused a very short, but extremely irregular delay effect that is simulated in flanger devices by sweeping a short delay (shorter than a chorus – about five to 10 milliseconds) over a wide range (from one to 10, or two to 20 milliseconds) with a certain amount of feedback, or recycling of the delay.

Don't confuse effects

Flangers are confused with phase shifters due to the similar sweeping sound. Phase shifters use an even shorter delay and almost no feedback; this acts like a filter, sweeping the tone of the signal

▶ The Small Faces made use of the distinctive 'jet-taking-off' flanging effect that was perfected in the early 1960s.

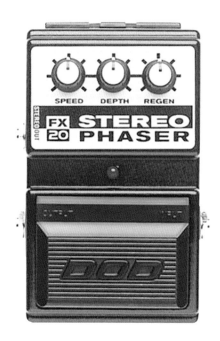

◄ A phaser has a characteristic swirling sound that can be varied with a speed control to provide colour to a rhythm–guitar part or increased to produce a bubbling effect.

continually from treble to bass and back. A phase shifter is desirable over flanging in cases where a more subtle effect is required, or where it is important that the pitch remains unaffected.

A distinctive sound

In addition to the speed or rate controls found on chorus pedals, flangers often have an added control marked feedback or regeneration. This recycles the delay back through itself. Here, it increases the 'metallic' sound of the effect. Extremely fast rate settings on both flangers and phasers can result in a kind of Leslie speaker effect, à la Stevie Ray Vaughan. Setting a flanger for a medium rate, a lower depth, and minimal feedback can mimic a mild chorus effect. A flanger set like this, rather than a chorus, helped define Andy Summers' sound in the Police. A slow sweep with more intense depth and feedback settings will get closer to the Hendrix or Van Halen sound. Eddie also uses a phaser for this type of effect.

Advanced functions

Some more upscale flanging and phasing units will allow you to tap in the time of the sweep to match the tempo of the song that you are playing; some even have a 'trigger' setting that starts the sweep anew each time you strike the strings; this can work well for funk applications.

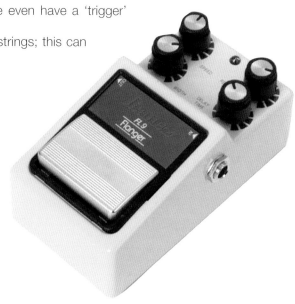

Stereo versions of these effects (including chorus) can work in one of two ways. One version sends the dry signal to one output and the effect to the other. The other version sends effects to both outputs but sweeping out of phase.

► As well as producing a whooshing sound, the flanger also produces a metallic warbling reminiscent of sci–fi ray guns.

Ambient Effects: Delay and Reverb

Your guitar sound does not exist in a vacuum but in the air around it. Musicians are often required to play and record in clubs and studios that are less than acoustically ideal. Luckily, engineers have invented methods of modifying the ambience artificially. (Ambience literally means 'the surrounding air'.)

Ambience

Room ambience is due in part to the time delay between a sound leaving its source (the amplifier) and its return from obstacles in its path. The ear hears the sound first from its source and then again – after various delays – bounced off walls, ceiling and floors. The amount, length and tone of these delays allows the brain to gauge the

▲ Some ambient effects will make it sound as if you are playing in a concert hall, even if you are in your bedroom.

size and nature of the room in which the sound is produced. To counteract the effect of close miking and dead-sounding rooms, engineers came up with some effects to restore a natural room ambience. These effects allow the guitar to sound like it is being played in a huge empty hall, even in a small basement-size club or recording room.

Tape delay

Les Paul (b. 1915) not only invented his legendary guitar, but was also one of the first to discover tape delay. Running a signal into a reel-to-reel tape recorder, he recorded it on the 'record' head and played it back as it passed over the same machine's 'playback' head. The signal coming off the playback head was delayed by the distance between the two heads. This delayed signal, added to the original signal on the main recording, creating a delay effect. By recycling the delayed signal over the record and playback heads, additional repeats were achieved.

Varying the length of tape delay is done in a number of ways. The speed of the tape can be changed from seven to 15 to 30 inches per second (ips), causing the delay to get shorter as the speed increases; or the playback head

can be moved further away from the record head to lengthen the delay. Multiple playback heads can also be used, allowing multiple delays. Recycling the repeats and mixing them further back is one way of creating the illusion of a much larger room.

The 'slap' echo used on early rockabilly recordings was also produced in this way. Used more as an effect than as a means of recreating ambience, it is one of the earliest examples of using 'effects' in recording.

▶ Elvis's early singles were noted for their slap–back echo.

Delays

As with flanging, the discovery of the tape delay effect in the studio created a tremendous demand for a unit that could recreate the effect live. Thus the Echoplex, a portable tape echo, was born. Alternatives quickly appeared in the form of analogue and digital delays.

Analogue delay

Tape and tape heads have certain attendant problems that caused researchers to seek a way of creating the effect using the budding chip technology. They quickly developed 'analogue' delays, eliminating tape by passing the signal along a series of IC chips. This 'bucket-brigade' technology allows tape-type effects using smaller devices (tape delays are about the size of a desktop stereo speaker, while analogue units are more the size of a trade paperback).

▲ Analogue delays appeared in the 1970s and are the link between tape and digital delays.

In analogue delays the sound quality of the echoes diminishes significantly as the delay times and number of repeats increases. They are usable only up to about half a second of delay, after which even the highest-quality units add so much noise and unpleasant distortion that they became pretty worthless. But for many purposes that is plenty. Many guitarists value analogue delays for their warmth, and the fact that the degradation of the signal with each repeat adds naturalness, as well as preventing the ensuing signal from obscuring the original. The Edge and Andy Summers used analogue delays to set up rhythmic patterns, while Adrian Belew placed one on a microphone stand and manipulated the feedback by hand to create insect sounds. Bucket-brigade chips have become increasingly rare, so newly manufactured analogue delays can be quite expensive.

Digital delay

Digital technology solved some of the problems inherent in analogue delays. The easiest way to grasp the difference between analogue and digital is to think about it like this: analogue deals with the signal itself, while digital breaks that signal down into a digital code. The code is then processed and translated back into a signal again before sending it to the output. Since the encoded signal is less subject to degradation, it allows longer delays with less distortion.

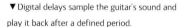

▼ Digital delays sample the guitar's sound and play it back after a defined period.

▲ You can hear The Edge's use of delay on 'Where The Streets Have No Name'.

Digital delays allow delay times of 16 seconds, 32 seconds, and beyond. These extremely long delay times have applications like playing along with yourself, much like Robert Fripp's (b. 1946) heavily effected guitar style, his self-styled Frippertronics. The other result is that shorter delay times are extremely clean, to the point where the delayed signal can be virtually indistinguishable from the original.

Using Delay

As we have already seen, delays have a number of uses. They can be used for ambience, for doubling, for creating rhythmic patterns, and for many other effects. Delay plays a subtle but distinct role in the sound of artists like Jeff Beck, David Gilmour, Eddie Van Halen and Robben Ford (b. 1951).

Confusion in using delay effects stems from an inability by manufacturers to agree on terminology. Most delays have three controls. One is delay length; this can be called delay time, effect, range or simply delay. Another control affects the number of repeats, from a single repetition of the signal to 'runaway' feedback; this knob can be called feedback, regen (regeneration) or repeat. The third controls the amount of effect added to the original or 'dry' signal (a signal with no effects is called dry; with effects it is wet). This may be called mix, blend, delay or effect, depending on the unit. Many delays will also have a dry output and an effect output, allowing an unaffected signal to be sent to one amplifier or recording track, and just the delay signal or a blend of dry and effected signal to another amplifier or track.

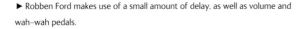
▶ Robben Ford makes use of a small amount of delay. as well as volume and wah–wah pedals.

▲ Ensure that you tailor the amount of delay you use to the room size you are playing. and to monitor this during performance.

Artificial ambience

To sound like you are playing in a garage or basement with concrete walls there are a couple of things to remember:

1. Use a short delay and a number of repeats, with quite a bit of effect signal in the mix.

2. Increasing the length of the delay increases the room size, but you should reduce the amount of effect or the repeats will obscure your original signal. Also, decrease the number of repeats as you increase the length of the delay or you will sound like you are playing in a cave (unless that is the effect you want).

Too much delay will sink your instrument into the mix, to an indistinguishable level. That said, when playing your guitar alone, it might seem that you have your mix right, but when the rest of the band is added the sound becomes too dry. Be prepared to add delay to your signal as a club fills up, since bodies will absorb the ambience.

Digital delays work well for a doubling effect. For this you need the delay to be as clean as possible since it will be mixed equally, or almost equally, with the original. The delay should be long enough to fatten the sound, but short enough so that it is not a rhythmic pattern. Use a single repeat or it will start to sound like reverb.

◀ When you are trying to create a natural ambience remember that delay is never louder than the direct signal.

Rhythmic Delays and Looping

Digital delays are also good for setting up rhythmic repeat patterns. They can turn your guitar into a sequencer, or result in polyrhythmic patterns like those created by Andy Summers or The Edge. Looping delays can provide a single guitarist with extra parts, or can create highly textured, atmospheric pads.

To use rhythmic delays with a live drummer, he or she must be able to hear you clearly because your delay time will set the tempo. Some digital delays allow you to set the delay length by tapping a switch, so you can make adjustments on the fly if the drummer wavers.

▲ When playing in a band with a large drum kit, ensure the drummer can hear the delays otherwise you will lose the beat.

▶ A looping device can add texture to your playing.

Looping effects

Digital delays with longer delay times (two seconds or more) allow you to create 'looping' effects by playing along with yourself, in the manner of Robert Fripp, Bill Frisell (b. 1951) and others. This can be done in one of two ways. The first is to set a very long delay time, with the mix at near equal, and the feedback at just below 'runaway'. This way, as old patterns fade, you can overlay new ones. The second method is to use the hold button (present on almost all digital delays) to lock in what you have played up until that point (called 'loops'), then perform improvisations that will not be recorded. These improvisations may sound very dry unless you are running your guitar signal through a second delay or reverb. Some delays include specific 'looping' functions, and some devices are meant for looping alone.

The sequencer effect

Emulating a sequencer requires only a short delay time and any sort of device will do.

1. Set the device for a single repeat.

2. Set your delay for 110 to 130 ms. If the device doesn't have a read-out use your ears to set a short slap.

3. Set the blend for the same level delay as original signal (50 per cent).

4. Play an arpeggio with one note on each beat.

5. The delay will double the note, creating a sequencer-like pattern.

6. If you wish to accent the original note, back off the delay blend a little.

Dedicated loopers or combination looper/delay pedals often permit the player to slow the recorded loop to half speed or jump it up to double speed. Some devices also allow the signal to be thrown into reverse, for 'backwards guitar' effects.

▶ Listen to *Exposure* by Robert Fripp to hear the first recorded evidence of his pioneering looping technique.

Reverb

From surf music to ECM jazz records, reverb plays a major role in defining a guitarist's sound. Even the lack of reverb makes a statement about the kind of music you are making. In general, it is an effect that moves the sound further away from the listener the more it is applied.

What is reverb?

Natural ambience is not the result of a single delay length or evenly spaced repeats. Sound is being constantly echoed back at us at various delay times, and the echoes are heard not as repeats, but as the ambience, size, type and emptiness or fullness of the room.

The distinction and the identical nature of their repeats limit delay units in their ability to reproduce ambience. Although they are adequate for sounds with little or no attack, like volume swells and lightly picked or strummed chords, the repeats become too distinct and the regularity of their spacing too pronounced when any hard picking or tight, funky chord work is required. The creation of a space around your sound is more the provenance of reverb.

◄ The Beach Boys' early recordings give great examples of the all-time classic use of reverb.

Spring reverb

An early type of mechanical reverb was the spring reverb. Found in many guitar amplifiers, it employs a transducer to convert the signal from electrical energy to mechanical energy, then sends it down a spring or springs to another transducer, where it is converted back to electrical energy. The time it takes to travel the length of the spring adds delay. The spring degrades the frequency response in a more uneven manner than analogue or digital delays, creating a more natural effect. More springs means a more natural effect, and longer springs create longer delays. Tube-driven spring reverbs offer extra warmth. Prone to a 'sproi-oi-oing' sound when subjected to hard attack, these are a must when searching for the true Duane Eddy surf tone.

▲ The spring reverb's sound is created from the physical reverberations of a spring built into the amplifier.

Digital reverb

The accuracy of digital reverbs allows them to simulate virtually any size and type of room, and place the sound anywhere in it. This technology gives us the airy ECM jazz sound (Pat Metheny, John Abercrombie (b. 1944), Bill Frisell et al). Similar to digital delays, digital reverbs take the signal and convert it to digital code, then add delays and frequency changes to simulate the desired room size and to place the sound in the desired location within it.

▶ As well as simulating the sound of different room spaces, digital reverb can also mimic the sound of artificial reverb devices, such as reverb plates and chambers used in studios.

Volume and Wah-Wah Pedals

By placing volume and/or tone controls, like those on your guitar, into a pedal, manufacturers have managed to make those quotidian items into creative effects. George Harrison (1943–2001) and Larry Carlton (b. 1948) have turned the simple volume pedal into an expressive tool, while the wah-wah has provided rhythmic and vocal-like effects from Isaac Hayes' 'Shaft' to Hendrix.

Volume pedal

The volume pedal is simply a passive potentiometer placed in a pedal. Simple though it is, it has myriad uses. At its most basic, it allows you to adjust your volume without interrupting play, maintaining the proper mix with the band. If you are experiencing hum, or buzz, from your guitar, it can act as a noise-gate by instantly lowering your sound during quiet passages.

Many guitarists were inspired to get creative with volume pedals by pedal-steel players, who constantly manipulate one while playing. You will find that your pedal-steel licks sound more authentic if you swell into them with a pedal. You can also create lush pads with a volume pedal and a delay: add distortion and play single low notes for a cello effect, or higher ones for a violin sound.

◄ George Harrison: master of the volume pedal?

▲ Mark Knopfler and Dire Straits had great success with a wah–wah pedal.

Getting pedal-steel effects

1. Plug your guitar into the volume pedal.

2. Plug the pedal into a delay and then into your amplifier.

3. Set the delay for a longer delay (500–700 ms), with six or seven repeats, and the blend at about 30 per cent delay.

4. Play a chord and gradually increase the volume with the pedal from zero to full.

5. If your guitar has a vibrato arm, gently rock it – this will cause modulation as the different pitched notes echo against one another.

Wah-wah

The wah-wah is similar to a volume pedal, but it has tone control. Unlike a guitar tone, the pedal has active circuitry that doesn't merely roll off high end, but actively boosts the highs at one end and the lows at the other. Often rocked in time for rhythmic effect, it can also be used for expressive tonal effects. The riff on the Dire Straits' hit 'Money for Nothing' is the sound of a partially backed-off wah-wah pedal. Accenting the treble on bent notes gives a distinct vocal effect, while slowing sweeping through the range as you play a rhythmic part can emulate a synthesizer filter.

Combining Effects

Once you understand the workings of individual effects you will want to combine them to create sounds you have heard, or to make some exciting new sounds of your own. Whether you just throw some pedals in a bag or use an elaborate rack system, multiple effects can enhance your music. Remember, though – what doesn't add, detracts.

Effects can be combined in a number of ways. Pedals can be thrown in a bag and set up for each gig, attached to a pedalboard, or placed in a rack pedal drawer and triggered remotely along with rack devices. Or, you may want to use one of the many multi-effects units available in either rack or pedal form. Let's examine some of the possibilities.

Carrying a bag of pedals is the most compact way to transport them, but setting up can be time consuming, and they can be jostled and disconnected. Attaching the pedals to a board of some sort can greatly speed up set-up time and add stability. Attaching the pedals with Velcro will allow you to experiment with different effects and orders.

▼ Securing your pedals to a board makes it easy to see exactly what you are working with.

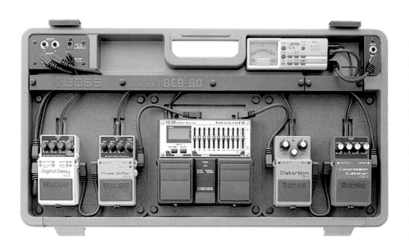

Pedals on a board

No matter how you combine pedals, the order does make a difference. Ultimately the only rule is what sounds good to you, but here is a good starting order for your effects (from the guitar to the amplifier):

1. Compressor
2. Tuner
3. Fuzz
4. Wah-wah
5. Distortion or overdrive
6. Chorus/flanger/tremolo
7. Volume
8. Delay
9. Reverb

Multi-effects unit

Many manufacturers offer multi-effects units containing all those effects that we have discussed – and more. These can come in a floorboard system or a rack unit that requires a separate controller, usually using MIDI, a protocol that allows devices to talk to one another. The advantage of a multi-effects unit is that you can program it to switch numerous effects on and off

▲ Pedal–board cases are a good idea if you are on the move: your effects will be far more portable as well as secure.

simultaneously. Thus, with one motion you could conceivably turn your distortion and delay on and your chorus and compressor off. The disadvantage is that modifying the settings of the effects is not as easy as bending down and turning a knob on a pedal. A common compromise is a rack with a drawer for pedals and a switcher that brings the pedals in and out of the signal path in pre-set combinations.

There is a wealth of sonic modifiers available that we have been unable to cover here, but the ones we have discussed are the basic building blocks of electric guitar tone.

The guitarists mentioned previously, as well as players as diverse as Steve Vai, John Scofield (b. 1951) and Pat Metheny have used these effects to craft their distinctive instrumental voices. You can use them to find yours.

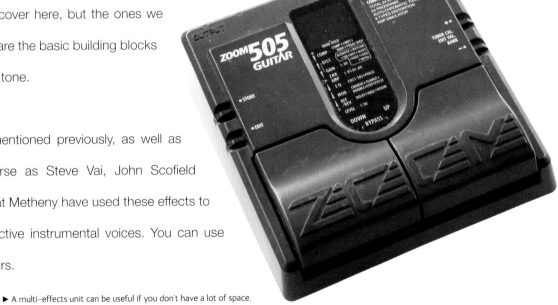

▶ A multi-effects unit can be useful if you don't have a lot of space.

Maintenance

To get the best out of a guitar, it is important to treat the instrument with the care and attention that it deserves. Guitars sometimes end up getting a bit of a rough ride – consider the tragic fates of most of Pete Townshend's early instruments – but even players who are constantly gigging and swapping their gear around need to keep up a certain level of guitar maintenance.

Players often find it useful to familiarize themselves with how the instrument is constructed and the various parts that make it up, from the headstock down to the tailpiece. It is a great help to know how a guitar fits together before attempting to take it apart for repairs, and variations in a guitar's anatomy can alter the sound it produces.

The electric guitar

The electric guitar is a marriage of twentieth-century technology and design with a simple plucked instrument from ancient Persia. These first gut-stringed instruments were carried along trade routes from Asia to Europe. The guitar as we recognize it now was developed from these first instruments, and electric versions of the acoustic guitar were made in the early 1900s. In the 1950s Leo Fender developed the first mass-produced and affordable electric guitar.

The electric guitar is the result of half a century of ideas and imagination. But the first commercially successful electric guitars – the Fender Stratocaster and Telecaster – are still produced today. Anyone transported in time from 1950 to today would see nothing unusual in a guitar built in a South Korean factory just the day before. The design classic has stood the test of time.

◄ First created in 1954 by Leo Fender, the Stratocaster is a design classic.

► The National Style O is the most famous style of guitar produced by the National (Dobro) company.

How do they work?

Electric guitars make sound by creating electromagnetic induction through pickups containing copper wire wrapped around a magnet. The discovery by Michael Faraday and Joseph Henry in 1831 of electro-magnetic induction brought about many technological benefits, including the invention of the telephone some 45 years later. Some say that it was not long before guitar players were experimenting with telephone receivers attached to acoustic guitars in an effort to become amplified.

The first electric guitars

True or not, guitar players have spent forever trying to find ways to get their acoustic guitars heard above the stomping 88-key acoustic piano and doghouse bass at gin joints somewhere in the Southern states of the US. Some players even tried to attach a gramophone horn to the front of the guitar. This development, turned inside out, became the 'Dobro' – an all-metal guitar with a resonator inside the body. During the 1940s, a magnetic guitar pickup was developed and finally mass produced by Leo Fender for the Telecaster (first called a Broadcaster) guitar in 1949 and the Stratocaster in 1954. These designs have become classics. Seth Lover patented his high powered 'PAF' (patent-applied-for) pickup in 1955.

Future developments

More recent developments in technology have brought us instruments such as the Line 6 Variax; a guitar with a computer inside able to instantly recreate the sound of any guitar you need to use at the time. Who knows what developments are around the corner? But one thing is for sure – guitar players will experiment for as long as the guitar is around.

▲ The future of guitar playing? Variax 500 guitars have computers inside them that recreate the sound of any guitar.

If the fundamental design and components of the electric guitar are so old fashioned, why is it still so popular? Why hasn't the guitar become another retro trademark like an old car or a toaster oven? The answer is that nobody ever created a heartbreaking tune on a toaster and that old cars just rust and die. The electric guitar is still young, fun and sexy after more than 50 years in mass production.

Anatomy of an Acoustic Guitar

The acoustic guitar in all its forms has been around for about as long as we have. From simple instruments made from gut and turtle shell to the highly ornamental seventeenth-century lute and chittara, our love affair with the most portable and still the most lyrical of all acoustic instruments remains undiminished.

Woods

The wood used for body, top and neck of the guitar has an enormous effect on the tone and performance of the instrument. Mahogany has been a traditional material for back and sides as it has strength and tone.

The top of the guitar can be made from spruce, which has a warm sound, maple with a brighter sound or koa wood, which has a similar sound to mahogany but with an enhanced mid-range. Rosewood, alder, poplar, basswood and even bamboo can all be used in the manufacture of acoustic instruments.

❶ Top

The top of the guitar is usually made of one piece of close-grained spruce, split in two and laid in half over the top. This process is called 'book-matching'. To enhance the appearance of the guitar a rosette may be inlaid around the soundhole or a thin strip of darker wood may sometimes be inlaid along the guitar behind the bridge.

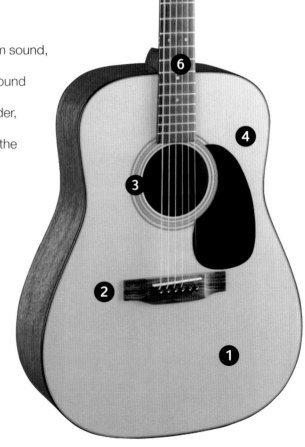

❷ Bridge

Steel string guitars have non-adjustable bridges fixed to the guitar top. The function of the bridge is to transmit the string vibrations to the guitar top, which will vibrate in turn and amplify the sound of the guitar. The bridge is often made of rosewood or ebony and is fitted with a bone or plastic saddle. The acoustic guitar bridge doesn't compensate for intonation.

❸ Bracing

Braces, or 'ribs', are thin pieces of wood glued to the top and back of the guitar inside the guitar body. The braces add strength to the guitar and, depending on the number and positioning of the ribs, can greatly affect the guitar tone. The steel string guitar uses the traditional 'X' brace pattern, with the centre of the X just below the soundhole.

❹ Body

The acoustic guitar has a hollow body, usually of mahogany. The body has waisted sides and, depending on the model, may also have a cutaway on the lower bout to enable access to the higher frets. Binding is inlaid around the body at the point where the top and back meet the sides of the guitar. The guitar is finished with polyester, polyurethane or nitro-cellulose lacquer depending on model and maker.

❺ Neck

Necks are traditionally made of the same wood as the guitar's back and sides. The neck has an adjustable truss rod running from the nut to the heel of the guitar where the body meets the neck. Nylon string acoustic guitars are not subject to as much tension as steel string guitars and so do not require a truss rod. Acoustic guitars are built to the same scale as the electric guitar, but the neck normally meets the body at the 14th fret.

❻ Frets and fingerboard

The rosewood or ebony fingerboard is laid on top of the neck and is fitted with 20 or 21 frets. As with the electric guitar, position markers are inlaid into the fingerboard to aid the guitarist. Dots are also laid into the edge of the fingerboard at the same position.

Anatomy of an Electric Guitar

The electric guitar is not complex, but the pieces of the electric guitar must fit together and match each other perfectly or the guitar will never reach its potential to move mountains. Here are some of the most important ingredients.

❶ Fingerboard

The fingerboard covers the face of the neck and provides a playing surface for the guitarist. The fingerboard can be made of any suitable material but they are usually made of rosewood or maple. Frets are set into the fingerboard to enable the guitarist to find and stop the string at the desired point quickly.

The fingerboard can have 21, 22 or 24 frets, depending on the model of guitar. Fingerboard material also influences the tone of the guitar. Maple and ebony produce a brighter tone while rosewood has a darker tone. Some manufacturers are making fingerboards from synthetic materials such as graphite these days.

❷ Body

This is usually wooden, made of ash, elder or basswood depending on the origin of your instrument. Expensive US-produced guitars are made of rare hardwoods such as mahogany and maple. As good-quality wood becomes harder to obtain, guitars are nearly always made of one or more pieces of wood sandwiched together to create a body of the required depth. Modern guitar manufacturers such as Ibanez have created guitars with no wooden parts, while Gibson has a range of 'Smart Wood' guitars made from wood cut from sustainable forests.

❸ Nut and frets

The nut of the guitar is placed at the end of the fingerboard just below the headstock, where it provides one of the two anchor points (the other being the bridge saddle) for the string. Nickel silver frets are fitted to the fingerboard underneath the strings. The frets are placed at precise points on the fingerboard to enable the guitarist to play in tune. Frets wear down over time and change the tone of the guitar as they do so. The distance between the nut and the bridge saddle is extremely important and dictates the scale of the guitar. Fender instruments have a 25-in (63.5-cm) scale while Gibson instruments have a slightly smaller 24-in (61-cm) scale.

❹ Hardware

Pickups, bridge and electronics are fundamental to the tone of the electric guitar. Single-coil pickups produce a very bright sound; twin-coil pickups have a warmer, less defined sound. Bridges are either fixed or vibrato models (aka tremolo). Vibrato models enable the player to produce amazing sounds by pressing on the vibrato arm to lower the tension in the strings. Tension is returned when the player releases the arm and springs pull the bridge back into place.

❺ Neck

The neck of the guitar is often made from dense maple or ash. The wood needs to be hard and stable as the neck is under tension. Depending on the model of guitar the neck may either be joined to the body with three or four long screws, or by a traditional wood joint and string glue. If the neck is screwed to the body it is called a 'bolt-on neck'. Necks that are jointed to the body are called 'set-in'. Bolted and jointed necks have different tonal characteristics: bolted necks are thought to be brighter while set-in neck guitars have a rounded tone.

Guitar Care

Your guitar is a living, breathing instrument. The wood of your guitar contains hundreds of thousands of tiny holes. These holes trap moisture, swell and contract, and can make your guitar change its mood overnight if not carefully looked after.

▲ A glass of water left in a centrally heated room can stop guitars drying out.

The golden rule is never keep your guitar anywhere that you would not be happy yourself. That means not storing it under the bed, hung on a wall above a radiator or put at the back of the garage for the winter. Seasonal change spells danger for the guitar. Your instrument can experience extreme changes in temperature just on the journey from the house to the car. Invest in a moulded case with a waterproof seal to check the ingress of moisture into the case (SKB and Hiscox have a fine selection). A packet or two of silica gel can be placed inside the case to absorb the moisture evaporating from the guitar. In winter, travel with your guitar in the car rather than the unheated boot.

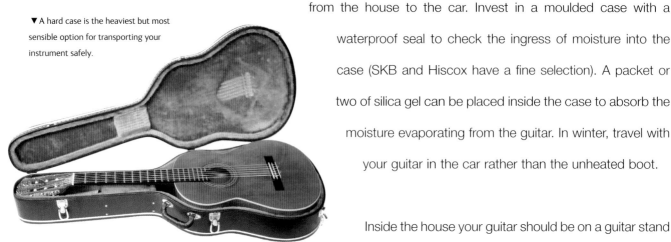

▼ A hard case is the heaviest but most sensible option for transporting your instrument safely.

Inside the house your guitar should be on a guitar stand away from radiators or sources of heat. In dry conditions place a glass of water near the guitar stand and, if you do have to leave the guitar in storage for more than a few months, do not take the strings off! Your guitar was made to be under tension and removing the strings will enable the neck to twist and warp. In short, make your guitar as comfortable as you would be yourself. But do not forget that the best thing you can do to keep your guitar in premium condition is to regularly pick it up and play it!

Keep it clean

When cleaning your guitar, use as little domestic cleaning product (furniture spray or silicone-based polish) as possible. Use a little white automotive polishing compound to take off the grease and grime, then use clean cotton cutting cloth to bring up the original finish. Use a tack rag (a cotton cloth moistened with light machine oil) to wipe down the bridge and other hardware. The tack rag will also do a good job on the metal pickup covers, but watch out for metal pieces that will stick to the magnets and fur up your tone. A clean tack rag moistened with a little WD-40 is as good as any shop-bought product when used along a dirty string. Unfinished fingerboards of ebony or rosewood can be helped with a little lemon oil or olive oil rubbed well into the grain. Finished maple fingerboards can be treated like the body of the guitar.

The plastic parts of your guitar can be treated with the same white automotive compound but may need a little silicone spray polish on a soft cloth when buffing back. Be careful with the control surfaces that may be screen printed 'Rhythm/ Treble' or similar. The printed words can be rubbed off if you use too much force and can't be rubbed back into view.

▲ Cleaning your guitar every time you play is an important habit to get into to prolong the life of your instrument.

▲ Wipe the strings down after every performance or practise.

Fret Care

Frets are both hardwearing and fragile at the same time. With normal use your guitar will last for years without needing a re-fret. Drop it on its face and those nickel frets will quickly acquire more grooves than your dad's record collection. Dented or badly worn frets can, with care, be brought back into line with a crowning file (available from any good luthier) and some fine needle files and steel wool.

▲ Fret files are used to sand down uneven or protruding frets.

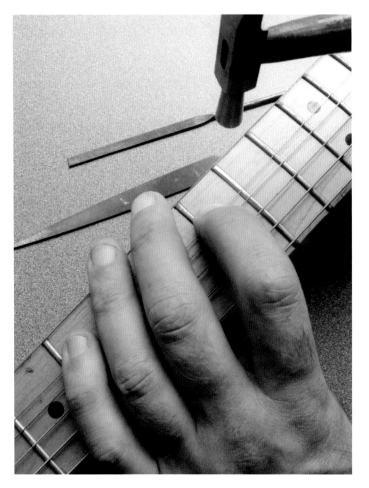

Replacing frets

The key is to carefully draw the needle files over the fret, taking as little material off the fret as possible. When the top of the fret is as smooth you can get it, take the crowning file over the top of the fret to bring back the rounded shoulder of the fret. Finish off with same fine steel wool. This process takes a lot of time and is not easy. The problem is that taking material off the fret means lowering its height. A string stopped at this fret will probably buzz on the fret in front because it can no longer clear it. If this is happening you have a choice. You could lower all the frets on the neck, but this is a bad choice as it will take a lot of time, is highly

◄ A loose fret can cause string buzzing. Tap the loose fret into place with a small hammer or remove carefully with pliers.

destructive, completely irreversible and will probably be disastrous for your guitar. The other thing to do is to raise or re-adjust the string height to clear all the frets. This is much simpler, is completely non-destructive and could even improve the sound of your guitar. It will be harder to play – but at least it will be playable and you can spend your time making enough money from all those gigs to pay for a complete re-fret.

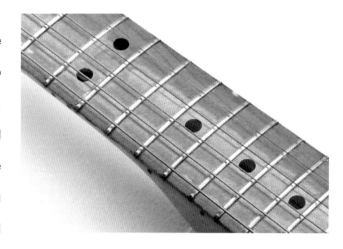

▲ Frets are metal strips placed across the radius of a guitar's fingerboard to mark out notes a half tone apart.

Cleaning frets

Polished frets are impressive and one of the best ways to get a great reaction from a customer is to make sure that when you open the case on their newly set-up instrument, the frets are polished enough to see your face in them. Shop polishes like this are simple to achieve and can look fantastic.

Start by taping between the frets with low-tack masking tape until you can't see the wooden fingerboard and only the crowns of each fret are exposed. Use a pad of very fine 000-grade synthetic steel wool, available from DIY stores. Wipe (do not rub) over the tops of the frets along the length of the guitar neck using minimal pressure. Brush off the grime that has collected by each fret and carefully polish the sides of each fret using a soft toothbrush if necessary. Do not be tempted to use any metal polish, particularly Brasso or anything with abrasive qualities. This kind of polish is too much for the nickel silver. Even worse, the residue will work its way on to the fingerboard – a

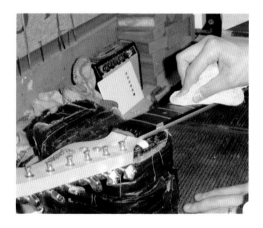

nightmare on an open-grained rosewood board. Use only hard cotton cutting cloth and some firm rubbing to bring the nickel silver right up.

Remove the tape, wipe the fingerboard over with lemon oil, wipe down again, restring, check action, intonation and relief … and you are done!

◀ Your guitar's fretboard can accumulate a lot of dirt and grease from your fingers, so it is important to clean it regularly.

Choosing Strings

Strings are the voice of your guitar. The right strings will make your guitar sound great, feel fantastic and last much longer than a cheaper set. The wrong strings will sound terrible, will turn your expensive guitar into an unplayable plank and, worst of all, will break just at the worst moment. So buy the most expensive set you can afford. Your guitar and your ears will thank you for it.

▼ Try different sets of strings for a week or two, to see if they are comfortable.

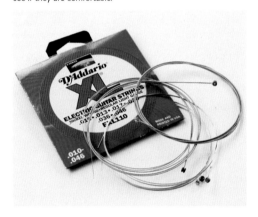

Strings for electric and acoustic guitars are either 'wound' (rhymes with round) or 'plain'. The difference is that wound strings are in fact two separate strings, one wound around the other. Plain strings are simply a single length of wire. Both wound and plain strings have a ball attached to one end of the string. This enables the string to be attached to the guitar bridge. Nylon strings mostly do not have this ball end, although some beginner's sets do have a ball as it makes the string easier to attach.

Strings for electric guitars

If playing an electric guitar choose a medium set of .009-gauge nickel-steel strings and play with them for a week or so. If they do not feel quite right change up a gauge to .010 or down a gauge to .008.

Strings are sold in packs of six and described by the weight of the first (thinnest or highest in pitch) string. A set of .009 gauge strings will have a top E just nine-thousandths of an inch thick. The other strings are graded to suit. Each of the strings in a .010-gauge set will be heavier than their equivalent in a .009 set and much heavier than in a .008-gauge set.

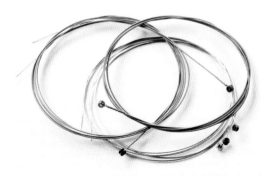

▶ The gauge of a string is the technical term for its width.

Ernie Ball and other manufacturers make hybrid sets. For instance, a 'heavy bottom/skinny top' set has the three highest strings from a light-gauge set (.008) and the lower strings from a heavier set. Some players like this bottom-heavy feel and sound. The trade-off is always feel against stability. Thinner .008 or even .007 strings feel easy on your fingers but quickly go out of tune and break. Heavier .010 or .011 strings are harder work but last much longer and sound louder. One thing that Jimi Hendrix, Stevie Ray Vaughan and many other fantastic players have in common is that they all had big, strong fingers and used heavy strings.

Strings for acoustic guitars

Acoustic guitar strings are also sold in light, medium and heavy sets. However, acoustic sets are always heavier than electric. An extra-light set of .010 acoustic strings is a medium-weight electric set and so on. Acoustic string sets have two other major differences. Firstly, the wound strings are usually made of bronze and steel alloy instead of nickel-silver. This has a brighter sound more suited to acoustic music. Secondly, the third string (G) is wound instead of the plain G in an electric set.

▲ Bronze string are usually used with acoustic guitars.

Nylon strings are used on classical guitars. Nylon produces a round, mellow sound which is preferred for classical, Latin and many pop/folk styles. This type of string requires a lower string tension, making a classical guitar easier to play than a steel-string acoustic. The longer string length from saddle to nut enhances the bass response and sustain.

◀ Nylon strings are used on classical guitars for a softer tone.

Fitting Strings: Acoustic

To fit new strings on an acoustic guitar, place the instrument on a clean, flat surface – a workbench, table or even your knee. Loosen the strings using the (tuning) machine heads until the end of the string can be pulled back through the centre hole. At the other end of the guitar remove the wooden or plastic bridge pin using a bridge–pin remover/string-winding tool and keep safely. The ball end can now be pulled out of the bridge and the string is free from the guitar.

▲ When changing a string on an acoustic guitar, first remove the pin that holds it in place.

Clean it up

Repeat this process for each string and discard the old set safely. Before fitting the new set, take a few minutes to wipe down the fingerboard. Use a soft cloth with some lemon or olive oil, or even a specialist fingerboard cleaner, to remove the dirt from between the frets. Buff the fingerboard and frets with a soft cloth but resist the urge to take metal cleaner or polish to the frets. If shiny frets are a must, wipe frets gently with 000-gauge synthetic steel wool and buff with cotton cutting cloth available from specialist carpentry or finishing suppliers (or an old cotton shirt will do).

Attach the string

Take the thickest string from the packet of new strings and uncoil. Bend the new string 30 degrees, one inch from the ball end and push the ball end into the first hole in the bridge. Seat the bridge pin in the hole and pull the string gently. Remember that the bridge pin is not there to hold the string down. The pin simply pushes the string against the side of the hole, thereby trapping the ball end under the bridge. If the pin keeps slipping out, buy a new set from your local guitar store. Wooden pins are always better than plastic.

Wind it through

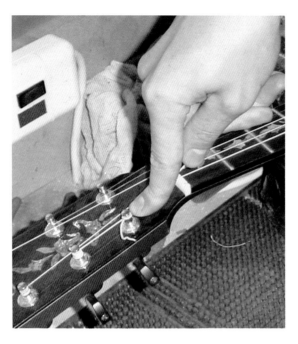

▲ Once the new string has been inserted through the capstan, ensure enough slack has been left to wind it round the post.

With the string attached under the bridge it's time to take the other end of the string over the bridge saddle, up the fingerboard, over the nut and then push it through the hole in the first machine-head. Turn the machine-head

▲ A fast winder is a simple device that lets you quickly wind the capstan of the tuning peg, winding the string evenly.

key until the hole is pointing towards the string, then pass the first few inches of string through the head. The actual amount of string to pass through the head depends on which string it is in the set, the scale of your guitar, the weight of the string and even the manufacturer. Only experience will give you that perfect 'one, three, three, five, eight, eight' winding – and even guitar players with many years experience get it badly wrong sometimes. Always aim for at least four windings on any plain string, two windings on any wound string. Ensure that the windings are neat and placed on top of each other; never leave so much loose that the new winding is lying on top of the string already wound round the post.

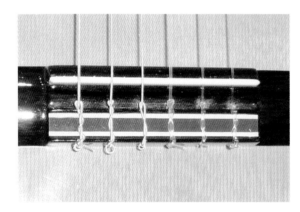

▲ This is how the strings on an acoustic guitar should appear once secured.

Finishing off

Finally, when all the strings are fitted to the guitar take a pair of side cutters and give your guitar a haircut. Six inches of wire in the eyeball is enough to take the edge off anyone's day!

Fitting Strings: Electric

Electric guitar players love to abuse and destroy their strings as quickly as possible. Unlike acoustic players, electric guitar players believe that two gigs is a very long time between string changes and that 'medium weight' .013 strings are best left to bass players. Fit your electric guitar strings so that they will come up to tune quickly, stay there and can be replaced just as quickly – ideally in the time it takes to sing a chorus of 'Living on a Prayer' and at the same time!

Attach the string

Pass the ball end through the bridge of the guitar, either from the back if you have a Stratocaster, Telecaster or some other model with a through-body bridge, or through the back of the bridge as fitted to Les Paul, PRS and other solid-top models. Tug the string firmly a couple of times to seat the ball end and pass the string up to the machine heads. As usual, turn the machine head key until the hole in the shaft is pointing down at the string.

▲ Push the string through the bridge block in the back of the guitar and up through the hole in the centre of the saddle.

▲ Fast winders can help you wind new strings round the post.

Wind it through

Pass the string through the machine head but leave enough slack to enable the string to be pulled about three inches from the fingerboard. Bring the loose end clockwise around the shaft and tuck it under the string as it enters the string post. Turn the key so the string is wound on to the post, trapping the loose end under the new winding. This is tricky but it comes with practise and when you have the knack you'll find that strings fitted like this are easier to tune and stay in tune. Repeat for each of the other strings. If your headstock is 'three a side', you'll need to pass the loose end clockwise around the post for the G, B and E strings to trap the end successfully.

▲ Stretching new strings once fitted helps tuning stability.

Stretch your strings

Stretch the new strings immediately after fitting. Place the guitar on your knee in the playing position and place the flat of your thumb under the low E string. Push the string firmly away from the guitar and repeat for each string. Now retune and stretch again. You should find that you can repeat this three or four times before the guitar remains roughly in tune after stretching. Replace any broken strings immediately. If a string is poor enough to break during this procedure, it's a safe bet that it would not have lasted until the end of your first song.

▼ Cleaning your strings helps reduce grime building up.

Making strings last longer

To increase the life of your new strings, as well as stretching them, you could try applying a very thin coat of three-in-one oil to each saddle before fitting the new strings. This fine layer of oil will prevent moisture from creeping between the string and the saddle. When you have fitted the new strings, wipe a soft cloth dipped in three-in-one over the strings

and saddle. This will prolong the life of your strings and also keep intonation and height adjustment screws from seizing up. After playing, wipe down the strings with a piece of soft cotton, and use a string-care product such as Fast Fret to remove grease and grime from the strings.

Setting the Action

Action is incorrectly known as the height of the string above the fingerboard. In truth, the 'action' of the guitar is a combination of string height, intonation and neck relief, and it refers to how the guitar feels when played.

The great majority of guitar players prefer a comfortable action, though some jazz players are proud of the difficult action of their instruments as it enables the purity of tone that jazz players prefer. Rock players could not use a heavily strung jazz instrument, as rock relies on super-fast playing with extreme hammering and pull-offs that are only possible on a guitar with a very low and comfortable action.

String height

String height on all electric and some acoustic guitars can be adjusted at the bridge. Optimum string height is dictated by player preference and the physical characteristics of the guitar, such as fret height or the angle of the neck. Generally, players prefer to have the strings as close as possible to the fingerboard without buzzing or false tones that are produced when the vibrating string meets the frets or even the top of the pickup.

Depending on the model of the guitar, the individual saddles or even the whole bridge can be adjusted to whatever height is suitable. Adjustments should always be made with

▲ The action of a guitar significantly affects the sound – the higher the action, the louder the volume.

▲ The gap between the bottom of the low E string and the top of the seventh fret should be about 0.013 inches.

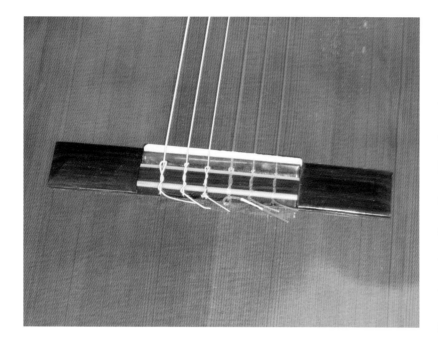

◄ The saddle is the place on a guitar's bridge for supporting the strings. Acoustic guitars tend to have a one–piece saddle.

the guitar tuned to concert pitch. Make small changes to the height of the bridge saddles before retuning and playing at the top of the neck close to the pickups. Listen closely for rattles caused by the strings meeting the frets and if possible, check with the guitar through an amplifier. Stratocasters and other guitars with individual bridge saddles, can be adjusted to produce a profile at the bridge that mirrors or closely resembles the camber (curved radius) of the fingerboard. Some guitars have bridges that may only be raised or lowered using wheels or screws at each bridge pillar. Height adjustment with this kind of bridge can only be a compromise and if you find that you are unable to get the adjustment you need it may be time to talk to a repairman about a more adjustable bridge for your guitar. Often the strings will appear to mysteriously rattle or buzz around the 13th or 14th fret. This is caused by fret wear or even a poorly fitted fret behind the point where the buzz is heard. If you do not have the tools or experience to put it right yourself, the only option is to raise the bridge until the string stops buzzing and make plans to take the guitar for a service.Guitar bridges trap muck and grease from your hands and if left for a while they will rust and eventually stick. Adjusting a stuck bridge saddle is difficult and sometimes destructive as the small grub screws inside the saddle are easily broken. Use a small amount of penetrating oil or 'Plus Gas' on the screws and other

moving parts, then set aside for a couple of hours before trying again. A stuck bridge probably needs more maintenance than just a simple wipe over with a little oil, but a can of WD-40 in the guitar case comes in handy for emergencies.

► Electric guitar saddles usually have six substructures. each with a groove over which a string passes.

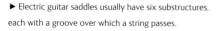

Setting the Bridge for Intonation

The electric guitar bridge has a moveable string saddle under each string. These saddles can be adjusted in two ways – backwards or forwards for intonation or up and down for string height. Bridge adjustment involves correctly setting both string height and intonation for each string to make the guitar comfortable to play and to play in tune.

▲ Raise or lower the height of the bridge by turning the milled thumb wheel under the bass or treble sides.

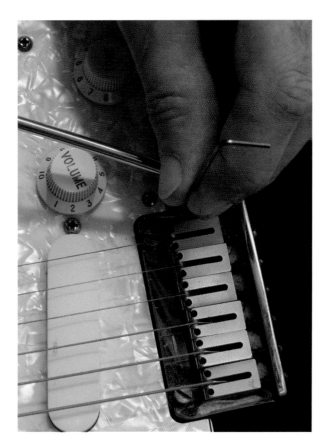

▲ Use a hex key to raise or lower the bass and treble side of the bridge by screwing or unscrewing each of the retaining pillars.

Some bridges do not have height-adjustable saddles. For these guitars the whole bridge must be moved up or down using screws set into the bridge posts. Height adjustment in this way is not as precise but it is easier than setting the height for each string.

Different bridges

Because each string is larger than the next, the distance between the string and the top of the fret is greater or smaller depending on the thickness of the string. This tiny difference causes the guitar to go gradually out of tune as the notes are fretted higher up the neck. Electric guitars have bridge saddles that can be moved forwards or backwards to compensate for this difference. Acoustic guitars have the same problem, but bridges with this kind of correction are not common on acoustic guitars as notes above the 12th fret are not as easy to play. It is important to correctly adjust the bridge as the guitar will permanently be 'out of tune' above the 12th fret if this is not done. This adjustment should also be checked each time the strings are changed as the new set may have different characteristics.

Check the intonation

To check the intonation you will need an electronic tuner and a screwdriver or 'Allen wrench', depending on the model of bridge. Prepare to move the string saddle using the screwdriver or key to turn the adjustment

▲ Adjusting the intonation should be done whenever changes are made to string gauge, neck relief or string height.

screw behind each string saddle. Play the harmonic note at the 12th fret and note the reading on the tuner. Tune to concert pitch (A=440Hz) if necessary and recheck the harmonic note – it should be reading dead centre on the tuner. Now play the fretted note at the 12th fret and check the reading. If the fretted note is lower (flat) the saddle must be moved forward by 1/16 in (1–2 mm). If the fretted note is sharp, the saddle must be moved back towards the bottom of the guitar. Retune and check that the harmonic and fretted notes are the same, then move on to the next string.

Tiny adjustments

Following this adjustment you may find that the string height has also changed. After adjusting the string height you will have to recheck the intonation. Either the string height or the intonation of the guitar will change each time the saddle or the bridge is moved. Optimum bridge adjustment involves making tiny adjustments and then checking both height and intonation. Eventually the bridge will be balanced and your guitar will play in tune and feel great. It is a hassle, and it may take some time, but it will be worth the trouble.

Adjusting the Neck Relief

The neck of the guitar has a slight concave bow in it. This bow is there by design to allow for the vibrating string at its widest excursion above the seventh fret. If the bow was not there, or if it was not deep enough, the vibrating string would catch on the frets causing the guitar to rattle as it was played.

The amount of bow set into the neck is called the 'relief'. The relief is held by a metal rod, which lies at tension under the fingerboard. This is called the truss rod. One end of the truss rod has a key or nut allowing for more or less tension to be applied to the neck. Neck relief is the third most important adjustment you have to make to your guitar. It must also be made in conjunction with string height and intonation and, most importantly, the bridge must be reset following adjustment of neck relief.

How much relief?

If your guitar is not rattling when played it may be that your neck relief is perfectly set. On the other hand if your guitar feels 'stiff' when playing around the seventh fret it may be that there is too much relief. To check the amount of relief you must tune the guitar to concert pitch and hold it in the playing position. Lay a steel ruler on its edge along the neck of the guitar between the low E and A strings. Examine the gap between the ruler and the seventh fret. There should be enough space to slip a thin piece of card or even a .010

▲ A Gibson Les Paul–style truss rod (pictured top) and a Fender Stratocaster–style truss rod (pictured bottom).

◄ Check for faults in the guitar's neck by looking along it.

flatpick between the ruler and the fret. Any thin material will do. If this gap appears to be too large you may be able to reduce the gap and so ease the playing of the guitar without causing string rattle.

Truss-rod adjustment

Depending on the model of your guitar, use a nut spinner or Allen wrench to loosen the truss-rod adjustment screw by a very small amount. The adjustment screw is normally found at the headstock just behind the nut and is often covered with a plastic plate. Check the measurement again, play the guitar and see how it has reacted to this adjustment. You may have to adjust and play several times before you have the optimum neck relief. Check string height (action) and intonation at the bridge following the final adjustment.

The truss-rod adjustment key may be stiff and difficult to turn. This could indicate that the guitar neck has suffered some damage (maybe from extreme changes in heat or humidity, causing warping) or it may be that the truss rod is damaged. If the adjustment cannot be made you must take the guitar to a professional repair shop. Truss-rod adjustment is always made with the guitar tuned to concert pitch and in the playing position. Allowances should also be made for further changes in the neck in the hours following adjustment; any adjustment that is made should always following a change in choice of string gauge.

► Measure the guitar's action with a ruler. It should be no more than 0.013 inches.

How the Electrics Work

The standard electric guitar contains a few relatively simple components. Electromagnetic pickups harness the vibrating metal string to produce energy, which is attenuated (made weaker) if desired by rotary controls called potentiometers further along the signal chain. These are called volume controls on the guitar.

▲ Switches and pickups are the basic electronic components of the electric guitar.

Very similar potentiometers attached to capacitors bleed more energy from the signal in the form of tone controls. If the guitar has more than one pickup, a switch is placed in the path between the pickups and the tone and volume controls to enable the guitarist to select which pickup is activated. Finally, the signal appears at a jack socket which mates very closely with a jack or 'phone' plug, which is attached to high-quality copper strands protected by a rubber or cloth sleeve. The other end of the copper is attached to another phone plug, which connects the guitar to an amplifier. The purpose of the amplifier is to take the signals from the guitar and make them into something you want to hear.

Active technology

Modern guitars take these basic principles and add more switching or tone controls to enable a wider range of tones to be achieved from the guitar. Active guitars boost the

▲ Most electric guitars have a selector switch that allows the player to choose whichever pickup is desired.

signal after it leaves the pickups using power from a battery situated in the guitar. Active pickups are fitted to non-active guitars to achieve the same thing. Some pickup manufacturers use high technology to produce clean, glassy sounds from the guitar (EMG, Actodyne). Many pickup manufacturers pride themselves on using very old equipment and NOS (New Old Stock) components to produce brand-new pickups that look, sound and feel exactly like pickups made 40 years ago (Seymour Duncan).

In with the new

During the 1980s some innovative manufacturers began to experiment with computer music technology to create guitars that were more like keyboards than stringed instruments (Bond guitars). In the early 1980s, Ned Steinberger produced the 'L-2' guitar with a wholly carbon-graphite composite body. Guitars such as the Parker Fly Mojo, featuring a mahogany body and composite neck, offer the best of traditional and modern.

In the new millennium the crown belongs to 'modelling' guitars such as Line 6 Variax. These computer-aided instruments create convincing real-time guitars using the characteristics of sounds stored in their memory blended with the artist's own performance. Because the sounds are created from a list of instructions held in the computer's memory the guitarist is able to produce a rock sound, then a country sound, even an acoustic guitar or banjo sound one after the other without having to put down a plectrum. Instruments like the Variax offer so much in the way of convenience to the player that it's difficult to believe guitarists will lose sight of these instruments in the way that previous innovations have gone by the wayside. But however popular the Variax might get, it's still never going to be as easy to fix or as much fun to customize as an old electric guitar. The pickup isn't dead yet!

◀ The Parker Fly Mojo guitar is made using an effective mix of traditional and modern.

▶ The Variax 500 may be the future for guitarists, but don't write off the Fender just yet.

Tools

Some say that all you need to fix an electric guitar is a sharp knife and a roll of gaffa tape. That's true up to a point, but lasting repairs are made by skilled technicians and these guys need a few simple tools to get the job done.

Screwdrivers

Get a Philips #2 and flat-bladed screwdriver with a high-quality tip that won't blunt and leave the tops of domed screws in a mess. Fender bolt-on necks need a larger Philips tip, while Gibson AB-1 bridges and stop-bar tailpieces need a large, good-quality flat-bladed tip. Rubber grips are much more pleasant to bounce off a glassy finish than hard plastic.

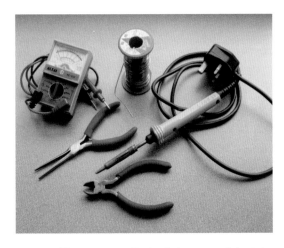

▲ It is possible to equip yourself to handle the majority of electrical tasks with just a few inexpensive tools.

Keys

A complete set of 'Allen' or hex keys in US (inches) and European (metric) sizes. Allen keys hold everything together, from bridges to locking nuts to control knobs. Many guitars have hex nuts at the truss rod too. Many US guitars need a 1/2-in (1.2-cm) key for bridge adjustment and a 1/8-in (3-mm) hex key for truss-rod adjustment. A set of nut drivers or box spanners is also useful for truss-rod adjustments on Gibson guitars and some others.

▲ You may need an Exacto saw to deepen the B and E string slots when replacing a nut.

Needle files

A set of fine modeller's files is vital for removing burrs from bridges and nuts. Other abrasives such as 000-gauge synthetic steel wool and glass paper are also useful for fretwork and for removing very shallow scratches. Deeper scratches and dents require filling with specialist materials available from luthier suppliers. A very fine modeller's saw is also useful for cutting nut slots.

Fillers and liquid abrasives

Holes can be filled with automotive fibreglass filler then rubbed smooth before spraying. Liquid abrasives are good for cutting back around shallow scratches but should never be used on unfinished wood such as fingerboards.

◄ Have the right tools to hand so you can make vital repairs.

Soldering iron

A good-quality soldering iron with variable heat is vital for perfect solder joints. Resin flux solder is required along with the hot iron to make the joint. Always use safety glasses when working with hot solder and a mask to avoid directly inhaling the fumes. If you are considering a lot of soldering, make a rig at the right height with enough light to see by, and ventilation to bring clean air into the room and to extract the fumes that may build up.

Side cutters and thin pliers or pincers

Side cutters are essential for trimming excess wire and snipping the untidy guitar strings from the headstock. Needle nose pliers are useful if you have to hold cables within a cavity. Crocodile clips or locking clamps can make tricky wiring jobs much easier.

Tape and glues

Low-tack masking tape is essential for masking areas around the working point. High-speed glue is occasionally useful for repairs to pickups or other parts inside the body, but has very low shear strength and doesn't stand up well to handling or moisture. High-speed glue repairs are often highly visible as well. If you need to join two plastic parts use Araldite and smooth the excess if you can with glass paper.

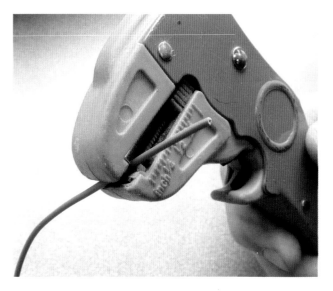

▲ A useful tool for cutting wires and trimming strings.

Pickups

Pickups create the sound of the electric guitar. Every guitar has at least one pickup placed under the strings and, depending on the model of the guitar, there may be two or even three pickups. The function of the pickup is to detect the vibrating string of the guitar and

▲ The Patent Applied For (PAF) humbucker pickup is perhaps the most sought-after of all Gibson electric guitar pickups.

turn the vibrations into electric current that can be amplified enough to move a speaker cone. The electric guitar pickup does this by electro-magnetic induction.

Each pickup is a coil of some 7,000 turns of copper wire wrapped around a magnet. The vibrating metal strings of the guitar push and pull the magnetic field created by the magnet and so create an alternating electric current in the coil of wire. Stronger magnets, combined with a greater number of turns of wire, will produce a more powerful pickup but will eventually lose definition. Smaller magnets and fewer turns produce a more musical sound but are lower in power. Pickup manufacturers use these characteristics to produce a range of pickups for country, rock or metal players. This simple explanation can't take into account the decades of experimentation and innovation that have produced the amazing electric guitar pickups available today. However, the principle of wires and magnets remains at the heart of every electric guitar.

◄ The inside view of a humbucker pickup.

Humbuckers

Electric guitar pickups have one or two coils of wire. Pickups with a single coil have a bright, clean sound which is full of detail and popular with country and blues players. Pickups with two coils are much more powerful and can overdrive an amplifier to produce a

▲ A humbucking pickup can translate vibrations into energy.

distorted sound which is associated with rock. Pickups are sensitive to electromagnetic noise or 'hum', which is amplified along with the strings causing the sound to be unclear. While working on ways to avoid this interference, an engineer working with the Gibson guitar corporation of America found that by reversing the polarity of one of the coils in a double-coil pickup, the hum would almost disappear. This became the famous 'humbucking' pickup, the design of which has been copied many times over.

Pickups for acoustic guitars

The sound of acoustic guitars, pianos, violins and every sort of acoustic instrument can also be amplified using transducers or contact microphones. This kind of pickup also uses electro-magnetism but, instead of relying on the strings to disturb the magnetic field, these pickups sense acoustic vibration. The magnet and coil is mounted underneath a small metal plate placed against the instrument's soundboard. When the soundboard vibrates, the vibrations are converted by the electromagnet into small electric currents, which are amplified in the same way as electric guitar pickups.

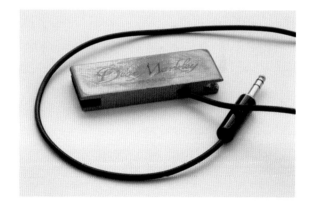

▲ Piezo pickup systems are fitted to most electro–acoustic and some purely electric guitars.

Magnetic magic

Inventors and engineers have stretched the simple principle of electro-magnetism almost to breaking point. Pickups can be single or twin coil at the touch of a switch. The electric guitar bridge can also be turned into a pickup by placing transducers below each bridge saddle. The pickups can be battery powered to produce massive distortion and can be placed underneath the wooden top of the guitar to aid its appearance.

Troubleshooting

Guitar electronics lend themselves to simple troubleshooting. Here are a few common problems and remedies....

Noisy switching

Pickup selector switches fail over time as the point of contact inside the switch becomes dirty or broken. This usually results in pickups not seeming to work, a big problem but one that can easily be resolved. Spray contact cleaner (Servisol) inside the switch and move the selector to work the fluid into the contacts. If the problem doesn't go away you will have to remove the rear cover or scratchplate and examine the switch. Check for loose or missing wiring. Finally, consider having the switch replaced with a new one.

Problems with the jack socket

The jack socket is a weak point on the guitar. If the instrument appears to work only when the barrel of the jack plug is pushed to one side you have a bent or corroded socket. Remove the control plate or scratchplate and gently squeeze the long spring arm towards the centre hole. Gently rub with a little fine glass paper to remove corrosion, then test.

▲ The jack sockets are the parts of your guitar most vulnerable to damage and should be replaced whenever necessary.

Dull or scratchy volume and tone control

Carbon tracks inside the tone control become worn with age and use. Remove the scratchplate or rear cover and apply contact cleaner to the inside of the potentiometer through the small space in the metal can above the solder connections. Work the control backwards and forwards to ease the fluid along the track. The pot will have to be replaced if this procedure fails to solve the problem.

Humming or noise that stops when the strings of the guitar are touched

This problem indicates poor grounding of the guitar. Remove the rear cover or scratchplate and look for a grounding wire connecting the metal can of the volume pot to the bridge of your guitar. Replace if this connection is missing or broken on your Stratocaster or Telecaster guitar. This ground wire is missing on Les Paul-style guitars. Unfortunately most copy Les Paul guitars have a hum problem because the electronics in these instruments are shielded with a metal can. Copy Les Paul guitars don't have the can and also don't have the ground wire.

▲ Copper tape can be used to deal with humming or any other noise that stops when the strings are touched.

Adding a ground wire between the bridge and ground will help protect your copy Les Paul from noise. Electric foil or conductive paint should completely cover the walls of the cavity containing the electronics. A few strips attached to the scratchplate won't be enough. Check out Stewart Macdonald or any good electronic parts supplier. Some players also add a 0.022uF capacitor to the ground wire. This will help to protect you from lethal mains voltage if your amplifier should have a poor or missing ground. Ensure that the capacitor is taped or wrapped in bubble wrap to avoid touching and shorting on any other components.

'Furry' pickups

Pickups attract metal particles from strings and other metal parts of the guitar. Over time these can cause the pickup to lose definition. Use Blu-Tack to remove the metal particles by dabbing around the pickups, paying attention to the small gaps between the cover and the pole pieces.

▲ Dab Blu-Tack around the pickups to remove accumulated metal particles.

Blues

The blues has played a larger role in the history of popular music than any other genre. It is a direct ancestor to music styles as diverse as rock 'n' roll, rock, heavy metal, soul, funk and pop. Without the blues there would have been no Beatles, Jimi Hendrix, Led Zeppelin, James Brown, Stevie Wonder or Oasis, to name but a few!

The blues emerged out of the hardships endured by generations of African-American slaves during the late nineteenth and early twentieth centuries. By 1900, the genre had developed into a three-line stanza, with a vocal style derived from southern work songs. These 'call and response' songs were developed further by early blues guitar players, who would sing a line and then answer it on the guitar. By the 1920s, rural African Americans had migrated to the big cities in search of work, bringing their music with them. Early street musicians such as Blind Lemon Jefferson (1893–1929), a guitar-playing blues singer, started to make recordings and these inspired the next generation of blues guitar players.

▲ Blind Lemon Jefferson's lack of sight resulted in expressive playing and vocals.

Delta blues

The 1930s were a crucial period in the development of the blues, for it was then that acoustic Mississippi Delta blues performers Charley Patton (1891–1934), Son House (1902–88) and Robert Johnson (1911–38) travelled throughout the southern states, singing about their woes, freedom, love and sex to community after community. Johnson, who allegedly made a mysterious pact with the devil to become a better guitar player, was the first true blues performance artist. Over on the East Coast, musicians such as Blind Boy Fuller (1907–41), Sonny Terry (1911–86) and Gary Davis (1896–1972) developed a more folky 'Piedmont' blues style.

◄ The intricate guitar work and unusual tunings of Robert Johnson were a revelation.

Chicago blues

By the 1940s, Chicago bluesmen took Mississippi Delta ideas and played them on electric guitars. Lone performers became more scarce while small bands sprang up everywhere. By the 1950s, electric blues was in full swing, with B. B. King, Muddy Waters, John Lee Hooker (1917–2001), T-Bone Walker and Howlin' Wolf (1910–76), all playing to packed houses in major cities. King pioneered across-the-string vibrato and note-bending techniques on his beloved guitar, 'Lucille', and these techniques are now used by all blues lead guitar players. Hooker developed a completely different style, in which he stomped continuously with his right foot while singing and playing. Wolf injected more power and frustration into the blues, and Walker jazzed things up, but it was perhaps Muddy Waters' passionate singing and biting guitar tones that popularized the style more than anyone else from this period. Some bluesmen, such as Big Bill Broonzy (1893–1958), visited England, where their performances inspired British musicians to adopt the style.

British blues

The 1960s witnessed a musical and cultural revolution when British guitar players such as Eric Clapton and Peter Green started to mimic American bluesmen. They used solidbody guitars and more powerful amplifiers to get a harder, more driving sound than their American mentors. Clapton's electric guitar sound led to the birth of a number of other styles, including blues-rock, hard rock and even heavy metal. From the 1970s onwards, artists including Stevie Ray Vaughan, Robert Cray and Robben Ford have added more voices and sounds to the blues repertoire, and the genre is still thriving today.

Playing the blues

Blues is based around the blues scale (see page 48), which is a pentatonic minor scale with an added flat fifth note (the 'blue' note). Blues music is usually played in the keys of A, D, E and G as they are all easy keys to play on the guitar. The style has an odd harmonic structure, as the blues scale is usually played or sung over chords that are all dominant sevenths (e.g. A7, D7 and E7 in the key of A) or chords derived from them.

▲ Buddy Guy was a leading exponent of the Chicago blues sound.

Acoustic blues

There are two main blues styles: traditional acoustic blues and urban electric blues. Acoustic blues normally requires a 'fingerstyle' approach, in which the thumb of the right hand – assuming the player is right-handed – plays a steady bass-note groove while the melody or licks are picked out by the first and second fingers. Most of this is performed quite forcefully, although acoustic blues players rest the side of their picking hand across the strings at times to make sure the bass notes don't ring out too loudly. Son House, Leadbelly (1889–1949) and Big Bill Broonzy were all masters of this style, so if you want to play it you should familiarize yourself with their recordings. It is important to realize, however, that a lot of their guitar playing was improvised and designed to accompany their own vocal phrasings.

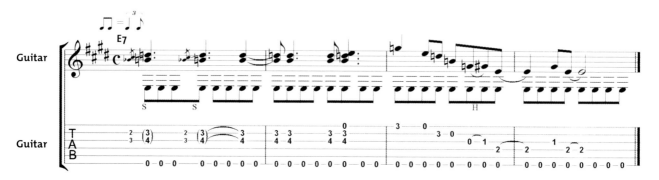

▲ Acoustic blues finger-style playing. The low E string is played repeatedly with the thumb, establishing a traditional blues rhythm.

Electric blues

Urban electric blues guitar is usually played within the context of a band, so it is normally restricted to lead or rhythm playing at any one time. Some electric guitar players use a plectrum to achieve accurate pick articulation, while others favour a more earthy fingerstyle approach. Electric blues guitarists play in a wider range of keys than their acoustic counterparts, as they often work with horn players who prefer to play in B♭ and C. Lauded electric blues guitar players include B. B. King, Freddie King, Albert Collins, Buddy Guy, Eric Clapton, Robben Ford and Stevie Ray Vaughan.

▲ An example of an electric blues solo. A 'lead-in' before the bar, and the use of string bends, makes this a typical Chicago-style solo.

◄ Bending strings is one of the oldest techniques of lead guitar playing. You can bend one, two, or even three strings at the same time.

Playing electric blues

Electric blues stylists often embellish their phrases with expressive techniques such as string bending, sliding and vibrato. String bending should simply be thought of as another way of moving from one pitch to another on the fretboard. To bend a string accurately, you must know your target note – this will usually be a note pitched a half step, a whole step or a step and a half above your unbent note. If your target note is a half step higher, for example, you can play the note behind the next fret up on the same string to hear what it should sound like. When you perform the bend, push the string over towards the bass strings until you hear your target note.

|| C7 | C7 | C7 | C7 |

| F7 | F7 | C7 | C7 |

| G7 | F7 | C7 | G7 :||

▲ Tens of thousands of blues songs are based around the most common chord-progression in the history of popular music: the 12-bar blues sequence.

You can produce a blues slide effect when you play a note on a string and, while holding the string firmly down, slide along the fingerboard to another note. You can even slide across two or more strings at a time by barring your fretting finger across the strings and moving it along the neck in the same way. To obtain a vibrato effect, play a fretted note and move the string from side to side – across the fingerboard – with your fretting finger. This makes a sustained note sound more expressive or even aggressive.

Going solo

There are many different approaches to soloing over a blues progression, but the simplest way to learn is to target the root notes of each chord in the progression. In the key of C, for example, the main blues chords are C7, F7 and G7. You can begin by playing the C pentatonic minor scale and targeting the notes C, F and G (which are all in the scale) over their respective chords. Try bending or sliding to these notes to make things sound more bluesy.

It is also a good idea to practise blues lead phrasing by using the 'call and response' approach favoured by early blues musicians; sing a phrase and then reply to it with a guitar line, and so on. This should help you to get an authentic blues feel, even if you're not a singer. It will enable you to put comfortable, natural rests between your phrases and notes so it all ends up sounding more musical and logical. You should also jam with other like-minded musicians, as this not only is fun but will also motivate you to become a better player.

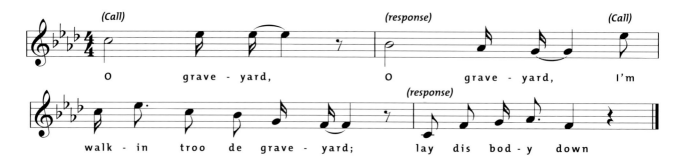

▲ Work songs such as this retain a strong African influence, with irregular rhythms that often follow speech patterns.

Using a bottleneck

Some blues players, including Elmore James (1918–63) and Duane Allman, have used a bottleneck made out of glass or metal to obtain a distinctive sliding effect between notes. Bottlenecks are inexpensive and fun to play with, but you'll need a little patience to master the technique properly. Special tunings such as D A D F# A D are often used for bottleneck pieces, as they enable the guitarist to play whole chords up the guitar neck with just one finger!

▶ Duane Allman of the Allman Brothers was renowned for his use of a bottleneck.

Getting a blues sound

To get an authentic blues sound you'll need an appropriate guitar. Almost any acoustic instrument will do for acoustic blues, although resonators, guitars that use thin aluminium cones to mechanically amplify their sound, will give you a particularly 'bluesy' tone. If you're after an authentic electric blues sound, you should pick an instrument similar to one played by your favourite blues artist. If you want to sound like B. B. King, for example, you should consider a Gibson ES-335, as this is the guitar he has favoured over the years, while a Fender Stratocaster will enable you to sound more like Robert Cray or Stevie Ray Vaughan, and a Telecaster would be essential for that biting Albert Collins sound.

Amplification is important too, and most blues artists favour valve amplifiers such as the Marshall Bluesbreaker combo or Fender's Twin and Deluxe models as they give a warm, fat sound with a big dynamic range.

Transistor amplifiers are cheaper but they sound more synthetic. If you're just playing guitar in your bedroom you should consider getting an amp modelling box such as a Line 6 POD, or a virtual amp software package such as IK Multimedia's AmpliTube or Steinberg's Warp VST. Each of these comes armed with a surprisingly authentic set of blues presets, and you can use them without upsetting the neighbours.

Tone control settings are important as well; boosting an amplifier's bass and mid-range will give a fat B. B. King sound, while boosting the treble will help to emulate the 'icy' tones of Albert Collins. All in all, it is important to find a guitar tone that you feel comfortable with – if you sound great, you'll play well!

▶ The IK Multimedia Amplitude, an amplifier simulator plug-in.

Classical

Although guitar-like instruments have been around since the Middle Ages, the 'classical' guitar as we know it today didn't appear until the middle of the nineteenth century. And its repertoire was non-existent until Andrés Segovia started performing 50 years later.

▼ Self-taught. Andrés Segovia plucked the strings with a combination of flesh and nail that helped him produce a wide range of tones.

Segovia was born in Grenada, Spain in 1893. He started playing guitar at an early age and quickly developed a virtuoso playing style. He created a basic classical guitar repertoire by adapting music composed for other instruments to his own and, by the time he was 20, had arranged pieces by Bach, Handel, Tarrega, Chopin, Schumann and Mozart. By the late 1920s, Segovia's arrangements had become standards and he was performing them in front of Spanish royalty. Composers of the period took note, and the likes of Villa-Lobos, Falla, Castelnuovo-Tedesco and Ponse began to write music specifically for the classical guitar.

Segovia put the classical guitar on the map as a 'serious' instrument and personally taught a further generation of classical virtuosos, including Alirio Diaz (b. 1923), Julian Bream (b. 1933), Christopher Parkening (b. 1947), Eliot Fisk (b. 1954), John Williams and Alexandre Lagoya (1929–99). These players took the classical technique to new heights and broadened its repertoire further by performing contributions from other new composers.

Playing classical guitar

To adopt the correct classical guitar posture, sit on a chair and rest the centre of your instrument's body on your left leg. Angle the neck upwards so that your left arm (assuming you're a right-handed

▲ Taught by Andrés Segovia, Julian Bream also studied piano, cello, harmony and composition at the Royal College of Music, London.

player) can reach the fingerboard without any obstructions. Rest your right arm on the upper edge of the guitar's body so that you can position your right hand's fingers directly over the strings near the sound hole. You might also want to place your left foot on a small footstool to bring your left leg up a little to better support the instrument. Practise picking up the guitar and getting into playing position so that it feels natural and easy. Make sure you feel relaxed and there is no tension in your limbs when you do this.

▶ The classical guitar was the first to feature struts – pieces of wood inside the body to improve volume and tonal response.

Classical techniques

The classical guitar is picked by the tips/nails of the thumb and first three fingers of the right hand (or left hand for left-handed players) so it is important to keep these tidy. These fingers are labelled as follows after their Spanish names: P = pulgar (thumb), I = indice (index finger), M = medio (middle finger) and A = anular (third finger).

To get a basic idea of how it all works, start to play the open sixth string (the

▲ Acoustic guitarists often prefer to use the fingers for picking the strings. as opposed to a plectrum.

thickest string) with a downward movement of the tip of your thumb, and then, while this low note is still ringing out, strike the open third, second and first strings consecutively with upward movements from your index, middle and third fingers respectively. Repeat this series of movements again and again so that you are following the pattern PIMA PIMA PIMA PIMA. Now start to reverse the order of your finger movements so that your thumb stroke is followed by your third finger, your middle finger and then your index finger: PAMI PAMI

◄ Student Eurico Pereira learns the correct technique from Eliot Fisk.

PAMI PAMI. Then combine the two exercises so that you alternate between the two: PIMA PAMI PIMA PAMI. Once you feel comfortable with these variations, you'll be in a position to start learning classical guitar music.

The fretting hand is equally important as it has to articulate the notes you are picking. With your thumb behind the neck, position your fingers so that they arch around and their fingertips are perpendicular to the strings. You must have very short fingernails on this hand so that you can press down on the strings and articulate notes cleanly and accurately. The fretting hand switches between chordal positions (for playing arpeggios) and a one-finger-per-fret style (for scalar melodies).

Tremolo

Classical guitarists also employ a tremolo technique which involves the I, M and A fingers playing a continuous, repeating pattern on a single note, a 'ligado' technique which involves striking a note and then hammering on to another note on the same string with a finger, and rubato, a technique involving the use of subtle tempo changes to accentuate and embellish specific parts of the music.

Reading music

Although you can learn how to play the classical guitar by ear, it is normally taught conventionally with traditional music notation. It is therefore a good idea to familiarize yourself with the notes on the conventional music stave, but bear in mind that to make guitar music easy to read, the notes on the fingerboard are often written one octave higher than their actual pitch. If you're serious about playing classical guitar, we recommend you see a tutor regularly to ensure that you learn to sight-read properly and do not develop any bad playing habits.

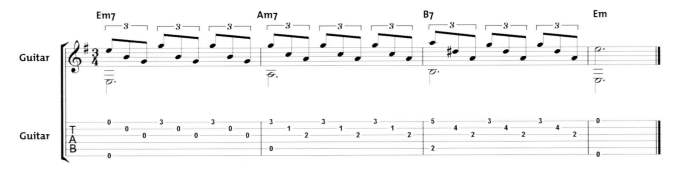

▲ If you can read music, try playing through this excerpt from Francisco Tárrega's *Étude* in E Minor, for a true idea of how music for a the classical guitar can sound.

Country

Country music originally grew out of American folk music and it now encompasses a variety of styles, including bluegrass, American folk, hillbilly, country-rock, zydeco (cajun music) and C&W (country and western). At its core, country is a simple music and most of its songs are built around simple chord progressions and melodies played on guitars, fiddles and other instruments.

The country genre was 'born' in the late 1920s when Jimmie Rodgers (1897–1933) and the Carter Family signed recording contracts with Victor Records. Rodgers had a unique voice and the Carters had an impressive repertoire of 'old-style' American folk tunes. They appeared regularly on the Grand Ole Opry, a legendary Nashville-based national radio show.

The first cowboy singers

By the 1930s, a number of other country music strands started to become popular: 'cowboy' singers such as Roy Rogers (1911–68) and Gene Autry (1907–98) appeared in popular films; western swing bands like Bob Wills' Texas Playboys successfully fused country-folk with big band, blues, Dixieland and Hawaiian steel sounds; and Bill Monroe introduced a more Celtic-influenced bluegrass style.

◄ Gene Autry had one of the most visually stunning Martin guitars. the D-45, made for him in 1932.

Honky tonk

In the 1940s, a style called 'honky tonk' defined two country music clichés: stories about drinking and losing the one you love. Hank Williams' (1923–53) 'Lovesick Blues' (1949) epitomizes this. Ironically his last hit, 'I'll Never Get Out Of This World Alive' was released just before his death on New Year's Day 1953, after a heart attack brought on by drinking.

▼ Willie Nelson and Waylon Jennings were the 'most wanted' of the outlaw movement.

Nashville

Another milestone was 'the Nashville sound', a blend of country and pop that appeared during the 1950s. It propelled artists such as Jim Reeves, Eddy Arnold and Patsy Cline into the limelight with well-recorded ballads and honky-tonk stories. Then 'outlaw' artists Johnny Cash (1932–2003) and Willie Nelson (b. 1933) added a little danger into the equation during the 1960s, and Lynyrd Skynyrd and Alabama fused country with rock in the 1970s.

Modern country

During the 1980s and 1990s, artists such as Garth Brooks (b. 1962), Ricky Skaggs (b. 1954), the Judds and Randy Travis (b. 1959) had considerable success, with some of their albums even outselling mainstream pop artists such as Michael Jackson and Madonna.

Country music has had its fair share of guitar virtuosos over the years, and these have included fingerpicking pioneers like Merle Travis (1917–83) and Doc Watson (b. 1923); Hawaiian steel specialists such as Sonny Garrish (b. 1943) and Lloyd Maines (b. 1951); and dynamic electric players like Albert Lee, Danny Gatton (1945–94) and Steve Morse (b. 1954). It is worth checking out recordings by all these great players.

Playing country

Much country music is based around the pentatonic major scale (see page 45). This scale is often confused with the pentatonic minor scale (used in blues) as they use the same finger patterns across the guitar neck, but they are in fact different modes in the same scale family.

To explain further, the A pentatonic minor shape between the fifth and eighth frets of the fingerboard is identical to the C pentatonic major shape in the same position. The reason for this is that they both consist of the same notes; C, D, E, G, A and C. The difference is that the A pentatonic minor uses A as its first (tonic) note while the C pentatonic major scale begins on the C note; playing the shape over an A bass note

▲ Randy Travis is a neo–traditionalist, and his music is built on foundations established by the likes of Merle Haggard.

will make it sound bluesy, whereas playing it over a C bass note will make it sound 'country'. The pentatonic major scale is actually the regular major scale ('do-re-mi') with the fourth and seventh notes removed. Because of this it is easier to play and it harmonizes better with the simple chord progressions used in country music.

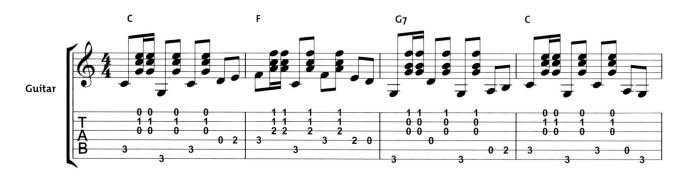

▲ The classic country music guitar figure would be played on an acoustic instrument, providing a simple but steady melodic and rhythmic structure.

◄ Violining: the little finger of the picking hand adjusts the volume while playing.

Electric Country

Electric country guitar players use a lot of note bends in their solos. Of particular importance is the 'harmony bend', a pedal-steel type effect where some notes are held while another is bent. Country players also use double-stops (two-note chords), hammer-ons, pull-offs and slides to add further colour to their solos. Another specialist country technique is 'chicken picking', a damped, staccato right-hand style employed by James Burton (b. 1939) and others for fast, funky phrases.

You can play a basic country rhythm guitar style by separating the bass notes in each chord you play from the rest of the notes in the chord; play the bass notes first and then follow with the rest. Another neat country trick is to use the guitar's volume control (or a volume pedal) to fade chords and notes in from nothing to give a nice, soft attack to the tone – a technique known as 'violining'.

The right guitar

If you're serious about playing electric country guitar, you should consider getting a Fender Telecaster as it produces a clean, twangy sound and has probably been favoured by more country players than any other electric guitar. If you haven't got a Telecaster, you can approximate its sound by choosing the bridge pickup on any single coil guitar, selecting a clean amplifier sound and cutting back on your bass and mid-range.

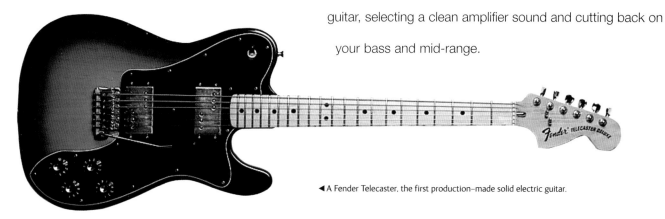

◄ A Fender Telecaster, the first production-made solid electric guitar.

Flamenco

Flamenco music can be traced back to mid-nineteenth century Spain, when Andalucian musicians developed a 'café cantante' guitar style to accompany singers and dancers at local cafés. Although the earliest Spanish guitar players had relatively unrefined skills, the style evolved over the next half century until Ramon Montoya emerged in the early twentieth century as the first celebrated modern flamenco player.

Ramon was born in Madrid in 1880. He spent his early years cattle trading with his gypsy parents and bought a guitar. Swiftly learning the instrument, he was accompanying singers in Madrid cafés by the time he was 14. He formed a musical allegiance with one of the greatest Spanish singers of the time, Antonio Chacon, and they became a famous act. By then Montoya had developed an unprecedented level of virtuosity on his instrument, and singers had to change the way they sang to accommodate his playing; modern flamenco was born!

Montoya made more than 700 recordings with top cantantes and was a huge influence on the next generation of flamenco guitarists, including his nephew, Carlos Montoya, who developed the style further between the 1940s and 1960s.

◄ Flamenco dancing was developed by Spanish gypsies in the fifteenth century.

Flamenco today

Today a number of talented flamenco guitarists are recognized worldwide, but the most respected of all these is Paco de Lucía. Born in 1947, Paco took up the guitar at an early age and was performing on Spanish radio by the time he was 12. As a teenager he toured with flamenco dancer José Greco and met Sabicas, an influential guitarist who encouraged Paco to pursue a more personal style. He took this advice and evolved into a highly individual player with a formidable technique, stretching well beyond the boundaries of traditional flamenco.

Paco also made a number of critically acclaimed acoustic guitar trio recordings with jazz-rock maestros Al Di Meola (b. 1954) and John McLaughlin including *Friday Night In San Francisco* (1980) and *The Guitar Trio* (1996). Despite this, his style has always remained decidedly Spanish: 'There was a time when I was concerned about losing myself,' he once said, 'but not now. I realize that, even if I wanted, I couldn't sound like anything other than flamenco.'

▲ Renowned flamenco guitarist Paco de Lucía has one of the fastest, most intricate finger-picking techniques in the world.

Playing flamenco

While classical guitarists aim for a clean, elegant style, flamenco players tend to favour a more earthy, powerful and dynamic sound. Flamenco guitarists use a number of specialist techniques, including rasgueado, tremolo and golpe. A rasgueado is a unique strumming technique created by fanning or brushing the fingers across the strings

▲ The guitar provides the accompaniment to strong, rhythmic, passionate dancing in traditional Flamenco.

to generate a circular effect. To achieve this, hold your strumming hand tightly closed and then strum the strings by releasing the fingers in quick succession. A tremolo involves playing a single note repeatedly and swiftly with the picking-hand fingers to produce long, sustained notes. To play a tremolo, pick a string with your third finger, then your middle finger and then your index finger of the picking hand in quick succession and repeat the pattern again and again. A golpe is a percussive effect performed by tapping the instrument's body with the picking hand to reinforce rhythms and accents in the music.

There are dozens of different flamenco styles and these are defined by characteristic melodic, rhythmic and harmonic structures. The most popular of these styles include bulerías, soleares, alegrías, fandangos, rondeña and tanguillos. Each one has a distinctive mood, although many are actually regional variants of each other. Flamenco guitarists also play a number of other folk and latin influenced styles including garrotín, farruca, guajiras and rhumba. The traditional flamenco posture has the guitar resting against the upper part of the body and held tightly between thigh and upper right arm.

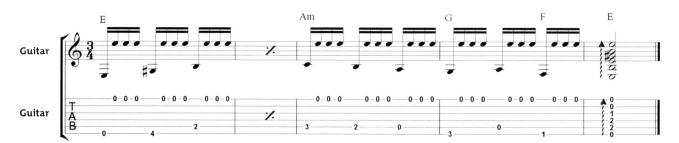

▲ In flamenco, the exact guitar lines played are normally improvized around a standard theme.

Techniques

While the capo is rarely used in classical guitar playing, it is commonly used in flamenco music as it allows the guitarist to change keys while preserving his or her favourite chord voicings. Flamenco players also use the capo because it shortens the vibrating string length and can thus brighten the instrument's sound. Flamenco guitarists also make greater use of their thumbs and

▲ A capo is a simple device that allows the pitch of the guitar's open strings to be changed.

fingers than classical players: in classical music, the thumb is usually limited to playing the bass notes, while the next three fingers concentrate on the higher strings; in flamenco, the thumb can range over all six strings and all four picking-hand fingers are usually employed. Flamenco players also mute the strings with their left hand while strumming with the right to produce a percussive rhythmic style.

Flamenco guitar

Although flamenco guitars look similar to classical instruments, they are actually quite different; classical guitars tend to have deep rosewood bodies while flamenco instruments are thinner and usually constructed from cypress. Flamenco guitars tend to produce a louder, more penetrating sound than classical instruments. They also have their strings set lower and feature a plastic shield on the soundboard to protect the body from damage caused by the energetic finger rasgueados and golpes employed by the players.

▶ A flamenco guitar is deceptively similar to but slightly smaller than a typical classical guitar.

Folk

Folk music can be described as 'the natural expression of a people'. It exists in every country, whether it comes in the form of African tribal chants, Irish reels, Indian ragas, nursery rhymes, Hungarian gypsy tunes or Native American ceremonial songs.

Folk music is rarely written for profit and it is passed down from generation to generation, musician to musician. Often lacking the technical sophistication and complexity found in other music styles, it can be extraordinarily beautiful and stirring.

Popular folk music, as we know it today, can be traced directly back to the singer-songwriter Woody Guthrie. Born in 1912 in Okemah, Oklahoma, Guthrie grew up in a poor but musical family. As a teenager he experienced first the tragic death of his older sister, Clara, and then his family's financial ruin when the town's boom period went bust. They moved to Pampa, Texas, where Woody fell in love, married and formed his first band, the Corn Cob Trio.

▲ Prolific songwriter and performer Woody Guthrie sang songs about economic, political and social problems.

Guthrie's influence

After a great dust storm hit the area (chronicled in John Steinbeck's novel *The Grapes of Wrath*) the Guthrie family headed west with a mass migration of refugees known as 'Okies'. These unemployed workers from Oklahoma,

Kansas, Tennessee and Georgia had all lost their homes and had set out in search of opportunities elsewhere. Penniless and hungry, Woody walked and hitchhiked over to California, where he wrote songs about his experiences. He later travelled all over the US and became a champion for oppressed migrant workers, as well as a controversial critic of politicians, lawyers and businessmen. He made a number of recordings during the 1940s and the honesty, humour and wit expressed in these influenced the likes of Bob Dylan (b. 1941), Joan Baez (b. 1941) and Paul Simon (b. 1941), who all had unprecedented chart success with folk-style songs during the

▲ Joan Baez and Bob Dylan were responsible for a folk revival in the 1960s.

1960s. Guthrie died after a long struggle with Huntington's Chorea in 1967, and has since been acknowledged as the most important folk artist of the first half of the twentieth century.

UK folk scene

Over in the UK, Renaissance lute music and American folk styles inspired the likes of Martin Carthy (b. 1941), Bert Jansch (b. 1943) and John Renbourn (b. 1944) to write strong, original guitar material during the 1960s. Ralph McTell (b. 1944) also helped to popularize English folk with his hit 'Streets of London' (1974).

Although traditional folk has always been popular, the global 'folk scene' has often been in a state of flux, with new musicians adding their own voices to the throng. John Martyn (b. 1948) and Christy Moore (b. 1945) had developed unique and earthy folk styles by the 1970s and influenced many other singer-songwriters, while today artists such as Ani DiFranco (b. 1970), the Levellers and Asian Dub Foundation are all fusing elements of folk with different popular music cultures.

Playing folk music

The acoustic guitar is the main instrument used in folk music, and it can either be fingerpicked or strummed with a plectrum. Typical folk fingerpickers will normally play the bass strings with the thumb and the treble strings with the index, middle and third fingers of their right hand (assuming they are right-handed), although some just use their index and middle fingers for the treble strings and rest their other two fingers on the guitar body for support.

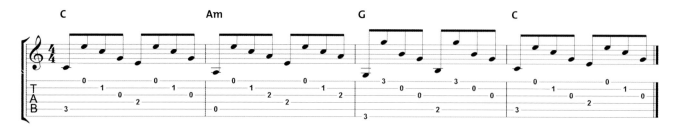

▲ With any folk song, the words are the main focus, leaving the melody and structure simple, as in this example.

Most folk tunes played in this way use the same fingerpicking pattern – or a series of variations of it – for the whole song. Some virtuoso players adopt a more elaborate style with all four fingers playing the treble strings, or separate contrapuntal harmonies being played on the bass and treble strings at the same time.

Flatpicking

There are also a number of folk flatpickers who use a plectrum to play chord arpeggios across the strings, along with scales and licks. Such players use strumming techniques to play the guitar in a rhythmic context and, like fingerpickers, they tend to keep the same rhythm for an entire song. To strum with a plectrum, finger your chord with your left hand and angle the plectrum in towards the strings and pointing slightly upwards with your right hand. Then stroke the plectrum across the strings, making sure that all the notes in the chord ring out cleanly.

▲ Flat-picking is a playing style where all notes, scalic and chordal, are articulated with a plectrum or thumb pick.

Some acoustic flatpickers can play extremely fast scalar solos with a plectrum by alternating between upstrokes and downstrokes of the right hand, while the left hand is fingering the notes. A number of bluegrass players and 'crossover' guitarists like Al Di Meola, Steve Morse and Ricky Skaggs have used this style to devastating effect.

▲ Typically, most traditional folk guitar playing is based on finger-picking. The bass strings are usually picked by the thumb, whilst the index, middle and ring fingers are used to pick the treble strings. It is very rare for the little finger to be used.

Amplification

While most traditional folk music can be performed without any amplification, anything in a more modern band context should be performed through a dedicated acoustic amplifier such as the Roland AC60, the Behringer Ultracoustic ACX1000 or one of Marshall's AS series amplifiers. These are specifically designed to bring out the natural characteristics of an acoustic guitar which is playing at a typical 'live band' volume.

► Folk singer Ani DiFranco started her own record label.

Jazz

► Before musicians such as Eddie Lang began to play single–line lead solos, guitars were just part of the rhythm section.

Eddie Lang is widely acknowledged as the first significant jazz guitarist. His single-note playing with jazz orchestras during the 1920s marked the beginning of the guitar as a solo instrument in the genre. He joined the Mound City Blue Blowers in 1924 and then Paul Whiteman's orchestra in 1929, before becoming Bing Crosby's accompanist. He was soon one of the best-paid musicians of the day but tragically died at the peak of his career in 1933.

Lang's legacy

Lang's pioneering guitar work in the 1920s paved the way for the two jazz guitar giants of the 1930s: Django Reinhardt (1910–53) and Charlie Christian (1916–42).

Reinhardt lost the use of two fingers in his left hand in a fire, but developed a way of playing the guitar with his remaining fingers. He formed the Quintette du Hot Club de France with violinist Stephane Grappelli in 1933; the band recorded more than 100 songs and toured all over Europe. Django's soloing set new standards and was greatly influential. Charlie Christian, meanwhile, emerged in the early 1940s as the first electric guitar virtuoso, playing saxophone-like lead lines at a volume that could compete with other jazz instruments.

Bebop

By the 1950s, a number of exciting bebop guitarists began to appear: Barney Kessel was an acclaimed soloist who became a session ace and played in bands fronted by Chico Marx and Oscar Peterson; Tal Farlow (1924–98) expanded the jazz guitar chord vocabulary and was one of the first guitarists to be able to play a harmonic note from every fret of the instrument. Johnny Smith (b. 1922) developed a subtle chord-oriented style and had a hit with the mellow 'Moonlight in Vermont' (1952).

Jazz superstars

Jim Hall (b. 1930), Wes Montgomery (1925–68) and Kenny Burrell (b. 1931) were the big jazz guitar names during the 1960s. Hall's phrases were lyrical, displaying a subtlety that few other guitarists have ever been able to achieve. Wes Montgomery used his thumb as a pick and was one of the first solo guitarists to mix single notes with octaves and chords, while Kenny Burrell forged a cool bop style that established him as one of the most popular instrumental voices in jazz. Joe Pass (b. 1929) was another great jazz guitar player to emerge during the 1960s; using a phenomenal right-handed finger technique, he was able to play melodies, chords and bass lines simultaneously. His album *Virtuoso* (1973) made him a jazz star and he later accompanied the likes of Ella Fitzgerald, Count Basie, Duke Ellington and Oscar Peterson.

▲ Joe Pass began playing the guitar aged nine and covered a huge range of styles, including jazz, bebop, blues and Latin.

Jazz fusion

During the 1970s, a number of guitar players began to fuse jazz with rock; the most influential of these were John McLaughlin, Al Di Meola and Allan Holdsworth (b. 1946). McLaughlin was the lead guitar player on Miles Davis's pioneering jazz-rock album *Bitches Brew* (1969), and he took the direction further with his own band the Mahavishnu Orchestra. Al Di Meola fused jazz with Latin and rock styles on his critically acclaimed albums *Elegant Gypsy* (1977) and *Casino* (1978), and Allan Holdsworth developed a truly unique style, characterized by spectacular chord voicings and legato solos.

A number of other great jazz guitar players have emerged during the past 30 years, including Pat Metheny, Larry Carlton, Martin Taylor (b. 1956), Stanley Jordan (b. 1959), John Scofield, Bill Frisell and Scott Henderson (b. 1954). Of all these, Pat Metheny has enjoyed the most commercial success, forging an earthy and mellow jazz style that appeals to both hardcore jazzers and easy listeners.

Playing jazz guitar

All accomplished jazz musicians have a thorough knowledge and understanding of chords and scales, which you will also need to master this most demanding of musical styles. Most jazz tunes are based around extended chords (sevenths, ninths, 11ths and 13ths) so make sure you know how to play these, and jazz composers also like to raise or lower the fifth and ninth intervals in chords, so it is a good idea to learn these chords as well. Another jazz trick is chord substitution, which is often done by taking a chord with a dominant seventh note and replacing it with another chord with a root note a tritone (a flattened fifth) higher – for example, substituting a D-flat 7 chord for a G minor chord.

Chord progression

The most common chord progression in jazz is the II-V-I, which uses chords based on the second, fifth and first notes of the major scale respectively. The II chord is a minor 7 chord, while the V is a dominant 7 and the I is a major 7 chord. So in the key of C, the basic II-V-I progression is Dm7, G7, CMaj7. You should familiarize yourself with this chord progression in different keys and in different positions on the fingerboard.

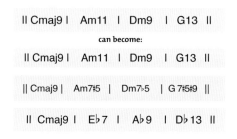

‖ Cmaj9 ‖ Am11 ‖ Dm9 ‖ G13 ‖

can become:

‖ Cmaj9 ‖ Am11 ‖ Dm9 ‖ G13 ‖

‖ Cmaj9 ‖ Am7♯5 ‖ Dm7♭5 ‖ G 7♯5♯9 ‖

‖ Cmaj9 ‖ E♭7 ‖ A♭9 ‖ D♭13 ‖

▲ Try playing through these examples of jazz chord extensions, substitutions and altered jazz chords.

Improvisation

To improvise a jazz solo you will need to know a variety of scales and understand which chords they complement. All the major scale modes can be used, but the Dorian, Mixolydian and Ionian modes are of particular importance as they complement the minor 7, dominant 7 and major 7 chords and extensions that are so frequently used in jazz. Most jazz tunes also feature key changes, so the big challenge is to play over them without interrupting the melodic flow of a solo. Other scales featured include the melodic and harmonic minor scales, the whole tone scale, the diminished scale and the chromatic scale. The latter is often used as it contains notes outside the key scale, which can be used to create extra tension in a melody or solo.

Improvisation within a set piece is best approached by starting with the basic melody of a tune and varying it. You should also jam regularly with other musicians as this will habituate you to playing over different chord progressions.

Start with simple progressions that allow you to improvise with one or two scales, and then work at jamming over key changes. If you like a real challenge, you can also try 'free improvisation' – trying to create music on the spot without any obvious chord progressions or grooves.

▲ Play through this example of chromatic playing in jazz improvisation, and then see if you can come up with your own.

Comping

Another important jazz guitar skill you should work on is 'comping' – playing chord progressions as an accompaniment while others improvise. When you're comping, try substituting different chords and using different strum patterns to create more harmonic and rhythmic interest.

Getting a jazz sound

Although jazz can be played on just about any type of guitar, you might want to try an electric archtop model such as the Gibson ES-175, as this produces a warm, mellow tone. A relatively clean amplifier such as a Polytone Mini Brute or Roland Jazz Chorus will complement this guitar perfectly. Set your amplifier to boost the low and mid-range frequencies, and cut back on the high frequencies. If you want to play

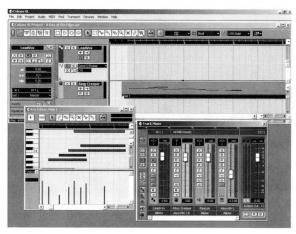

▲ Cubase has long been one of the most popular MIDI and audio sequencers for home recording.

jazz-rock, try a solidbody or semi-solid guitar with a rock amplifier as this will allow you to play soaring, sustained solos with minimal feedback. You can also use a chorus pedal to smoothen your chords, and an overdrive unit to make your solos sound more dynamic. Another effect worth trying is the ring modulator, a pedal that produces metallic, atonal sounds. You can also use an amp modelling box like the Line 6 POD, or a virtual amp software package such as IK Multimedia's AmpliTube to create a realistic jazz amp sound. If you're using a software sequencer package such as Cubase SX, Logic or Sonar to make recordings on your computer, you can also use the sequencer's built-in effects to add more colour and spice to your guitar sound.

Metal

Although the term 'heavy metal' did not become firmly established until the late 1970s, the roots for this popular genre were firmly planted when Led Zeppelin and Black Sabbath formed a decade earlier in the UK.

▲ Iron Maiden's trademark galloping rhythms and lyrics about fantasy or the devil have changed little over the years.

Led Zeppelin was assembled by guitarist Jimmy Page, after he left the Yardbirds. Influenced by Clapton and Hendrix, Page came up with a heavy riff style, as heard featured alongside Robert Plant's screaming vocals in Zeppelin's 'Whole Lotta Love' (1969). Black Sabbath formed that same year and comprised guitarist Tony Iommi, singer Ozzy Osbourne, bassist Geezer Butler and drummer Bill Ward. They developed a more basic heavy riff style, used on 'Paranoid' and 'Iron Man' (both 1970). The band's themes of death, destruction and mental illness were soon adopted by other bands such as Motörhead, Rainbow and the leather-clad Judas Priest, and heavy metal was born!

NWOBHM

In the late 1970s, a number of new British bands emerged, including Iron Maiden, Def Leppard and Samson. Although they did not match the depth, range and invention of their predecessors, their music, categorized as the New Wave Of British Heavy Metal (NWOBHM) was a huge commercial success. In the US Van Halen introduced a

new style of heavy rock, showcasing the two-handed tapping techniques of guitarist Eddie Van Halen (b. 1955) and showmanship of singer David Lee Roth, while over in Australia, school uniform-clad guitarist Angus Young (b. 1955) and his pals forged their own brand of 'no-nonsense rock 'n' roll' in AC/DC.

◄ Metallica were the most successful of the thrash metal bands, gradually developing their sound into heavy metal.

Thrash

By the middle of the 1980s, guitarists decided that they wanted to spice things up by playing harder and faster, resulting in the thrash metal sound made popular by Metallica, Slayer, Anthrax, Megadeth, Sepultura and Pantera. Metallica were by far the most successful of these bands; their first few albums, *Kill 'Em All* (1983), *Ride the Lightning* (1984) and *Master of Puppets* (1986), expanded the limits of metal by introducing intricately structured compositions played at an unheard-of speed. Slayer developed an even faster style, delivering a stream of full-throttle metal with manic solos and deranged lyrics. Their fifth album, *Reign in Blood* (1986), is widely regarded as a metal classic. Various other sub-styles later evolved out of thrash, including death metal and black metal.

A solo effort

While Kirk Hammett (b. 1962) of Metallica and Kerry King (b. 1964) of Slayer were thrashing their way around the globe, a handful of other heavy rock soloists such as Steve Vai and Yngwie Malmsteen adopted a more 'arty' approach to their soloing. Vai released a series of solo albums featuring his whammy bar pyrotechnics and sublime modal soloing, and, along with his former mentor, Joe Satriani (b. 1956), raised the standard for rock guitar virtuosity. Malmsteen fused metal with the classical styles of Bach and Paganini, pioneering the 'baroque and roll' style.

Nu-metal and the return of thrash

As the 1980s drew to an end, young audiences veered away from thrash and 'flash', but in the early 1990s nu-metal bands such as Korn and Slipknot took the best elements of metal and grunge, donned seven-string guitars and developed a subversive riff style that was hugely popular and spawned several successful offshoot bands such as System of a Down and Linkin Park. As nu-metal began to wane, thrash suddenly became cool again and the genre seemed to turn full circle as new American bands such as Shadows Fall, Chimaira, Killswitch Engage and Lamb of God fronted the unimaginatively named New Wave Of American Heavy Metal, while across the Atlantic the likes of Rhapsody, Soilwork, Lacuna Coil, In Flames and Nightwish have kept the European metal flag flying.

Playing metal

Although most metal guitarists know a variety of chords, you can play a lot of music in this style with power chords. The most basic of these are two-note chords consisting of the first and fifth notes of the major scale and played on any two adjacent strings, with your index finger fretting the root note and your third finger fretting the fifth note. To play a G power chord on the sixth and fifth strings (E and A), for example, place your index finger behind the third fret on the sixth string and your third finger behind the fifth fret on the fifth string, and then strum those strings only. To play an A power chord on the same two strings, simply move the shape two frets further up the guitar neck.

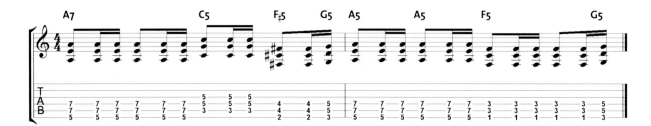

▲ Try this example of metal rhythm playing which uses sixteenth notes and power chords.

Add power to power chords

You can strengthen your power chords by adding the note an octave higher than your root note on the next string along; to play a three-note G power chord on the sixth, fifth and fourth strings, adopt the fingering position already described, and add your fourth finger, placed behind the fifth fret on the fourth string. Bear in mind, though, that when you're playing any power chords, you should only strum the strings you are fretting.

You should also learn the barred versions of the open A and E shapes and the open Am and Em shapes, as these can be used anywhere on the fingerboard to allow you to play full major or minor chords in any key you want. Diminished and augmented chords can also be useful for a dissonant metal sound.

Getting in rhythm

Rhythmically, metal is usually relentless, with emphasis on insistent eighth- or sixteenth-note rhythms and a heavy accent on the first and other beats. Strumming is usually performed with downstrokes, although more intricate rhythms sometimes require alternating downstrokes and upstrokes. Metal guitarists also perform muted versions of their riffs by resting the side of their picking hand against the strings.

You should learn the pentatonic scales and all the common major scale modes. If you want to play a thrash-related style you will have to learn to play them fast with alternate picking. Practise hammer-ons and pull-offs, as these can easily be combined with picked notes to create rapid phrases. Another common technique is sweep-picking (also called economy-picking). By applying this technique to notes on adjacent strings, you can play an ascending line with a downstroke or a descending line with an upstroke.

Getting an authentic metal sound

For an authentic metal sound you'll need a solidbody electric guitar and an amplifier with preamp distortion capabilities. Solidbody guitars produce a sustained, overdriven tone with minimal feedback at reasonably high volumes; all the classic Gibson models are suitable but there is a range of dedicated metal instruments available, including the ESP JH2, BC Rich Warlock, PRS Singlecut, Jackson Kelly and Washburn Dime models. These guitars have humbucking pickups, which are ideal for an aggressive metal sound, but you can also use guitars fitted with traditional single coil pickups if you use a distortion pedal.

A thick pick (0.9 mm/0.003 in or thicker) is essential for metal music as it will make firmer contact with your strings. Try out several different picks before you decide.

▲ Buying the right equipment is vital if you're trying to achieve an authentic metal sound. Pictured here is a Washburn special edition and a marshall head amplifier.

Which amplifier is best?

Amp-wise, there are a number of dedicated metal amplifiers, including valve-style models such as the Mesa Boogie Dual Rectifier, Marshall Mode 4, Hughes & Kettner Warp 7, Peavey 5150 and Randall Warhead models. If you want to play without upsetting your neighbours, try an amp modelling box such as a Linc 6 POD, or a virtual amp software package like IK Multimedia's AmpliTube or Steinberg's Warp VST. These feature metal presets, and can be used at any volume.

Rock

By the late 1960s, many popular acts had grown tired of producing chart songs, and injected more attitude, experimentation and social conscience into their music. 'Rock' was born. The pioneers of this new style included Eric Clapton, the Rolling Stones and Jimi Hendrix (1942–70), whose music appealed to record buyers who saw mainstream pop as tame.

Clapton first made a name for himself with John Mayall's Bluesbreakers in 1965 when he turned his amp up loud to get a more aggressive, sustained guitar tone. He formed Cream two years later with bassist Jack Bruce and drummer Ginger Baker, and they were the first popular group to feature extended virtuoso solos in their music. By 1967, Hendrix had also extended the range of the electric guitar by coaxing sounds out of it that hadn't been heard before. Clapton and Hendrix based their playing around the blues scale and their solos were often long improvisations. Pop guitar solos were usually brief instrumental fills between vocal passages, but 'classic rock' solos would often take up half of the song.

▼ In the 1970s, the Rolling Stones moved from their blues roots to a more polished rock sound.

Birth of the riff

Another prominent feature in early rock music was the riff – a repeated note or chord phrase over which the vocals and solos were projected. A classic example of this is Cream's 'Sunshine of Your Love' (1968), a whole song based upon a simple, grinding riff. Other players such as Jimmy Page, Ritchie Blackmore and Tony Iommi (b. 1948) latched on to the sheer power of this device and started to create even more powerful riffs, such as Led Zeppelin's 'Whole Lotta Love' (1969), Deep Purple's 'Speed King' (1970) and Black Sabbath's 'Paranoid' (1970).

Rock music marked a shift away from singles and towards albums; projects such as Led Zeppelin's acclaimed *Led Zeppelin II* (1969), Pink Floyd's psychedelic *Dark Side of the Moon* (1973) and Mike Oldfield's instrumental *Tubular Bells* (1973) were all bestselling albums by artists who rarely recorded singles.

Punk

In 1976, punk suddenly appeared and bands like the Sex Pistols, the Clash and the Damned introduced a basic rock style that relied more on attitude than technique. However, it was a short-lived trend and by the late 1970s rock began to fragment into a number of sub-genres, including new wave (an offshoot from punk), stadium rock (the likes of Bruce Springsteen and Queen) and the various strands of heavy metal that were beginning to develop in the US and UK.

▲ For many, the Clash were the ultimate punk rock band.

New wave was essentially a generic term used for the wide range of British bands that followed on from punk. These included idiosyncratic artists such as Elvis Costello (b. 1954) and XTC, straight-ahead rockers like the Pretenders and the Cars, white reggae or ska pop bands including Madness and the Police, and a legion of synthesizer-driven bands. The genre died out when new bands such as the Smiths and REM began to appeal to more alternative rock fans.

Indie

The Smiths were the dominant British 'indie' rock band of the 1980s, and this was mainly down to the unique combination of singer Morrissey's forlorn crooning and the uncluttered rhythm guitar work of Johnny Marr (b. 1963). They recorded a number of hit singles and albums that laid down the foundations for the next generation of British guitar bands, before splitting up in 1987. REM also boasted a unique singer/guitarist combination – Michael Stipe's cryptic vocals and the ringing guitar hooks of Peter Buck (b. 1956). They are still going strong today.

Grunge

Despite the influx of fresh indie bands into the album and singles charts during the 1980s, most of the popular bands from this period, including Bon Jovi and Guns N' Roses, were purveyors of straight-ahead rock. By the end of the decade, however, grunge – a vibrant mixture of punk and heavy metal – became a prominent movement with Nirvana, a Seattle-based band, at the helm. Nirvana's success was down to a combination of strong material, stop-start dynamics, and the manic intensity of singer-guitarist Kurt Cobain (1967–94). Unfortunately, Cobain suffered from drug addiction and manic depression, a combination that ended in suicide.

Variety of rock styles

A number of major song-orientated rock styles emerged during the 1990s including Britpop, which mixed songwriting – inspired by bands like the Beatles – with the more indie vibe of the Smiths. Suede, fronted by the quasi-glam vocals of Brett Anderson and sweeping guitar of Bernard Butler (b. 1970), pioneered this style, and they paved the way for the huge success of Oasis and Blur, bands from the north and south of England respectively. The decade also saw the rise of inventive alternative rock bands including Radiohead, who combined intense guitar sounds with electronic drones and angst-driven lyrics. Today there is an unprecedented variety of rock styles and this range is still growing.

Playing rock

If you want to be a proficient rock guitarist, you'll need to know a variety of basic chord shapes. The most common open chords (ones that include open strings as well as fretted ones) are A, Am, B7, C, C7, D, Dm, D7, E, E7, F, G and G7, which will allow you to play songs in the popular rock keys of A, C, D, E and G. The barre chords you should know are the barred versions of the A and E shapes (major barre chords) and Am and Em shapes (minor barre chords). These will allow you to play in any key you want, as barre shapes can be played anywhere on the fingerboard. Open chords are good for earthy strumming and would suit, for example, an Oasis-style song, while barre chords can be used to create a more powerful, aggressive sound for punk and hard-rock styles. Major chords are ideal for upbeat rock riffs, while minor ones are more suitable for ballads.

▲ Fifth chords are often referred to as 'power chords' because of their solid sound.

Power chords

You should also familiarize yourself with the basic 'power chords' used in grunge and hard rock. These are two note chords consisting of the first and fifth notes of the major scale, played on any two adjacent strings (such as the sixth and fifth strings, or fourth and third strings) with your index finger fretting the root note (on the thicker string) and your third finger fretting the fifth note (on the lighter string) two frets further up the fingerboard. To play an A power chord on the sixth and fifth strings (E and A strings), for example, place your index finger behind the fifth fret on the sixth string and your third finger behind the seventh fret on the fifth string and then strum those strings only. To play a B power chord on the same two strings, simply move the shape two frets further up the guitar neck and so on.

Strumming and picking

Rhythmically, rock is fairly straightforward, with emphasis mainly on the first and third beats of the bar. Strumming is usually performed with downstrokes, as these supply more power, although more intricate rhythms might require alternating downstrokes and upstrokes. Many rock guitarists also play chords as arpeggios (playing all the separate notes in ascending or descending order) with a plectrum or the fingers of their picking hand, to produce a more melodious sound. This is used to great effect in rock classics such as Led Zeppelin's 'Stairway to Heaven' and the Animals' 'House of the Rising Sun'.

▲ In classic rock, repetitive guitar riffs such as this one, often open and then form the basis of the songs.

▲ Chords in grunge rhythm playing are largely played as fifth chords in order to achieve a controlled, tighter sound.

All rock solos feature the pentatonic minor and blues scales (pages 46–48), and you should familiarize yourself with these scales if you want to play basic rock lead guitar. If you want to take things further, the major scale and the Mixolydian mode (pages 44–45 and 51) will add greater depth to your upbeat solos, and the Aeolian mode will come in handy for those haunting rock ballads.

Getting an authentic rock sound

If you want to get a good rock guitar sound you'll need an electric guitar and some sort of amplifier. The guitar can be a solidbody instrument (one made out of solid wood) or a semi-solid model (hollowed out). Solidbody guitars are great for producing a clear, sustained tone with minimal feedback, while semi-solid instruments produce a fat, warm sound but tend to feedback more when used at higher volumes.

▼ The Gibson SG produces a truly great rock sound from its humbuckers. Combine it with a great valve amp like this Fender deluxe, and you're really rocking.

▶ Some people are advocates of effects pedals like the Line 6 POD which can replicate the sounds of different amplifiers.

Choosing the right amplifier

When it comes to amplifiers, you have a number of options, the most traditional of which would be a hardware amp. These come in two flavours: valve amps, which are expensive but produce a fat, warm sound; and transistor amps, which are more affordable and reliable but not ideal if you're after a 'vintage' tone. If you do choose to buy a hardware amp, make sure it has a built-in preamp so you can optimize the amount of distortion in your guitar sound.

Hardware amps can get loud, and playing through one at home might upset your neighbours. In such a case, you should consider using an amplifier modelling box such as a Line 6 POD, or a virtual amp software package such as IK Multimedia's AmpliTube. These come with an arsenal of realistic and ready-to-go rock presets, and you can use them at any volume you like. You can even gig with them, as long as the venue at which you're playing has a PA system.

The right effects

Effects pedals have been used extensively by rock players over the years and you too can use them to colour your guitar sound. A wah-wah pedal will come in handy for Hendrix-style soloing, while a phaser or flanger can be used to create psychedelic textures and tones. An overdrive pedal might be useful for adding extra distortion during solos, and a compressor can be great for ironing out excessively loud or quiet sounds so you end up with a more consistent signal. Most virtual amps come with a selection of built-in effects that you can use, so don't forget to try them out if you've got such equipment!

▶ Queen, with Freddie Mercury at the helm, are a classic rock act, with soaring guitars and vocals competing for space.

Chord Dictionary

The chord fretboxes in this section will help you learn the shapes of hundreds of chords, and will be a useful reference guide when you are playing and composing your own music. These next few pages are by no means comprehensive, but should contain enough chord formations for you, whatever your needs.

While learning the fingerings might not seem particularly interesting, you should remember that the wider your chord vocabulary becomes, the more you will be able to vary your compositions and your playing style. If you jam with other musicians, it is very important to know your chords – you don't want to be struggling to find the right fingering when the leader shouts 'G'!

The chords are divided by key, from A to G#, with the key's notes shown at the end of the key's section. There are two double-page spreads devoted to each key. The first spread outlines the main chords you will need to learn, each shown in three different fingerings or positions. It can be useful to know a variety of positions for each chord, especially when fitting them into a progression – when you are playing in high fingerboard positions, you do not want to have to stop and scramble about, trying to find a chord position back on the first few frets.

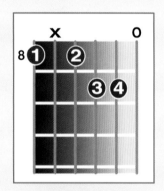

C7#5   C Dominant 7th #5
1st (C), 3rd (E), #5th (G#), ♭7th (B♭)

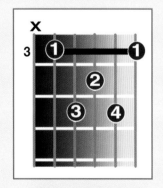

Cmaj7   C Major 7th
1st (C), 3rd (E), 5th (G), 7th (B)

The second spread shows some of the more advanced chords that can be useful when playing progressions, for linking chords or for use when you are improvising. There are only two positions shown for these, so as to include a greater variety of chords.

All the diagrams show the guitar fretboard in an upright position, with high E on the right. The nut appears at the top if the chord is played on the lower frets. If the chord is in a higher position, the fret number on which it begins is given to the left of the diagram.

The notes to be played are shown as circles, with the finger number that should be used for each note (❶= index finger; ❷ = middle finger; ❸ = ring finger; ❹ = little finger). An **X** above the string indicates that the string should not be played in the chord and should be muted to prevent it sounding accidentally. An **O** above the string shows that it should be played as an open string.

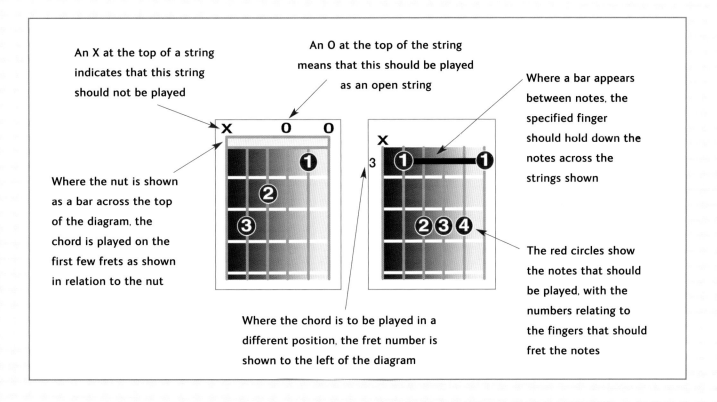

An X at the top of a string indicates that this string should not be played

An O at the top of the string means that this should be played as an open string

Where a bar appears between notes, the specified finger should hold down the notes across the strings shown

Where the nut is shown as a bar across the top of the diagram, the chord is played on the first few frets as shown in relation to the nut

Where the chord is to be played in a different position, the fret number is shown to the left of the diagram

The red circles show the notes that should be played, with the numbers relating to the fingers that should fret the notes

This section should not be difficult to use. Where there is a choice of note name (e.g. C♯ or D♭) we have selected the one that you are more likely to come across in your playing.

Where a chord contains a flattened (♭) or sharpened (♯) interval (e.g. ♯5th), you can find the notes by playing a fret lower (for a flat) or a fret higher (for a sharp) than the interval note indicated at the top of the page. In the keys that contain a large number of sharps or flats, double flats (♭♭) and double sharps (x) sometimes occur in the augmented or diminished chords. A double flat is the note two frets below the named note, while a double sharp is two frets up.

A Main Chords

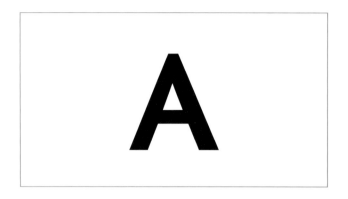

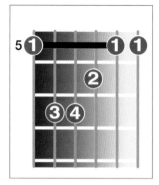

A A Major
1st (A), 3rd (C#), 5th (E)

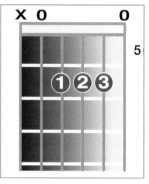

A A Major
1st (A), 3rd (C#), 5th (E)

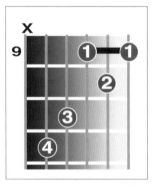

A A Major
1st (A), 3rd (C#), 5th (E)

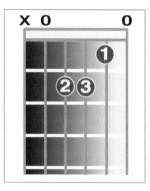

Am A Minor
1st (A), ♭3rd (C), 5th (E)

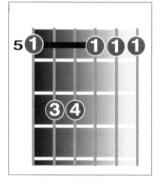

Am A Minor
1st (A), ♭3rd (C), 5th (E)

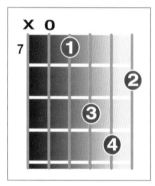

Am A Minor
1st (A), ♭3rd (C), 5th (E)

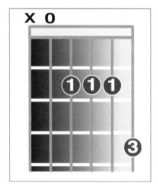

Amaj7 A Major 7th
1st (A), 3rd (C#), 5th (E), 7th (G#)

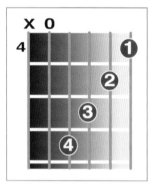

Amaj7 A Major 7th
1st (A), 3rd (C#), 5th (E), 7th (G#)

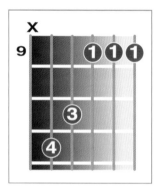

Amaj7 A Major 7th
1st (A), 3rd (C#), 5th (E), 7th (G#)

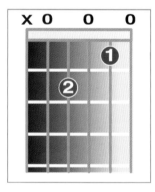

Am7 A Minor 7th
1st (A), ♭3rd (C), 5th (E), ♭7th (G)

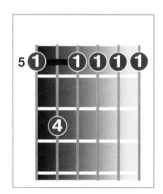

Am7 A Minor 7th
1st (A), ♭3rd (C) 5th (E), ♭7th (G)

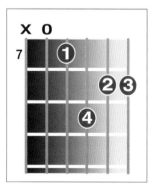

Am7 A Minor 7th
1st (A), ♭3rd (C), 5th (E), ♭7th (G)

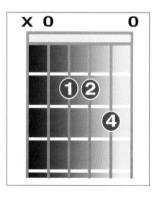

Asus4 A Suspended 4th
1st (A), 4th (D), 5th (E)

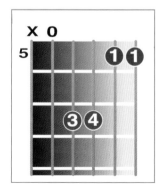

Asus4 A Suspended 4th
1st (A), 4th (D), 5th (E)

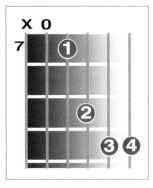

Asus4   A Suspended 4th
1st (A), 4th (D), 5th (E)

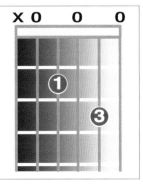

A7sus4   A Dominant 7th sus4
1st (A), 4th (D), 5th (E), ♭7th (G)

A7sus4   A Dominant 7th sus4
1st (A), 4th (D), 5th (E), ♭7th (G)

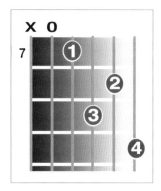

A7sus4   A Dominant 7th sus4
1st (A), 4th (D), 5th (E), ♭7th (G)

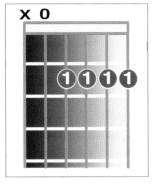

A6   A Major 6th
1st (A), 3rd (C#), 5th (E), 6th (F#)

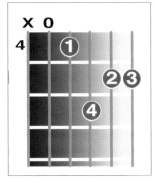

A6   A Major 6th
1st (A), 3rd (C#), 5th (E), 6th (F#)

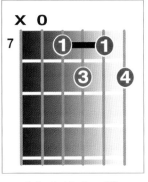

A6   A Major 6th
1st (A), 3rd (C#), 5th (E), 6th (F#)

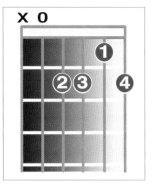

Am6   A Minor 6th
1st (A), ♭3rd (C), 5th (E), 6th (F#)

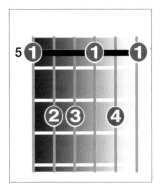

Am6   A Minor 6th
1st (A), ♭3rd (C), 5th (E), 6th (F#)

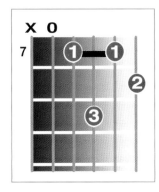

Am6   A Minor 6th
1st (A), ♭3rd (C), 5th (E), 6th (F#)

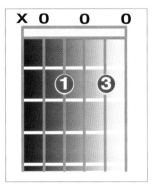

A7   A Dominant 7th
1st (A), 3rd (C#), 5th (E), ♭7th (G)

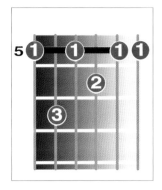

A7   A Dominant 7th
1st (A), 3rd (C#), 5th (E), ♭7th (G)

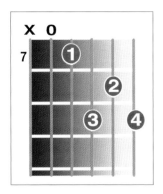

A7   A Dominant 7th
1st (A), 3rd (C#), 5th (E), ♭7th (G)

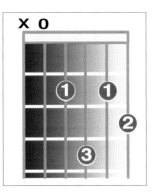

A9   A Dominant 9th
1st (A), 3rd (C#), 5th (E), ♭7th
(G), 9th (B)

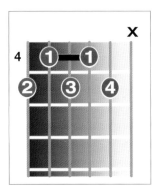

A9   A Dominant 9th
1st (A), 3rd (C#), 5th (E), ♭7th
(G), 9th (B)

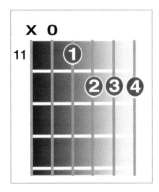

A9   A Dominant 9th
1st (A), 3rd (C#), 5th (E), ♭7th
(G), 9th (B)

A Advanced Chords

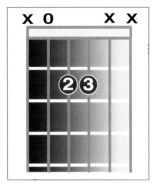

A5 **A 5th (power chord)**
1st (A), 5th (E)

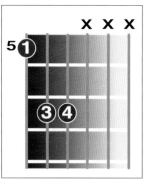

A5 **A 5th (power chord)**
1st (A), 5th (E)

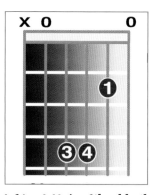

A 6/9 **A Major 6th add 9th**
1st (A), 3rd (C#), 5th (E),
6th (F#), 9th (B)

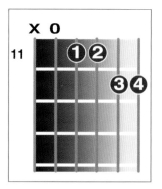

A 6/9 **A Major 6th add 9th**
1st (A), 3rd (C#), 5th (E),
6th (F#), 9th (B)

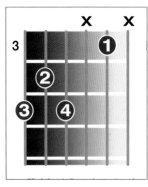

A11 **A Dominant 11th**
1st (A), 3rd (C#), 5th (E), b7th (G),
9th (B), 11th (D)

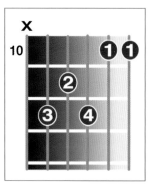

A11 **A Dominant 11th**
1st (A), 3rd (C#), 5th (E), b7th (G),
9th (B), 11th (D)

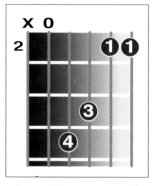

A13 **A Dominant 13th**
1st (A), 3rd (C#), 5th (E), b7th (G),
9th (B), 13th (F#)

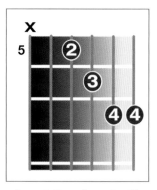

A13 **A Dominant 13th**
1st (A), 3rd (C#), 5th (E), b7th (G),
9th (B), 13th (F#)

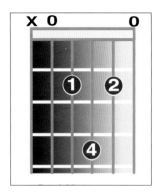

Aadd9 **A Major add 9th**
1st (A), 3rd (C#), 5th (E), 9th (B)

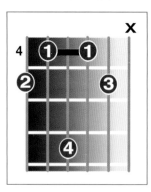

Aadd9 **A Major add 9th**
1st (A), 3rd (C#), 5th (E), 9th (B)

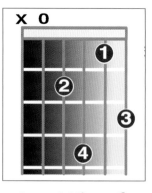

Am9 **A Minor 9th**
1st (A), b3rd (C), 5th (E), b7th
(G), 9th (B)

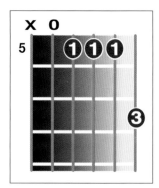

Am9 **A Minor 9th**
1st (A), b3rd (C), 5th (E), b7th
(G), 9th (B)

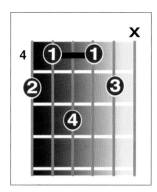

Amaj9 **A Major 9th**
1st (A), 3rd (C#),
5th (E), 7th (G#), 9th (B)

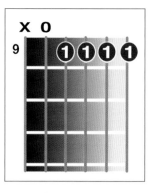

Amaj9 **A Major 9th**
1st (A), 3rd (C#),
5th (E), 7th (G#), 9th (B)

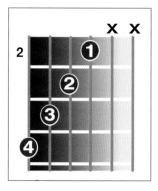

A+ **A Augmented**
1st (A), 3rd (C#), #5th (E#)

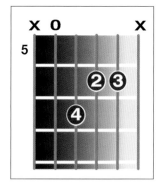

A+ **A Augmented**
1st (A), 3rd (C#), #5th (E#)

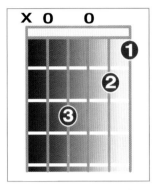

A7#5 A Dominant 7th #5
1st (A), 3rd (C#), #5th (E#), ♭7th (G)

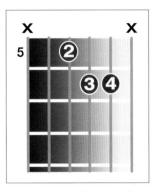

A7#5 A Dominant 7th #5
1st (A), 3rd (C#), #5th (E#), ♭7th (G)

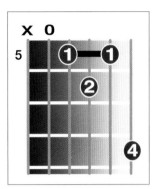

A7#9 A Dominant 7th #9
1st (A), 3rd (C#),
5th (E), ♭7th (G), #9th (B#)

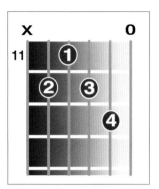

A7#9 A Dominant 7th #9
1st (A), 3rd (C#),
5th (E), ♭7th (G), #9th (B#)

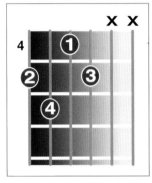

Ao7 A Diminished 7th
1st (A), ♭3rd (C), ♭5th (E♭), ♭♭7th (G♭)

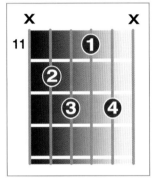

Ao7 A Diminished 7th
1st (A), ♭3rd (C), ♭5th (E♭), ♭♭7th (G♭)

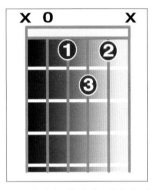

Ao A Diminished triad
1st (A), ♭3rd (C), ♭5th (E♭)

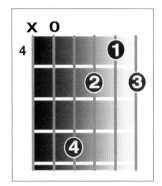

Ao A Diminished triad
1st (A), ♭3rd (C), ♭5th (E♭)

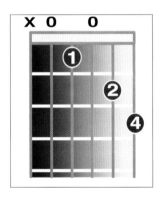

A7♭5 A Dominant 7th ♭5
1st (A), 3rd (C#), ♭5th (E♭), ♭7th (G)

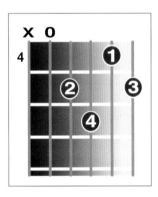

A7♭5 A Dominant 7th ♭5
1st (A), 3rd (C#), ♭5th (E♭), ♭7th (G)

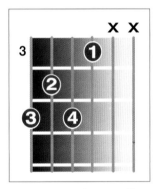

A7♭9 A Dominant 7th ♭9
1st (A), 3rd (C#),
5th (E), ♭7th (G), ♭9th (B♭)

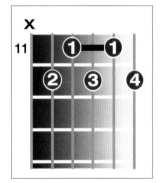

A7♭9 A Dominant 7th ♭9
1st (A), 3rd (C#),
5th (E), ♭7th (G), ♭9th (B♭)

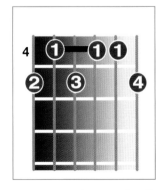

A9♭5 A Dominant 9th ♭5th
1st (A), 3rd (C#),
♭5th (E♭), ♭7th (G), 9th (B)

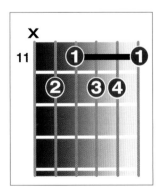

A9♭5 A Dominant 9th ♭5th
1st (A), 3rd (C#),
♭5th (E♭), ♭7th (G), 9th (B)

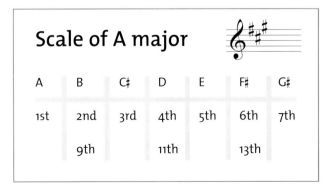

Scale of A major

A	B	C#	D	E	F#	G#
1st	2nd	3rd	4th	5th	6th	7th
	9th		11th		13th	

B♭/A♯ Main Chords

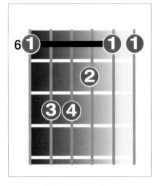

B♭ B♭ major
1st (B♭), 3rd (D), 5th (F)

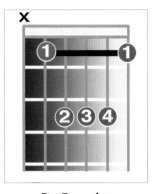

B♭ B♭ major
1st (B♭), 3rd (D), 5th (F)

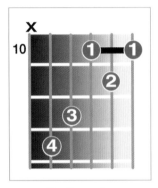

B♭ B♭ major
1st (B♭), 3rd (D), 5th (F)

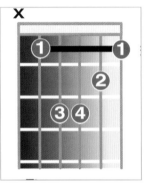

B♭m B♭ Minor
1st (B♭), ♭3rd (D♭), 5th (F)

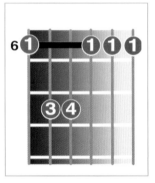

B♭m B♭ Minor
1st (B♭), ♭3rd (D♭), 5th (F)

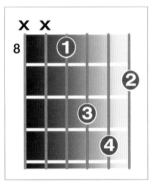

B♭m B♭ Minor
1st (B♭), ♭3rd (D♭), 5th (F)

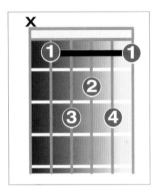

B♭maj7 B♭ Major 7th
1st (B♭), 3rd (D), 5th (F), 7th (A)

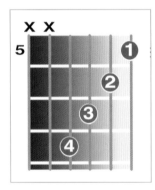

B♭maj7 B♭ Major 7th
1st (B♭), 3rd (D), 5th (F), 7th (A)

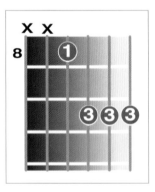

B♭maj7 B♭ Major 7th
1st (B♭), 3rd (D), 5th (F), 7th (A)

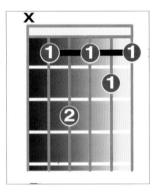

B♭m7 B♭ Minor 7th
1st (B♭), ♭3rd (D♭), 5th (F), ♭7th (A♭)

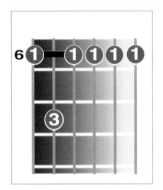

B♭m7 B♭ Minor 7th
1st (B♭), ♭3rd (D♭), 5th (F), ♭7th (A♭)

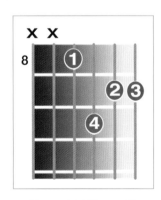

B♭m7 B♭ Minor 7th
1st (B♭), ♭3rd (D♭), 5th (F), ♭7th (A♭)

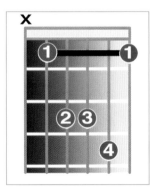

B♭sus4 B♭ Suspended 4th
1st (B♭), 4th (E♭), 5th (F)

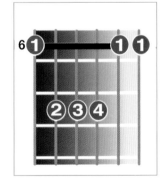

B♭sus4 B♭ Suspended 4th
1st (B♭), 4th (E♭), 5th (F)

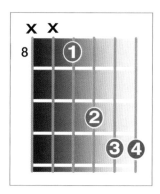

B♭sus4 B♭ Suspended 4th
1st (B♭), 4th (E♭), 5th (F)

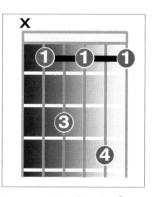

B♭7sus4 B♭ Dominant 7th sus4
1st (B♭), 4th (E♭), 5th (F), ♭7th (A♭)

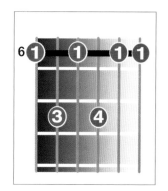

B♭7sus4 B♭ Dominant 7th sus4
1st (B♭), 4th (E♭), 5th (F), ♭7th (A♭)

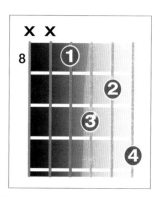

B♭7sus4 B♭ Dominant 7th sus4
1st (B♭), 4th (E♭), 5th (F), ♭7th (A♭)

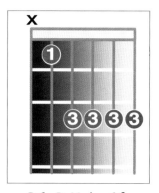

B♭6 B♭ Major 6th
1st (B♭), 3rd (D), 5th (F), 6th (G)

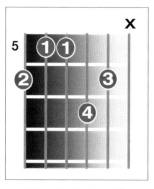

B♭6 B♭ Major 6th
1st (B♭), 3rd (D), 5th (F), 6th (G)

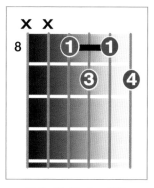

B♭6 B♭ Major 6th
1st (B♭), 3rd (D), 5th (F), 6th (G)

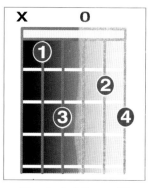

B♭m6 B♭ Minor 6th
1st (B♭), ♭3rd (D♭), 5th (F), 6th (G)

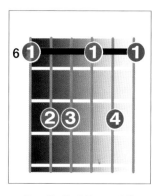

B♭m6 B♭ Minor 6th
1st (B♭), ♭3rd (D♭), 5th (F), 6th (G)

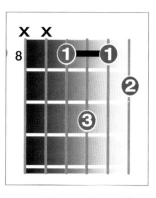

B♭m6 B♭ Minor 6th
1st (B♭), ♭3rd (D♭), 5th (F), 6th (G)

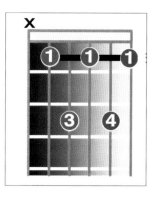

B♭7 B♭ Dominant 7th
1st (B♭), 3rd (D),
5th (F), ♭7th (A♭)

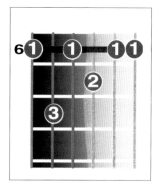

B♭7 B♭ Dominant 7th
1st (B♭), 3rd (D),
5th (F), ♭7th (A♭)

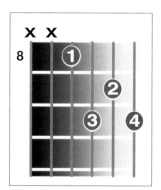

B♭7 B♭ Dominant 7th
1st (B♭), 3rd (D),
5th (F), ♭7th (A♭)

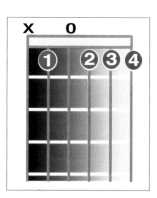

B♭9 B♭ Dominant 9th
1st (B♭), 3rd (D), 5th (F),
♭7th (A♭), 9th (C)

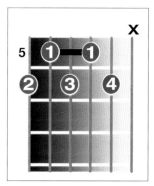

B♭9 B♭ Dominant 9th
1st (B♭), 3rd (D), 5th (F),
♭7th (A♭), 9th (C)

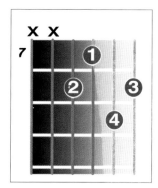

B♭9 B♭ Dominant 9th
1st (B♭), 3rd (D),
5th (F), ♭7th (A♭), 9th (C)

B♭/A♯ Advanced Chords

B♭5 **B♭ 5th (power chord)**
1st (B♭), 5th (F)

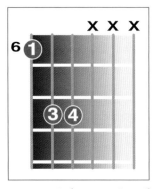

B♭5 **B♭ 5th (power chord)**
1st (B♭), 5th (F)

B♭6/9 **B♭ Major 6th add 9th**
1st (B♭), 3rd (D), 5th (F),
6th (G), 9th (C)

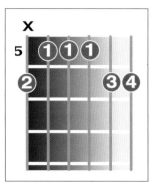

B♭6/9 **B♭ Major 6th add 9th**
1st (B♭), 3rd (D), 5th (F),
6th (G), 9th (C)

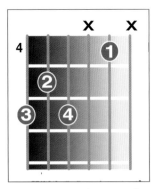

B♭11 **B♭ Dominant 11th**
1st (B♭), 3rd (D), 5th (F),
♭7th (A♭), 9th (C), 11th (E♭)

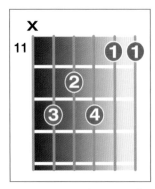

B♭11 **B♭ Dominant 11th**
1st (B♭), 3rd (D), 5th (F),
♭7th (A♭), 9th (C), 11th (E♭)

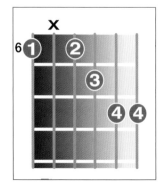

B♭13 **B♭ Dominant 13th**
1st (B♭), 3rd (D), 5th (F),
♭7th (A♭), 9th (C), 13th (G)

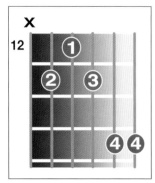

B♭13 **B♭ Dominant 13th**
1st (B♭), 3rd (D), 5th (F),
♭7th (A♭), 9th (C), 13th (G)

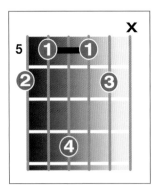

B♭add9 **B♭ Major add 9th**
1st (B♭), 3rd (D), 5th (F), 9th (C)

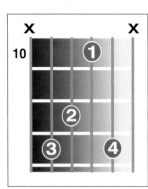

B♭add9 **B♭ Major add 9th**
1st (B♭), 3rd (D), 5th (F), 9th (C)

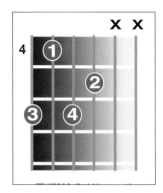

B♭m9 **B♭ Minor 9th**
1st (B♭), ♭3rd (D♭), 5th (F),
♭7th (A♭), 9th (C)

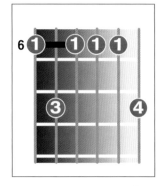

B♭m9 **B♭ Minor 9th**
1st (B♭), ♭3rd (D♭), 5th (F),
♭7th (A♭), 9th (C)

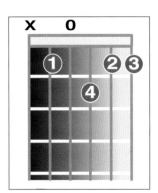

B♭maj9 **B♭ Major 9th**
1st (B♭), 3rd (D), 5th (F),
7th (A), 9th (C)

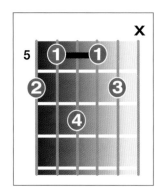

B♭maj9 **B♭ Major 9th**
1st (B♭), 3rd (D), 5th (F),
7th (A), 9th (C)

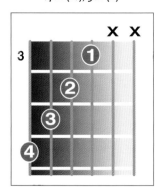

B♭+ **B♭ Augmented**
1st (B♭), 3rd (D), ♯5th (F♯)

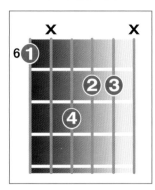

B♭+ **B♭ Augmented**
1st (B♭), 3rd (D), ♯5th (F♯)

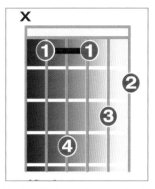

B♭7♯5   **B♭ Dominant 7th ♯5**
1st (B♭), 3rd (D), ♯5th (F♯), ♭7th (A♭)

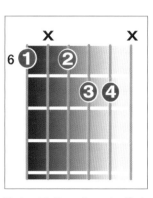

B♭7♯5   **B♭ Dominant 7th ♯5**
1st (B♭), 3rd (D), ♯5th (F♯), ♭7th (A♭)

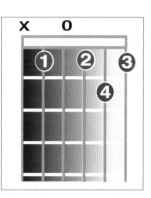

B♭7♯9   **B♭ Dominant 7th ♯9**
1st (B♭), 3rd (D), 5th (F),
♭7th (A♭), ♯9th (C♯)

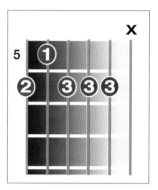

B♭7♯9   **B♭ Dominant 7th ♯9**
1st (B♭), 3rd (D), 5th (F),
♭7th (A♭), ♯9th (C♯)

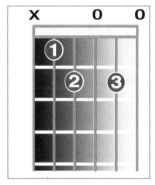

B♭o7   **B♭ Diminished 7th**
1st (B♭), ♭3rd (D♭), ♭5th (F♭), ♭♭7th (A♭♭)

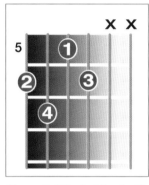

B♭o7   **B♭ Diminished 7th**
1st (B♭), ♭3rd (D♭), ♭5th (F♭), ♭♭7th (A♭♭)

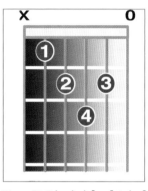

B♭o   **B♭ Diminished triad**
1st (B♭), ♭3rd (D♭), ♭5th (F♭)

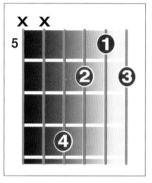

B♭o   **B♭ Diminished triad**
1st (B♭), ♭3rd (D♭), ♭5th (F♭)

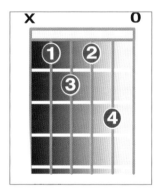

B♭7♭5   **B♭ Dominant 7th ♭5**
1st (B♭), 3rd (D), ♭5th (F♭), ♭7th (A♭)

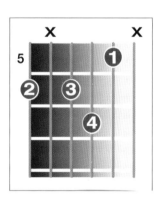

B♭7♭5   **B♭ Dominant 7th ♭5**
1st (B♭), 3rd (D), ♭5th (F♭), ♭7th (A♭)

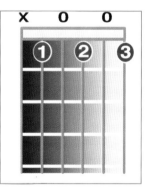

B♭7♭9   **B♭ Dominant 7th ♭9**
1st (B♭), 3rd (D), 5th (F),
♭7th (A♭), ♭9th (C♭)

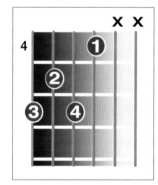

B♭7♭9   **B♭ Dominant 7th ♭9**
1st (B♭), 3rd (D), 5th (F),
♭7th (A♭), ♭9th (C♭)

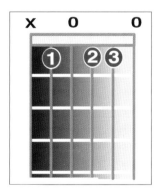

B♭9♭5   **B♭ Dominant 9th ♭5th**
1st (B♭), 3rd (D), ♭5th (F♭),
♭7th (A♭), 9th (C)

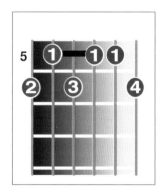

B♭9♭5   **B♭ Dominant 9th ♭5th**
1st (B♭), 3rd (D), ♭5th (F♭),
♭7th (A♭), 9th (C)

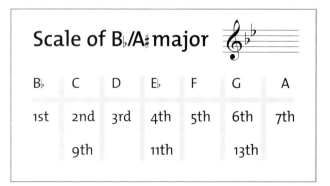

Scale of B♭/A♯ major

B♭	C	D	E♭	F	G	A
1st	2nd	3rd	4th	5th	6th	7th
	9th		11th		13th	

B Main Chords

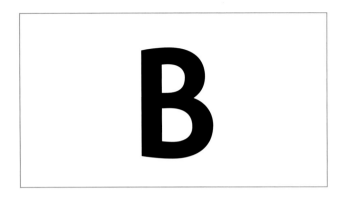

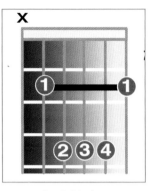

B   B Major
1st (B), 3rd (D#), 5th (F#)

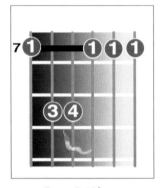

B   B Major
1st (B), 3rd (D#), 5th (F#)

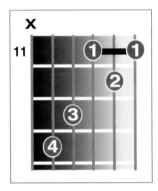

B   B Major
1st (B), 3rd (D#), 5th (F#)

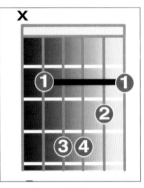

Bm   B Minor
1st (B), b3rd (D), 5th (F#)

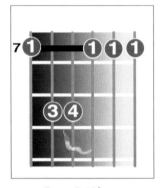

Bm   B Minor
1st (B), b3rd (D), 5th (F#)

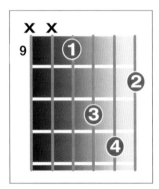

Bm   B Minor
1st (B), b3rd (D), 5th (F#)

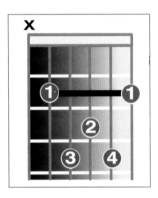

Bmaj7   B Major 7th
1st (B), 3rd (D#),
5th (F#), 7th (A#)

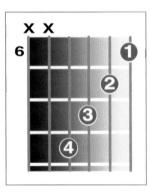

Bmaj7   B Major 7th
1st (B), 3rd (D#),
5th (F#), 7th (A#)

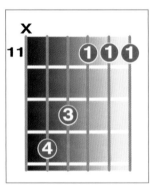

Bmaj7   B Major 7th
1st (B), 3rd (D#),
5th (F#), 7th (A#)

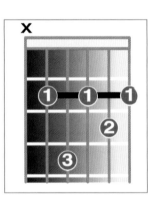

Bm7   B Minor 7th
1st (B), b3rd (D),
5th (F#), b7th (A)

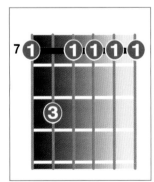

Bm7   B Minor 7th
1st (B), b3rd (D),
5th (F#), b7th (A)

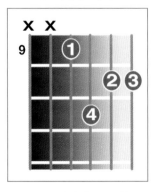

Bm7   B Minor 7th
1st (B), b3rd (D),
5th (F#), b7th (A)

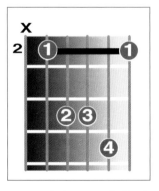

Bsus4   B Suspended 4th
1st (B), 4th (E), 5th (F#)

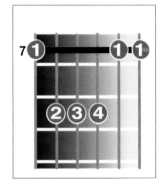

Bsus4   B Suspended 4th
1st (B), 4th (E), 5th (F#)

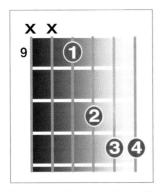

Bsus4   B Suspended 4th
1st (B), 4th (E), 5th (F#)

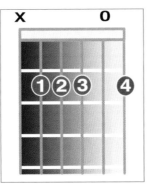

B7sus4   B Dominant 7th sus4
1st (B), 4th (E), 5th (F#), b7th (A)

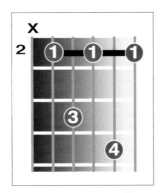

B7sus4   B Dominant 7th sus4
1st (B), 4th (E), 5th (F#), b7th (A)

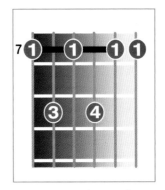

B7sus4   B Dominant 7th sus4
1st (B), 4th (E), 5th (F#), b7th (A)

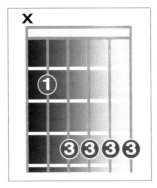

B6   B Major 6th
1st (B), 3rd (D#), 5th (F#), 6th (G#)

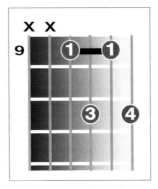

B6   B Major 6th
1st (B), 3rd (D#), 5th (F#), 6th (G#)

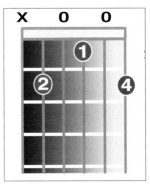

B6   B Major 6th
1st (B), 3rd (D#), 5th (F#), 6th (G#)

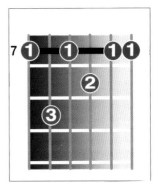

Bm6   B Minor 6th
1st (B), b3rd (D), 5th (F#), 6th (G#)

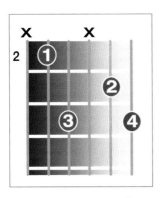

Bm6   B Minor 6th
1st (B), b3rd (D), 5th (F#), 6th (G#)

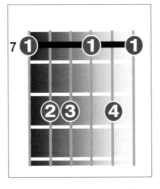

Bm6   B Minor 6th
1st (B), b3rd (D), 5th (F#), 6th (G#)

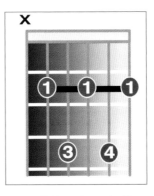

B7   B Dominant 7th
1st (B), 3rd (D#), 5th (F#), b7th (A)

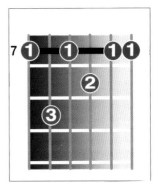

B7   B Dominant 7th
1st (B), 3rd (D#), 5th (F#), b7th (A)

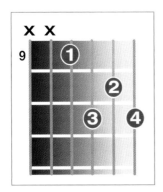

B7   B Dominant 7th
1st (B), 3rd (D#), 5th (F#), b7th (A)

B9   B Dominant 9th
1st (B), 3rd (D#), 5th (F#),
b7th (A), 9th (C#)

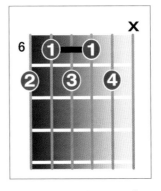

B9   B Dominant 9th
1st (B), 3rd (D#), 5th (F#),
b7th (A), 9th (C#)

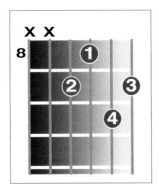

B9   B Dominant 9th
1st (B), 3rd (D#), 5th (F#),
b7th (A), 9th (C#)

B Advanced Chords

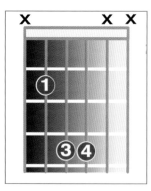

B5   **B 5th (power chord)**
1st (B), 5th (F#)

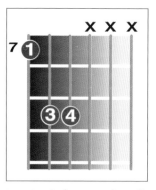

B5   **B 5th (power chord)**
1st (B), 5th (F#)

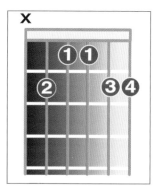

B 6/9   **B Major 6th add 9th**
1st (B), 3rd (D#), 5th (F#),
6th (G#), 9th (C#)

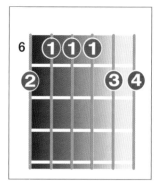

B 6/9   **B Major 6th add 9th**
1st (B), 3rd (D#), 5th (F#),
6th (G#), 9th (C#)

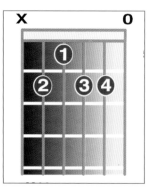

B11   **B Dominant 11th**
1st (B), 3rd (D#), 5th (F#),
♭7th (A), 9th (C#), 11th (E)

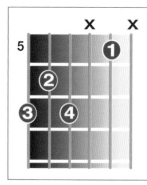

B11   **B Dominant 11th**
1st (B), 3rd (D#), 5th (F#),
♭7th (A), 9th (C#), 11th (E)

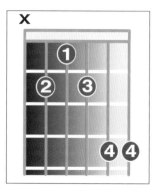

B13   **B Dominant 13th**
1st (B), 3rd (D#), 5th (F#),
♭7th (A), 9th (C#), 13th (G#)

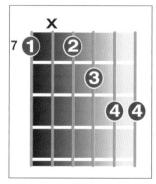

B13   **B Dominant 13th**
1st (B), 3rd (D#), 5th (F#),
♭7th (A), 9th (C#), 13th (G#)

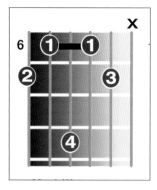

Badd9   **B Major add 9th**
1st (B), 3rd (D#), 5th (F#), 9th (C#)

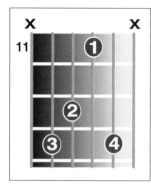

Badd9   **B Major add 9th**
1st (B), 3rd (D#), 5th (F#), 9th (C#)

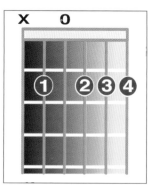

Bm9   **B Minor 9th**
1st (B), ♭3rd (D), 5th (F#),
♭7th (A), 9th (C#)

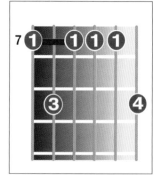

Bm9   **B Minor 9th**
1st (B), ♭3rd (D), 5th (F#),
♭7th (A), 9th (C#)

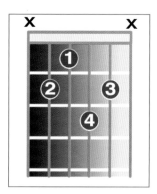

Bmaj9   **B Major 9th**
1st (B), 3rd (D#), 5th (F#),
7th (A#), 9th (C#)

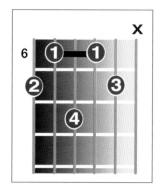

Bmaj9   **B Major 9th**
1st (B), 3rd (D#), 5th (F#),
7th (A#), 9th (C#)

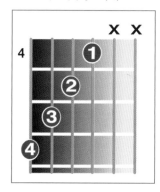

B+   **B Augmented**
1st (B), 3rd (D#), #5th (Fx)

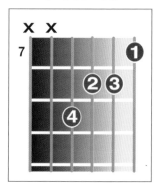

B+   **B Augmented**
1st (B), 3rd (D#), #5th (Fx)

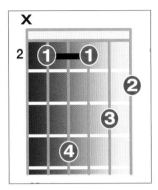

B7#5 B Dominant 7th #5
1st (B), 3rd (D#), #5th (Fx), b7th (A)

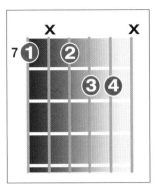

B7#5 B Dominant 7th #5
1st (B), 3rd (D#), #5th (Fx), b7th (A)

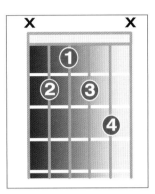

B7#9 B Dominant 7th #9
1st (B), 3rd (D#), 5th (F#),
b7th (A), #9th (Cx)

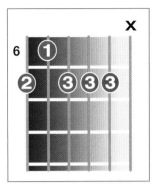

B7#9 B Dominant 7th #9
1st (B), 3rd (D#), 5th (F#),
b7th (A), #9th (Cx)

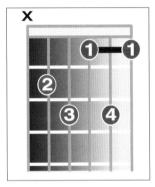

Bo7 B Diminished 7th
1st (B), b3rd (D), b5th (F), bb7th (Ab)

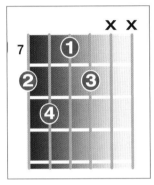

Bo7 B Diminished 7th
1st (B), b3rd (D), b5th (F), bb7th (Ab)

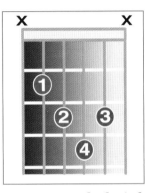

Bo B Diminished triad
1st (B), b3rd (D), b5th (F)

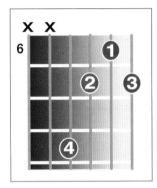

Bo B Diminished triad
1st (B), b3rd (D), b5th (F)

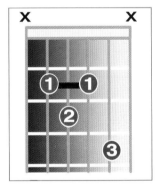

B7b5 B Dominant 7th b5
1st (B), 3rd (D#), b5th (F), b7th (A)

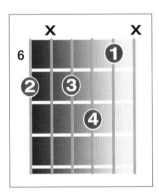

B7b5 B Dominant 7th b5
1st (B), 3rd (D#), b5th (F), b7th (A)

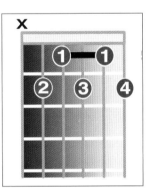

B7b9 B Dominant 7th b9
1st (B), 3rd (D#), 5th (F#),
b7th (A), b9th (C)

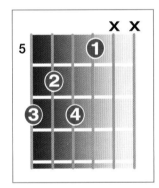

B7b9 B Dominant 7th b9
1st (B), 3rd (D#), 5th (F#),
b7th (A), b9th (C)

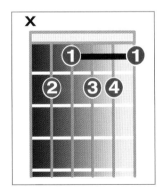

B9b5 B Dominant 9th b5th
1st (B), 3rd (D#), b5th (F),
b7th (A), 9th (C#)

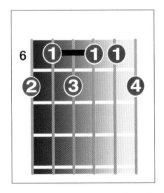

B9b5 B Dominant 9th b5th
1st (B), 3rd (D#), b5th (F),
b7th (A), 9th (C#)

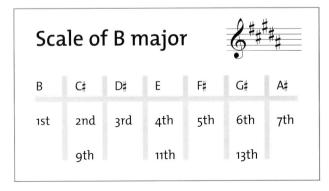

Scale of B major

B	C#	D#	E	F#	G#	A#
1st	2nd	3rd	4th	5th	6th	7th
	9th		11th		13th	

C Main Chords

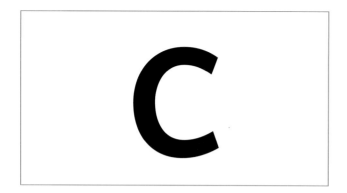

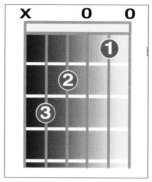

C   C Major
1st (C), 3rd (E), 5th (G)

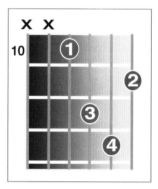

C   C Major
1st (C), 3rd (E), 5th (G)

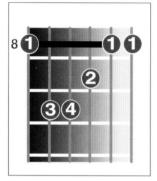

C   C Major
1st (C), 3rd (E), 5th (G)

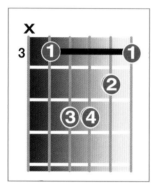

Cm   C Minor
1st (C), ♭3rd (E♭), 5th (G)

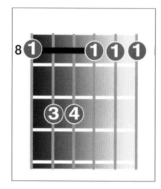

Cm   C Minor
1st (C), ♭3rd (E♭), 5th (G)

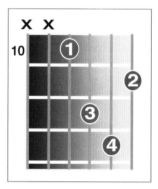

Cm   C Minor
1st (C), ♭3rd (E♭), 5th (G)

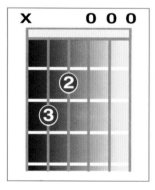

Cmaj7   C Major 7th
1st (C), 3rd (E), 5th (G), 7th (B)

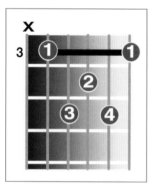

Cmaj7   C Major 7th
1st (C), 3rd (E), 5th (G), 7th (B)

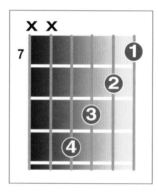

Cmaj7   C Major 7th
1st (C), 3rd (E), 5th (G), 7th (B)

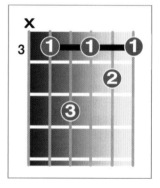

Cm7   C Minor 7th
1st (C), ♭3rd (E♭),
5th (G), ♭7th (B♭)

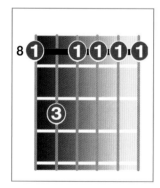

Cm7   C Minor 7th
1st (C), ♭3rd (E♭),
5th (G), ♭7th (B♭)

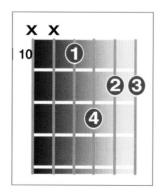

Cm7   C Minor 7th
1st (C), ♭3rd (E♭),
5th (G), ♭7th (B♭)

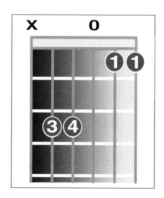

Csus4   C Suspended 4th
1st (C), 4th (F), 5th (G)

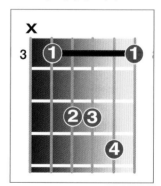

Csus4   C Suspended 4th
1st (C), 4th (F), 5th (G)

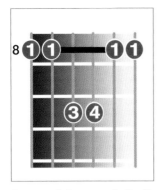

Csus4   C Suspended 4th
1st (C), 4th (F), 5th (G)

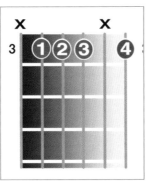

C7sus4   C Dominant 7th sus4
1st (C), 4th (F), 5th (G), ♭7th (B♭)

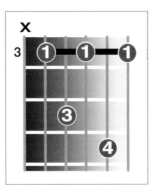

C7sus4   C Dominant 7th sus4
1st (C), 4th (F), 5th (G), ♭7th (B♭)

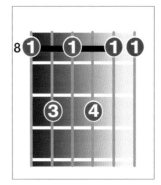

C7sus4   C Dominant 7th sus4
1st (C), 4th (F), 5th (G), ♭7th (B♭)

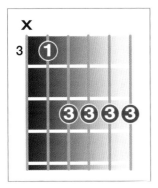

C6   C Major 6th
1st (C), 3rd (E), 5th (G), 6th (A)

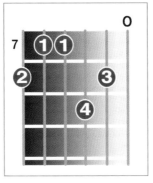

C6   C Major 6th
1st (C), 3rd (E), 5th (G), 6th (A)

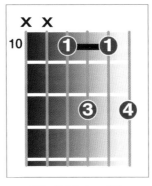

C6   C Major 6th
1st (C), 3rd (E), 5th (G), 6th (A)

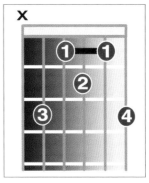

Cm6   C Minor 6th
1st (C), ♭3rd (E♭), 5th (G), 6th (A)

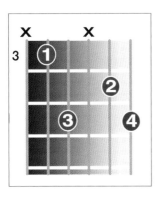

Cm6   C Minor 6th
1st (C), ♭3rd (E♭), 5th (G), 6th (A)

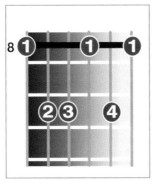

Cm6   C Minor 6th
1st (C), ♭3rd (E♭), 5th (G), 6th (A)

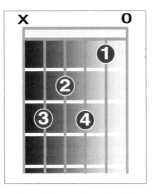

C7   C Dominant 7th
1st (C), 3rd (E), 5th (G), ♭7th (B♭)

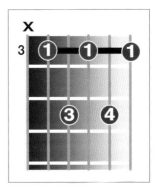

C7   C Dominant 7th
1st (C), 3rd (E), 5th (G), ♭7th (B♭)

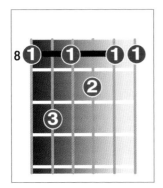

C7   C Dominant 7th
1st (C), 3rd (E), 5th (G), ♭7th (B♭)

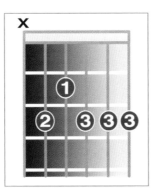

C9   C Dominant 9th
1st (C), 3rd (E), 5th (G),
♭7th (B♭), 9th (D)

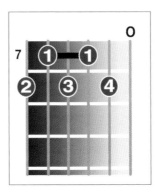

C9   C Dominant 9th
1st (C), 3rd (E), 5th (G),
♭7th (B♭), 9th (D)

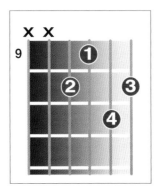

C9   C Dominant 9th
1st (C), 3rd (E), 5th (G),
♭7th (B♭), 9th (D)

C Advanced Chords

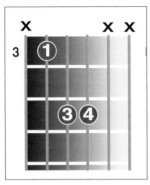

C5 C 5th (power chord)
1st (C), 5th (G)

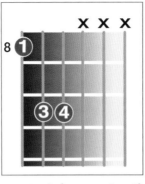

C5 C 5th (power chord)
1st (C), 5th (G)

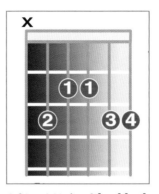

C 6/9 C Major 6th add 9th
1st (C), 3rd (E), 5th (G),
6th (A), 9th (D)

C 6/9 C Major 6th add 9th
1st (C), 3rd (E), 5th (G),
6th (A), 9th (D)

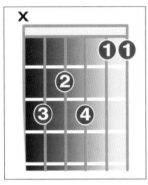

C11 C Dominant 11th
1st (C), 3rd (E), 5th (G),
♭7th (B♭), 9th (D), 11th (F)

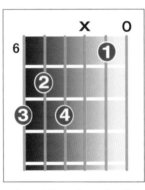

C11 C Dominant 11th
1st (C), 3rd (E), 5th (G),
♭7th (B♭), 9th (D), 11th (F)

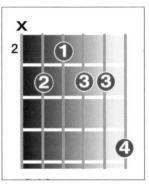

C13 C Dominant 13th
1st (C), 3rd (E), 5th (G),
♭7th (B♭), 9th (D), 13th (A)

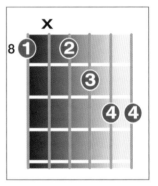

C13 C Dominant 13th
1st (C), 3rd (E), 5th (G),
♭7th (B♭), 9th (D), 13th (A)

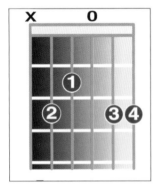

Cadd9 C Major add 9th
1st (C), 3rd (E), 5th (G), 9th (D)

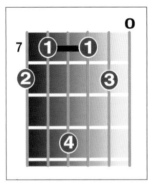

Cadd9 C Major add 9th
1st (C), 3rd (E), 5th (G), 9th (D)

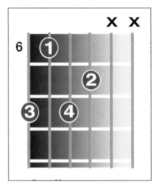

Cm9 C Minor 9th
1st (C), ♭3rd (E♭), 5th (G),
♭7th (B♭), 9th (D)

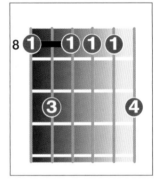

Cm9 C Minor 9th
1st (C), ♭3rd (E♭), 5th (G),
♭7th (B♭), 9th (D)

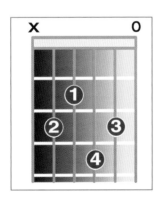

Cmaj9 C Major 9th
1st (C), 3rd (E), 5th (G),
7th (B), 9th (D)

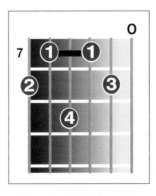

Cmaj9 C Major 9th
1st (C), 3rd (E), 5th (G),
7th (B), 9th (D)

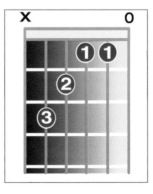

C+ C Augmented
1st (C), 3rd (E), #5th (G#)

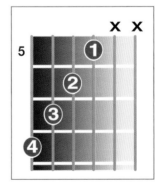

C+ C Augmented
1st (C), 3rd (E), #5th (G#)

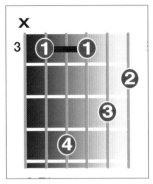

C7#5 C Dominant 7th #5
1st (C), 3rd (E), #5th (G#), ♭7th (B♭)

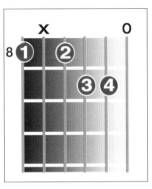

C7#5 C Dominant 7th #5
1st (C), 3rd (E), #5th (G#), ♭7th (B♭)

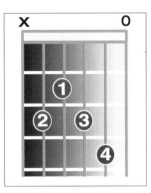

C7#9 C Dominant 7th #9
1st (C), 3rd (E), 5th (G), ♭7th (B♭), #9th (D#)

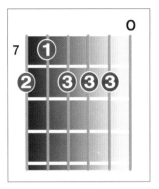

C7#9 C Dominant 7th #9
1st (C), 3rd (E), 5th (G), ♭7th (B♭), #9th (D#)

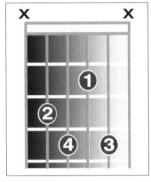

Co7 C Diminished 7th
1st (C), ♭3rd (E♭), ♭5th (G♭), ♭♭7th (B♭♭)

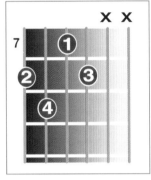

Co7 C Diminished 7th
1st (C), ♭3rd (E♭), ♭5th (G♭), ♭♭7th (B♭♭)

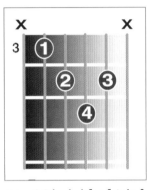

Co C Diminished triad
1st (C), ♭3rd (E♭), ♭5th (G♭)

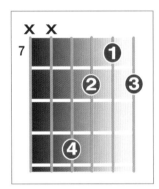

Co C Diminished triad
1st (C), ♭3rd (E♭), ♭5th (G♭)

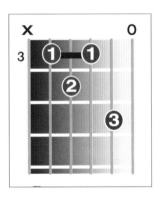

C7♭5 C Dominant 7th ♭5
1st (C), 3rd (E), ♭5th (G♭), ♭7th (B♭)

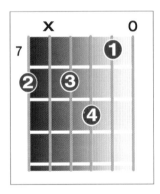

C7♭5 C Dominant 7th ♭5
1st (C), 3rd (E), ♭5th (G♭), ♭7th (B♭)

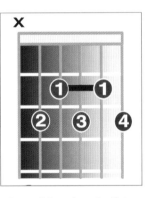

C7♭9 C Dominant 7th ♭9
1st (C), 3rd (E), 5th (G), ♭7th (B♭), ♭9th (D♭)

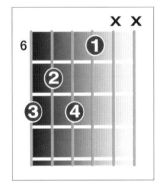

C7♭9 C Dominant 7th ♭9
1st (C), 3rd (E), 5th (G), ♭7th (B♭), ♭9th (D♭)

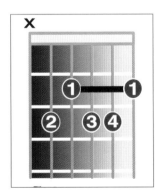

C9♭5 C Dominant 9th ♭5th
1st (C), 3rd (E), ♭5th (G♭), ♭7th (B♭), 9th (D)

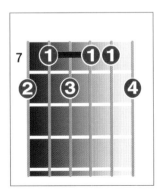

C9♭5 C Dominant 9th ♭5th
1st (C), 3rd (E), ♭5th (G♭), ♭7th (B♭), 9th (D)

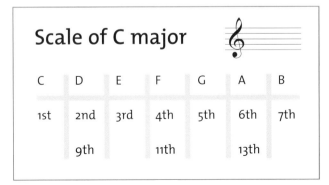

Scale of C major

C	D	E	F	G	A	B
1st	2nd	3rd	4th	5th	6th	7th
	9th		11th		13th	

C♯/D♭ Main Chords

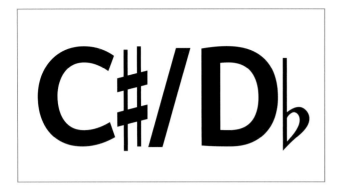

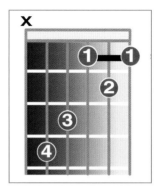

C♯ C♯ Major
1st (C♯), 3rd (E♯), 5th (G♯)

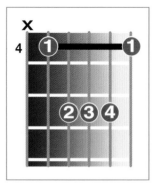

C♯ C♯ Major
1st (C♯), 3rd (E♯), 5th (G♯)

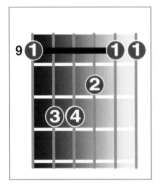

C♯ C♯ Major
1st (C♯), 3rd (E♯), 5th (G♯)

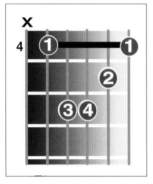

C♯m C♯ Minor
1st (C♯), ♭3rd (E), 5th (G♯)

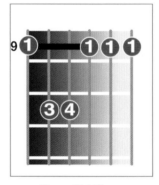

C♯m C♯ Minor
1st (C♯), ♭3rd (E), 5th (G♯)

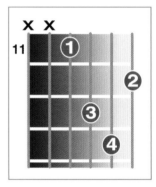

C♯m C♯ Minor
1st (C♯), ♭3rd (E), 5th (G♯)

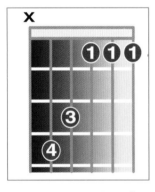

C♯maj7 C♯ Major 7th
1st (C♯), 3rd (E♯), 5th (G♯), 7th (B♯)

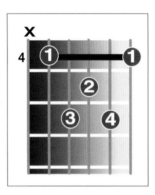

C♯maj7 C♯ Major 7th
1st (C♯), 3rd (E♯), 5th (G♯), 7th (B♯)

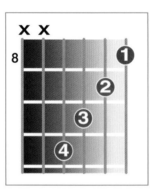

C♯maj7 C♯ Major 7th
1st (C♯), 3rd (E♯), 5th (G♯), 7th (B♯)

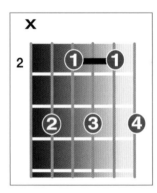

C♯m7 C♯ Minor 7th
1st (C♯), ♭3rd (E),
5th (G♯), ♭7th (B)

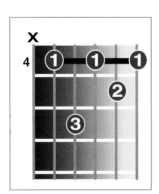

C♯m7 C♯ Minor 7th
1st (C♯), ♭3rd (E),
5th (G♯), ♭7th (B)

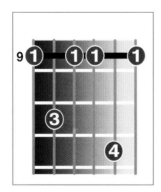

C♯m7 C♯ Minor 7th
1st (C♯), ♭3rd (E),
5th (G♯), ♭7th (B)

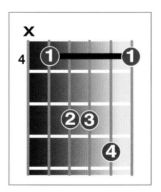

C♯sus4 C♯ Suspended 4th
1st (C♯), 4th (F♯), 5th (G♯)

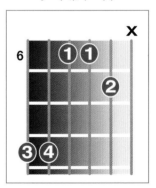

C♯sus4 C♯ Suspended 4th
1st (C♯), 4th (F♯), 5th (G♯)

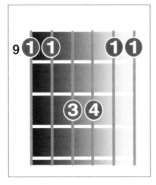

C♯sus4   C♯ Suspended 4th
1st (C♯), 4th (F♯), 5th (G♯)

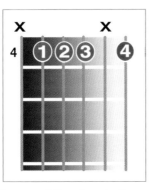

C♯7sus4   C♯ Dominant 7th sus4
1st (C♯), 4th (F♯), 5th (G♯), ♭7th (B)

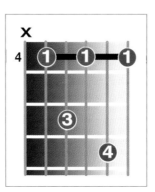

C♯7sus4   C♯ Dominant 7th sus4
1st (C♯), 4th (F♯), 5th (G♯), ♭7th (B)

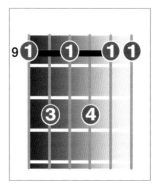

C♯7sus4   C♯ Dominant 7th sus4
1st (C♯), 4th (F♯), 5th (G♯), ♭7th (B)

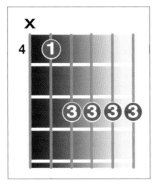

C♯6   C♯ Major 6th
1st (C♯), 3rd (E♯),
5th (G♯), 6th (A♯)

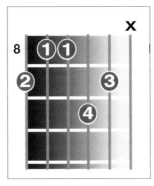

C♯6   C♯ Major 6th
1st (C♯), 3rd (E♯),
5th (G♯), 6th (A♯)

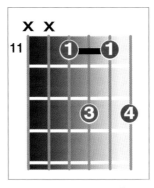

C♯6   C♯ Major 6th
1st (C♯), 3rd (E♯),
5th (G♯), 6th (A♯)

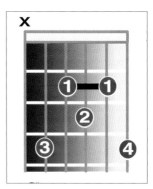

C♯m6   C♯ Minor 6th
1st (C♯), ♭3rd (E),
5th (G♯), 6th (A♯)

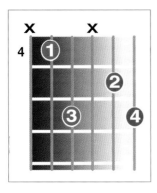

C♯m6   C♯ Minor 6th
1st (C♯), ♭3rd (E),
5th (G♯), 6th (A♯)

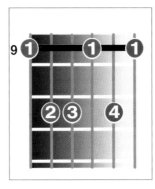

C♯m6   C♯ Minor 6th
1st (C♯), ♭3rd (E),
5th (G♯), 6th (A♯)

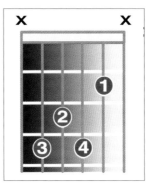

C♯7   C♯ Dominant 7th
1st (C♯), 3rd (E♯),
5th (G♯), ♭7th (B)

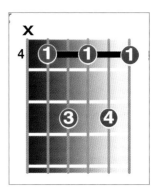

C♯7   C♯ Dominant 7th
1st (C♯), 3rd (E♯),
5th (G♯), ♭7th (B)

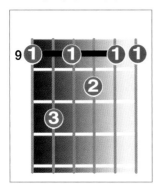

C♯7   C♯ Dominant 7th
1st (C♯), 3rd (E♯),
5th (G♯), ♭7th (B)

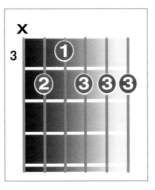

C♯9   C♯ Dominant 9th
1st (C♯), 3rd (E♯), 5th (G♯),
♭7th (B), 9th (D♯)

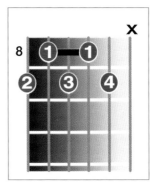

C♯9   C♯ Dominant 9th
1st (C♯), 3rd (E♯), 5th (G♯),
♭7th (B), 9th (D♯)

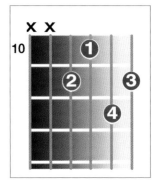

C♯9   C♯ Dominant 9th
1st (C♯), 3rd (E♯), 5th (G♯),
♭7th (B), 9th (D♯)

C♯/D♭ Advanced Chords

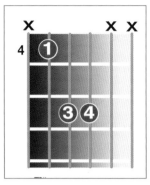

C#5 C♯ 5th (power chord)
1st (C♯), 5th (G♯)

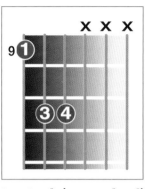

C#5 C♯ 5th (power chord)
1st (C♯), 5th (G♯)

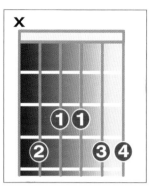

C# 6/9 C♯ Major 6th add 9th
1st (C♯), 3rd (E♯), 5th (G♯),
6th (A♯), 9th (D♯)

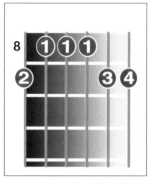

C# 6/9 C♯ Major 6th add 9th
1st (C♯), 3rd (E♯), 5th (G♯),
6th (A♯), 9th (D♯)

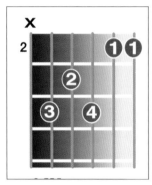

C#11 C♯ Dominant 11th
1st (C♯), 3rd (E♯), 5th (G♯),
♭7th (B), 9th (D♯), 11th (F♯)

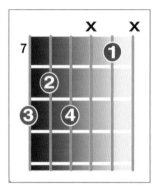

C#11 C♯ Dominant 11th
1st (C♯), 3rd (E♯), 5th (G♯),
♭7th (B), 9th (D♯), 11th (F♯)

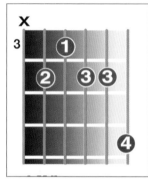

C#13 C♯ Dominant 13th
1st (C♯), 3rd (E♯), 5th (G♯),
♭7th (B), 9th (D♯), 13th (A♯)

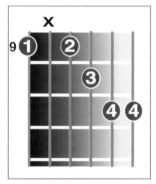

C#13 C♯ Dominant 13th
1st (C♯), 3rd (E♯), 5th (G♯),
♭7th (B), 9th (D♯), 13th (A♯)

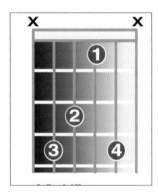

C#add9 C♯ Major add 9th
1st (C♯), 3rd (E♯), 5th (G♯), 9th (D♯)

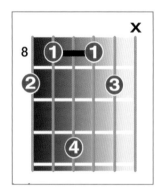

C#add9 C♯ Major add 9th
1st (C♯), 3rd (E♯), 5th (G♯), 9th (D♯)

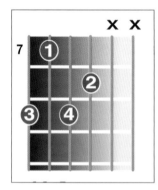

C#m9 C♯ Minor 9th
1st (C♯), ♭3rd (E), 5th (G♯),
♭7th (B), 9th (D♯)

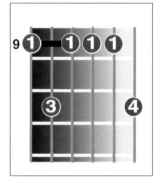

C#m9 C♯ Minor 9th
1st (C♯), ♭3rd (E), 5th (G♯),
♭7th (B), 9th (D♯)

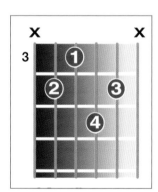

C#maj9 C♯ Major 9th
1st (C♯), 3rd (E♯), 5th (G♯),
7th (B♯), 9th (D♯)

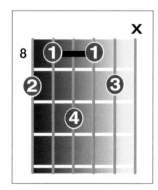

C#maj9 C♯ Major 9th
1st (C♯), 3rd (E♯), 5th (G♯),
7th (B♯), 9th (D♯)

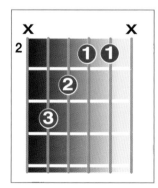

C#+ C♯ Augmented
1st (C♯), 3rd (E♯), #5th (Gx)

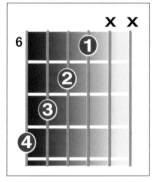

C#+ C♯ Augmented
1st (C♯), 3rd (E♯), #5th (Gx)

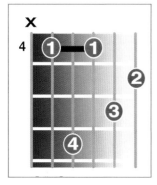

C♯7♯5   C♯ Dominant 7th ♯5
1st (C♯), 3rd (E♯), ♯5th (Gx), ♭7th (B)

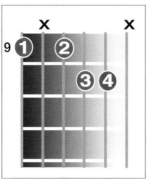

C♯7♯5   C♯ Dominant 7th ♯5
1st (C♯), 3rd (E♯), ♯5th (Gx), ♭7th (B)

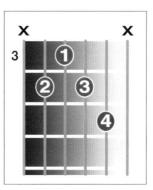

C♯7♯9   C♯ Dominant 7th ♯9
1st (C♯), 3rd (E♯), 5th (G♯),
♭7th (B), ♯9th (Dx)

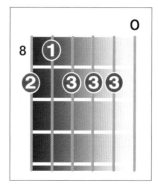

C♯7♯9   C♯ Dominant 7th ♯9
1st (C♯), 3rd (E♯), 5th (G♯),
♭7th (B), ♯9th (Dx)

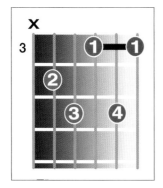

C♯°7   C♯ Diminished 7th
1st (C♯), ♭3rd (E), ♭5th (G), ♭♭7th (B♭)

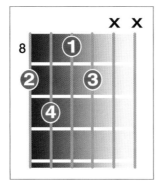

C♯°7   C♯ Diminished 7th
1st (C♯), ♭3rd (E), ♭5th (G), ♭♭7th (B♭)

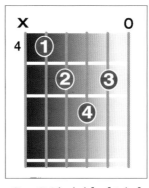

C♯o   C♯ Diminished triad
1st (C♯), ♭3rd (E), ♭5th (G)

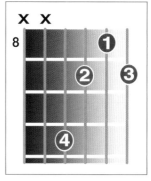

C♯o   C♯ Diminished triad
1st (C♯), ♭3rd (E), ♭5th (G)

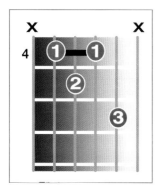

C♯7♭5   C♯ Dominant 7th ♭5
1st (C♯), 3rd (E♯), ♭5th (G), ♭7th (B)

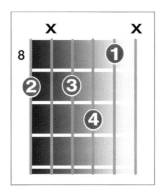

C♯7♭5   C♯ Dominant 7th ♭5
1st (C♯), 3rd (E♯), ♭5th (G), ♭7th (B)

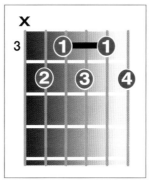

C♯7♭9   C♯ Dominant 7th ♭9
1st (C♯), 3rd (E♯), 5th (G♯),
♭7th (B), ♭9th (D)

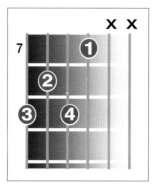

C♯7♭9   C♯ Dominant 7th ♭9
1st (C♯), 3rd (E♯), 5th (G♯),
♭7th (B), ♭9th (D)

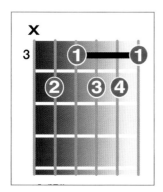

C♯9♭5   C♯ Dominant 9th ♭5th
1st (C♯), 3rd (E♯), ♭5th (G),
♭7th (B), 9th (D♯)

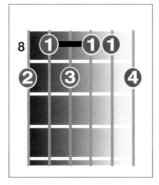

C♯9♭5   C♯ Dominant 9th ♭5th
1st (C♯), 3rd (E♯), ♭5th (G),
♭7th (B), 9th (D♯)

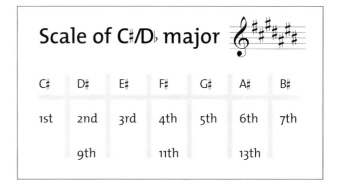

Scale of C♯/D♭ major

C♯	D♯	E♯	F♯	G♯	A♯	B♯
1st	2nd	3rd	4th	5th	6th	7th
	9th		11th		13th	

D Main Chords

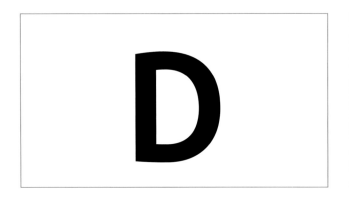

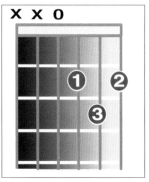

D   D Major
1st (D), 3rd (F#), 5th (A)

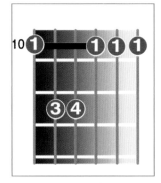

D   D Major
1st (D), 3rd (F#), 5th (A)

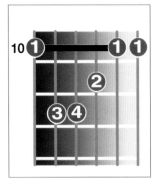

D   D Major
1st (D), 3rd (F#), 5th (A)

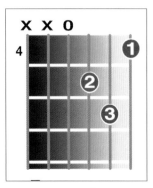

Dm   D Minor
1st (D), ♭3rd (F), 5th (A)

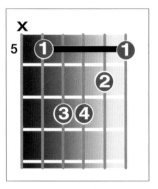

Dm   D Minor
1st (D), ♭3rd (F), 5th (A)

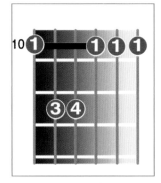

Dm   D Minor
1st (D), ♭3rd (F), 5th (A)

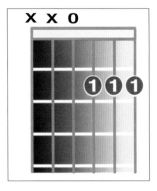

Dmaj7   D Major 7th
1st (D), 3rd (F#), 5th (A), 7th (C#)

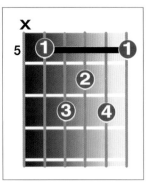

Dmaj7   D Major 7th
1st (D), 3rd (F#), 5th (A), 7th (C#)

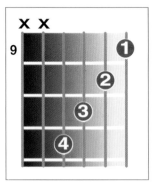

Dmaj7   D Major 7th
1st (D), 3rd (F#), 5th (A), 7th (C#)

Dm7   D Minor 7th
1st (D), ♭3rd (F), 5th (A), ♭7th (C)

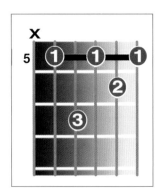

Dm7   D Minor 7th
1st (D), ♭3rd (F), 5th (A), ♭7th (C)

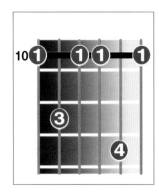

Dm7   D Minor 7th
1st (D), ♭3rd (F), 5th (A), ♭7th (C)

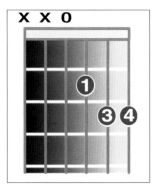

Dsus4   D Suspended 4th
1st (D), 4th (G), 5th (A)

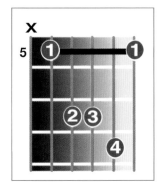

Dsus4   D Suspended 4th
1st (D), 4th (G), 5th (A)

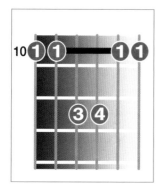

Dsus4   **D Suspended 4th**
1st (D), 4th (G), 5th (A)

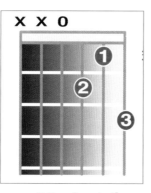

D7sus4   **D Dominant 7th sus4**
1st (D), 4th (G), 5th (A), ♭7th (C)

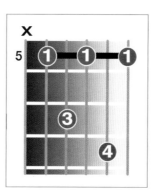

D7sus4   **D Dominant 7th sus4**
1st (D), 4th (G), 5th (A), ♭7th (C)

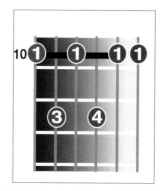

D7sus4   **D Dominant 7th sus4**
1st (D), 4th (G), 5th (A), ♭7th (C)

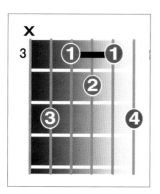

D6   **D Major 6th**
1st (D), 3rd (F♯), 5th (A), 6th (B)

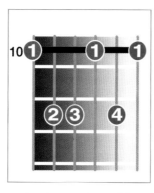

D6   **D Major 6th**
1st (D), 3rd (F♯), 5th (A), 6th (B)

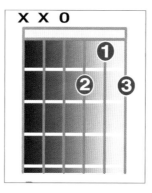

D6   **D Major 6th**
1st (D), 3rd (F♯), 5th (A), 6th (B)

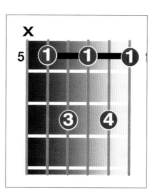

Dm6   **D Minor 6th**
1st (D), ♭3rd (F), 5th (A), 6th (B)

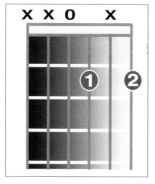

Dm6   **D Minor 6th**
1st (D), ♭3rd (F), 5th (A), 6th (B)

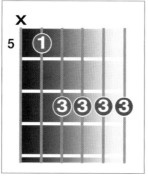

Dm6   **D Minor 6th**
1st (D), ♭3rd (F), 5th (A), 6th (B)

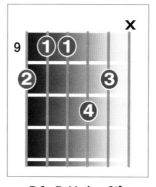

D7   **D Dominant 7th**
1st (D), 3rd (F♯),
5th (A), ♭7th (C)

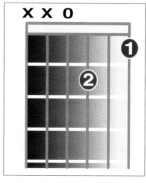

D7   **D Dominant 7th**
1st (D), 3rd (F♯),
5th (A), ♭7th (C)

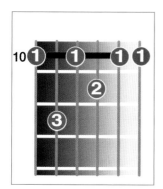

D7   **D Dominant 7th**
1st (D), 3rd (F♯),
5th (A), ♭7th (C)

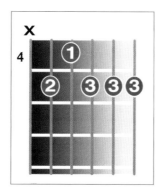

D9   **D Dominant 9th**
1st (D), 3rd (F♯), 5th (A),
♭7th (C), 9th (E)

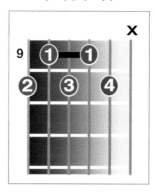

D9   **D Dominant 9th**
1st (D), 3rd (F♯), 5th (A),
♭7th (C), 9th (E)

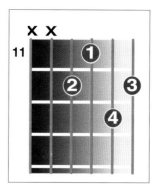

D9   **D Dominant 9th**
1st (D), 3rd (F♯), 5th (A),
♭7th (C), 9th (E)

D Advanced Chords

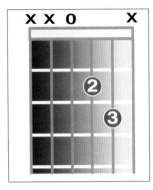

D5 D 5th (power chord)
1st (D), 5th (A)

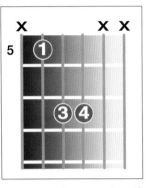

D5 D 5th (power chord)
1st (D), 5th (A)

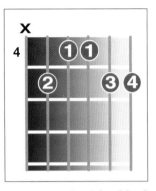

D 6/9 D Major 6th add 9th
1st (D), 3rd (F#), 5th (A),
6th (B), 9th (E)

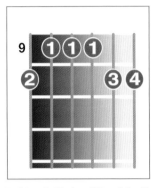

D 6/9 D Major 6th add 9th
1st (D), 3rd (F#), 5th (A),
6th (B), 9th (E)

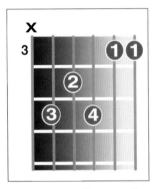

D11 D Dominant 11th
1st (D), 3rd (F#), 5th (A),
♭7th (C), 9th (E), 11th (G)

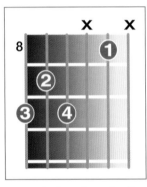

D11 D Dominant 11th
1st (D), 3rd (F#), 5th (A),
♭7th (C), 9th (E), 11th (G)

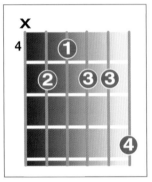

D13 D Dominant 13th
1st (D), 3rd (F#), 5th (A),
♭7th (C), 9th (E), 13th (B)

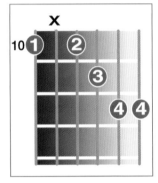

D13 D Dominant 13th
1st (D), 3rd (F#), 5th (A),
♭7th (C), 9th (E), 13th (B)

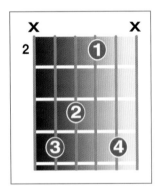

Dadd9 D Major add 9th
1st (D), 3rd (F#), 5th (A), 9th (E)

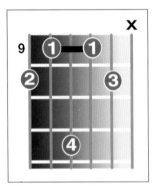

Dadd9 D Major add 9th
1st (D), 3rd (F#), 5th (A), 9th (E)

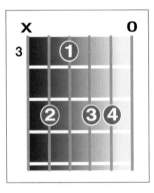

Dm9 D Minor 9th
1st (D), ♭3rd (F), 5th (A),
♭7th (C), 9th (E)

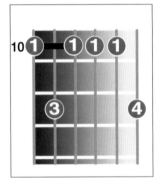

Dm9 D Minor 9th
1st (D), ♭3rd (F), 5th (A),
♭7th (C), 9th (E)

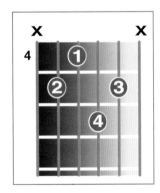

Dmaj9 D Major 9th
1st (D), 3rd (F#), 5th (A),
7th (C#), 9th (E)

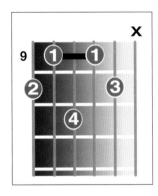

Dmaj9 D Major 9th
1st (D), 3rd (F#), 5th (A),
7th (C#), 9th (E)

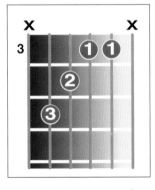

D+ D Augmented
1st (D), 3rd (F#), #5th (A#)

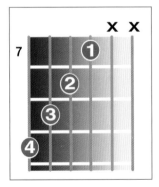

D+ D Augmented
1st (D), 3rd (F#), #5th (A#)

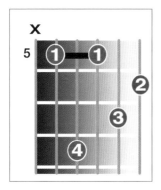

D7♯5 D Dominant 7th ♯5
1st (D), 3rd (F♯), ♯5th (A♯), ♭7th (C)

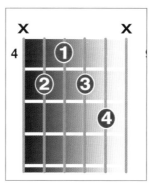

D7♯5 D Dominant 7th ♯5
1st (D), 3rd (F♯), ♯5th (A♯), ♭7th (C)

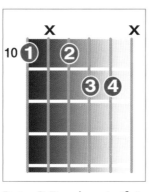

D7♯9 D Dominant 7th ♯9
1st (D), 3rd (F♯), 5th (A), ♭7th (C), ♯9th (E♯)

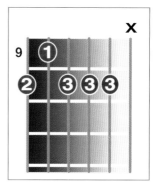

D7♯9 D Dominant 7th ♯9
1st (D), 3rd (F♯), 5th (A), ♭7th (C), ♯9th (E♯)

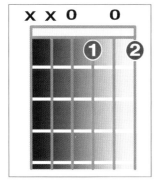

Do7 D Diminished 7th
1st (D), ♭3rd (F), ♭5th (A♭), ♭♭7th (C♭)

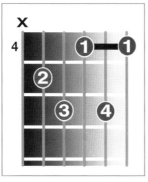

Do7 D Diminished 7th
1st (D), ♭3rd (F), ♭5th (A♭), ♭♭7th (C♭)

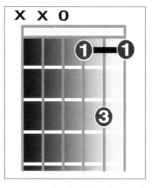

Do D Diminished triad
1st (D), ♭3rd (F), ♭5th (A♭)

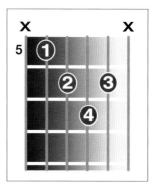

Do D Diminished triad
1st (D), ♭3rd (F), ♭5th (A♭)

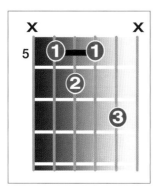

D7♭5 D Dominant 7th ♭5
1st (D), 3rd (F♯), ♭5th (A♭), ♭7th (C)

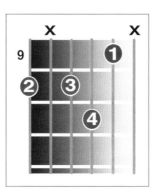

D7♭5 D Dominant 7th ♭5
1st (D), 3rd (F♯), ♭5th (A♭), ♭7th (C)

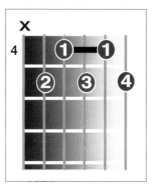

D7♭9 D Dominant 7th ♭9
1st (D), 3rd (F♯), 5th (A), ♭7th (C), ♭9th (E♭)

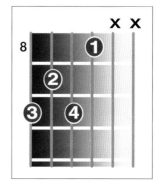

D7♭9 D Dominant 7th ♭9
1st (D), 3rd (F♯), 5th (A), ♭7th (C), ♭9th (E♭)

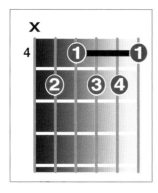

D9♭5 D Dominant 9th ♭5th
1st (D), 3rd (F♯), ♭5th (A♭), ♭7th (C), 9th (E)

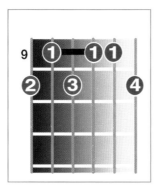

D9♭5 D Dominant 9th ♭5th
1st (D), 3rd (F♯), ♭5th (A♭), ♭7th (C), 9th (E)

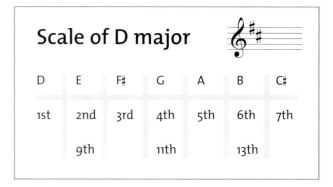

Scale of D major

D	E	F♯	G	A	B	C♯
1st	2nd	3rd	4th	5th	6th	7th
	9th		11th		13th	

E♭/D# Main Chords

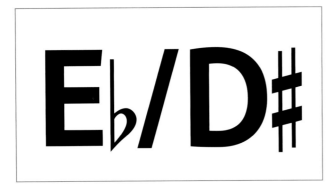

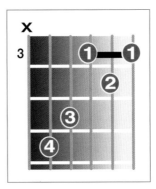

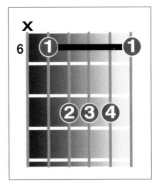

E♭ E♭ Major
1st (E♭), 3rd (G), 5th (B♭)

E♭ E♭ Major
1st (E♭), 3rd (G), 5th (B♭)

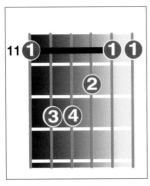

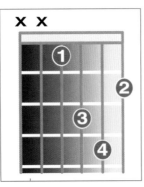

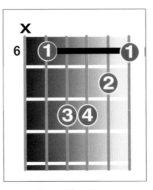

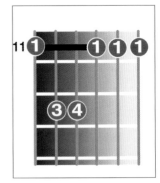

E♭ E♭ major
1st (E♭), 3rd (G), 5th (B♭)

E♭m E♭ Minor
1st (E♭), ♭3rd (G♭), 5th (B♭)

E♭m E♭ Minor
1st (E♭), ♭3rd (G♭), 5th (B♭)

E♭m E♭ Minor
1st (E♭), ♭3rd (G♭), 5th (B♭)

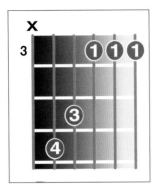

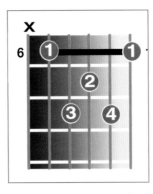

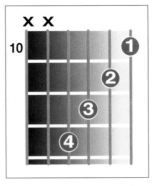

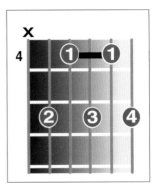

E♭maj7 E♭ Major 7th
1st (E♭), 3rd (G),
5th (B♭), 7th (D)

E♭maj7 E♭ Major 7th
1st (E♭), 3rd (G),
5th (B♭), 7th (D)

E♭maj7 E♭ Major 7th
1st (E♭), 3rd (G),
5th (B♭), 7th (D)

E♭m7 E♭ Minor 7th
1st (E♭), ♭3rd (G♭), 5th (B♭), ♭7th (D♭)

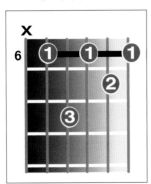

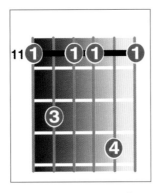

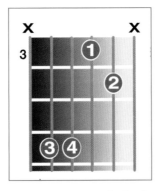

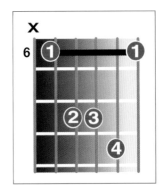

E♭m7 E♭ Minor 7th
1st (E♭), ♭3rd (G♭), 5th (B♭), ♭7th (D♭)

E♭m7 E♭ Minor 7th
1st (E♭), ♭3rd (G♭), 5th (B♭), ♭7th (D♭)

E♭sus4 E♭ Suspended 4th
1st (E♭), 4th (A♭), 5th (B♭)

E♭sus4 E♭ Suspended 4th
1st (E♭), 4th (A♭), 5th (B♭)

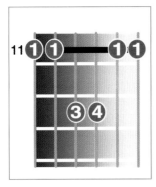

E♭sus4   E♭ Suspended 4th
1st (E♭), 4th (A♭), 5th (B♭)

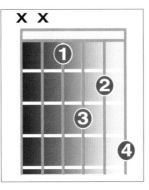

E♭7sus4   E♭ Dominant 7th sus4
1st (E♭), 4th (A♭), 5th (B♭), ♭7th (D♭)

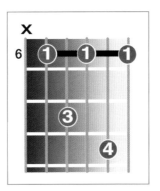

E♭7sus4   E♭ Dominant 7th sus4
1st (E♭), 4th (A♭), 5th (B♭), ♭7th (D♭)

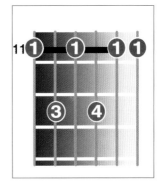

E♭7sus4   E♭ Dominant 7th sus4
1st (E♭), 4th (A♭), 5th (B♭), ♭7th (D♭)

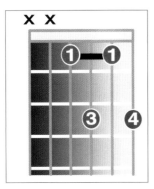

E♭6   E♭ Major 6th
1st (E♭), 3rd (G),
5th (B♭), 6th (C)

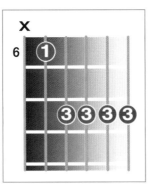

E♭6   E♭ Major 6th
1st (E♭), 3rd (G),
5th (B♭), 6th (C)

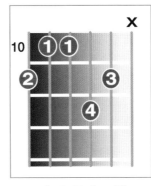

E♭6   E♭ Major 6th
1st (E♭), 3rd (G),
5th (B♭), 6th (C)

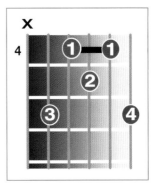

E♭m6   E♭ Minor 6th
1st (E♭), ♭3rd (G♭),
5th (B♭), 6th (C)

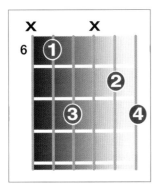

E♭m6   E♭ Minor 6th
1st (E♭), ♭3rd (G♭),
5th (B♭), 6th (C)

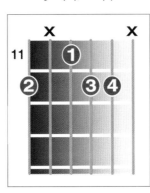

E♭m6   E♭ Minor 6th
1st (E♭), ♭3rd (G♭),
5th (B♭), 6th (C)

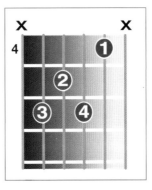

E♭7   E♭ Dominant 7th
1st (E♭), 3rd (G), 5th (B♭), ♭7th (D♭)

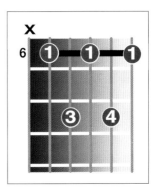

E♭7   E♭ Dominant 7th
1st (E♭), 3rd (G), 5th (B♭), ♭7th (D♭)

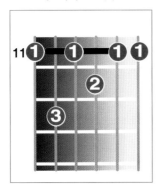

E♭7   E♭ Dominant 7th
1st (E♭), 3rd (G), 5th (B♭), ♭7th (D♭)

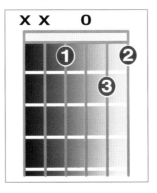

E♭9   E♭ Dominant 9th
1st (E♭), 3rd (G), 5th (B♭),
♭7th (D♭), 9th (F)

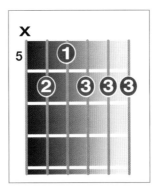

E♭9   E♭ Dominant 9th
1st (E♭), 3rd (G), 5th (B♭),
♭7th (D♭), 9th (F)

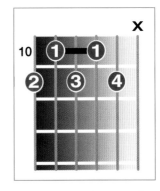

E♭9   E♭ Dominant 9th
1st (E♭), 3rd (G), 5th (B♭),
♭7th (D♭), 9th (F)

E♭/D♯ Advanced Chords

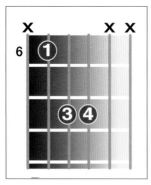

E♭5 E♭ 5th (power chord)
1st (E♭), 5th (B♭)

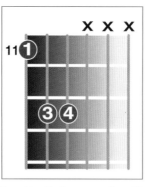

E♭5 E♭ 5th (power chord)
1st (E♭), 5th (B♭)

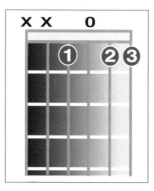

E♭6/9 E♭ Major 6th add 9th
1st (E♭), 3rd (G), 5th (B♭),
6th (C), 9th (F)

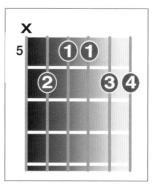

E♭6/9 E♭ Major 6th add 9th
1st (E♭), 3rd (G), 5th (B♭),
6th (C), 9th (F)

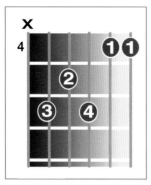

E♭11 E♭ Dominant 11th
1st (E♭), 3rd (G), 5th (B♭),
♭7th (D♭), 9th (F), 11th (A♭)

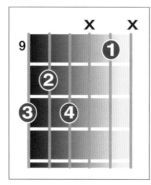

E♭11 E♭ Dominant 11th
1st (E♭), 3rd (G), 5th (B♭),
♭7th (D♭), 9th (F), 11th (A♭)

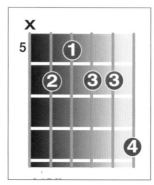

E♭13 E♭ Dominant 13th
1st (E♭), 3rd (G), 5th (B♭),
♭7th (D♭), 9th (F), 13th (C)

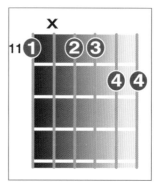

E♭13 E♭ Dominant 13th
1st (E♭), 3rd (G), 5th (B♭),
♭7th (D♭), 9th (F), 13th (C)

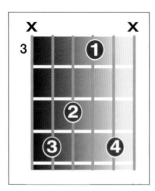

E♭add9 E♭ Major add 9th
1st (E♭), 3rd (G), 5th (B♭), 9th (F)

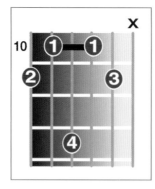

E♭add9 E♭ Major add 9th
1st (E♭), 3rd (G), 5th (B♭), 9th (F)

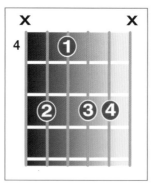

E♭m9 E♭ Minor 9th
1st (E♭), ♭3rd (G♭), 5th (B♭),
♭7th (D♭), 9th (F)

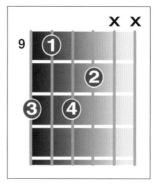

E♭m9 E♭ Minor 9th
1st (E♭), ♭3rd (G♭), 5th (B♭),
♭7th (D♭), 9th (F)

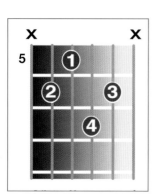

E♭maj9 E♭ Major 9th
1st (E♭), 3rd (G), 5th (B♭),
7th (D), 9th (F)

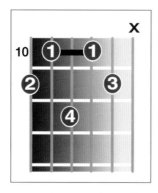

E♭maj9 E♭ Major 9th
1st (E♭), 3rd (G), 5th (B♭),
7th (D), 9th (F)

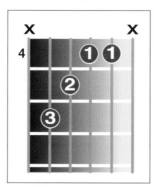

E♭+ E♭ Augmented
1st (E♭), 3rd (G), ♯5th (B)

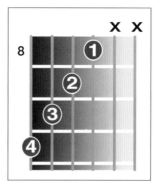

E♭+ E♭ Augmented
1st (E♭), 3rd (G), ♯5th (B)

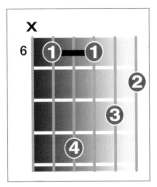

E♭7♯5 **E♭ Dominant 7th ♯5**
1st (E♭), 3rd (G),
♯5th (B), ♭7th (D♭)

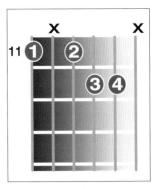

E♭7♯5 **E♭ Dominant 7th ♯5**
1st (E♭), 3rd (G),
♯5th (B), ♭7th (D♭)

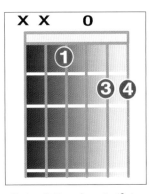

E♭7♯9 **E♭ Dominant 7th ♯9**
1st (E♭), 3rd (G), 5th (B♭),
♭7th (D♭), ♯9th (F♯)

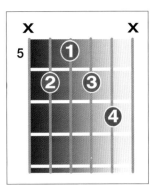

E♭7♯9 **E♭ Dominant 7th ♯9**
1st (E♭), 3rd (G), 5th (B♭),
♭7th (D♭), ♯9th (F♯)

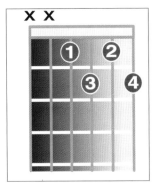

E♭○7 **E♭ Diminished 7th**
1st (E♭), ♭3rd (G♭),
♭5th (B♭♭), ♭♭7th (D♭♭)

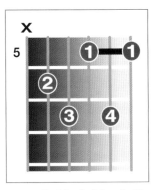

E♭○7 **E♭ Diminished 7th**
1st (E♭), ♭3rd (G♭),
♭5th (B♭♭), ♭♭7th (D♭♭)

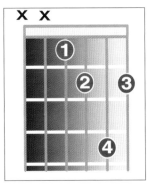

E♭○ **E♭ Diminished triad**
1st (E♭), ♭3rd (G♭), ♭5th (B♭♭)

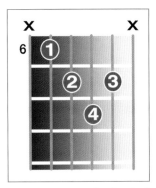

E♭○ **E♭ Diminished triad**
1st (E♭), ♭3rd (G♭), ♭5th (B♭♭)

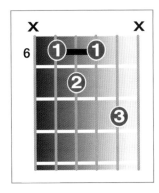

E♭7♭5 **E♭ Dominant 7th ♭5**
1st (E♭), 3rd (G), ♭5th (B♭♭), ♭7th (D♭)

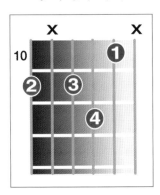

E♭7♭5 **E♭ Dominant 7th ♭5**
1st (E♭), 3rd (G), ♭5th (B♭♭), ♭7th (D♭)

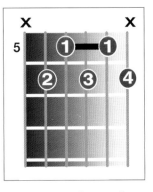

E♭7♭9 **E♭ Dominant 7th ♭9**
1st (E♭), 3rd (G), 5th (B♭),
♭7th (D♭), ♭9th (F♭)

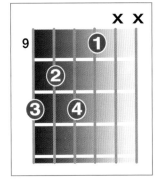

E♭7♭9 **E♭ Dominant 7th ♭9**
1st (E♭), 3rd (G), 5th (B♭),
♭7th (D♭), ♭9th (F♭)

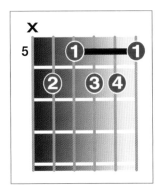

E♭9♭5 **E♭ Dominant 9th ♭5th**
1st (E♭), 3rd (G), ♭5th (B♭♭),
♭7th (D♭), 9th (F)

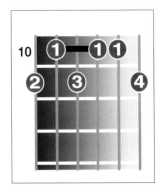

E♭9♭5 **E♭ Dominant 9th ♭5th**
1st (E♭), 3rd (G), ♭5th (B♭♭),
♭7th (D♭), 9th (F)

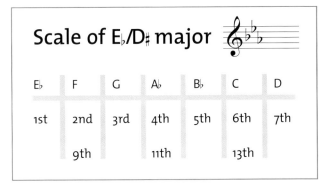

Scale of E♭/D♯ major

E♭	F	G	A♭	B♭	C	D
1st	2nd	3rd	4th	5th	6th	7th
	9th		11th		13th	

E Main Chords

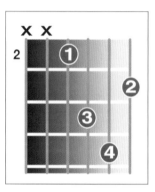

E   E Major
1st (E), 3rd (G#), 5th (B)

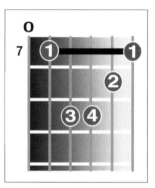

E   E Major
1st (E), 3rd (G#), 5th (B)

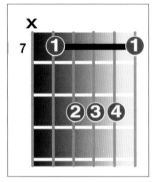

E   E Major
1st (E), 3rd (G#), 5th (B)

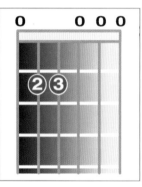

Em   E Minor
1st (E), ♭3rd (G), 5th (B)

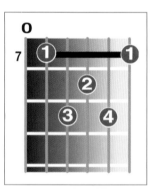

Em   E Minor
1st (E), ♭3rd (G), 5th (B)

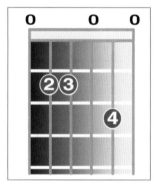

Em   E Minor
1st (E), ♭3rd (G), 5th (B)

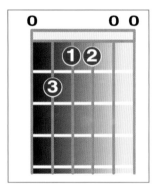

Emaj7   E Major 7th
1st (E), 3rd (G#), 5th (B), 7th (D#)

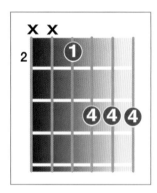

Emaj7   E Major 7th
1st (E), 3rd (G#), 5th (B), 7th (D#)

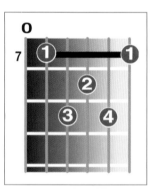

Emaj7   E Major 7th
1st (E), 3rd (G#), 5th (B), 7th (D#)

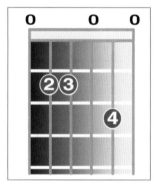

Em7   E Minor 7th
1st (E), ♭3rd (G),
5th (B), ♭7th (D)

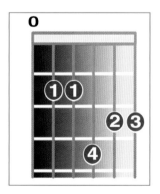

Em7   E Minor 7th
1st (E), ♭3rd (G),
5th (B), ♭7th (D)

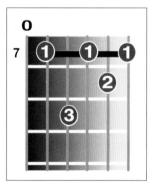

Em7   E Minor 7th
1st (E), ♭3rd (G),
5th (B), ♭7th (D)

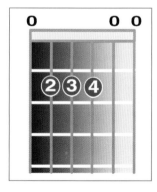

Esus4   E Suspended 4th
1st (E), 4th (A), 5th (B)

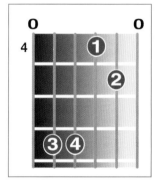

Esus4   E Suspended 4th
1st (E), 4th (A), 5th (B)

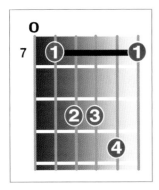

Esus4   E Suspended 4th
1st (E), 4th (A), 5th (B)

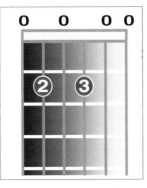

E7sus4   E Dominant 7th sus4
1st (E), 4th (A), 5th (B), ♭7th (D)

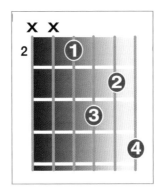

E7sus4   E Dominant 7th sus4
1st (E), 4th (A), 5th (B), ♭7th (D)

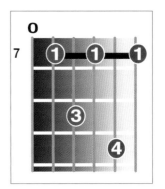

E7sus4   E Dominant 7th sus4
1st (E), 4th (A), 5th (B), ♭7th (D)

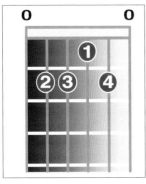

E6   E Major 6th
1st (E), 3rd (G♯),
5th (B), 6th (C♯)

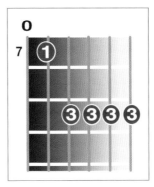

E6   E Major 6th
1st (E), 3rd (G♯),
5th (B), 6th (C♯)

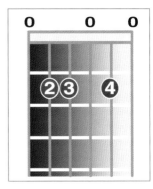

E6   E Major 6th
1st (E), 3rd (G♯),
5th (B), 6th (C♯)

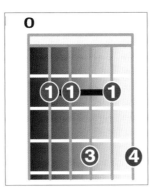

Em6   E Minor 6th
1st (E), ♭3rd (G), 5th (B), 6th (C♯)

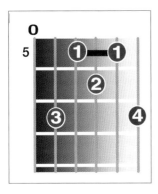

Em6   E Minor 6th
1st (E), ♭3rd (G), 5th (B), 6th (C♯)

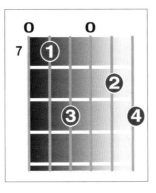

Em6   E Minor 6th
1st (E), ♭3rd (G), 5th (B), 6th (C♯)

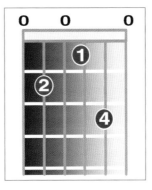

E7   E Dominant 7th
1st (E), 3rd (G♯),
5th (B), ♭7th (D)

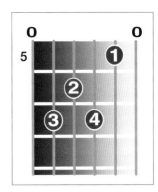

E7   E Dominant 7th
1st (E), 3rd (G♯),
5th (B), ♭7th (D)

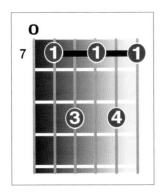

E7   E Dominant 7th
1st (E), 3rd (G♯),
5th (B), ♭7th (D)

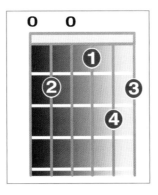

E9   E Dominant 9th
1st (E), 3rd (G♯), 5th (B),
♭7th (D), 9th (F♯)

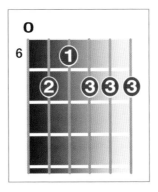

E9   E Dominant 9th
1st (E), 3rd (G♯), 5th (B),
♭7th (D), 9th (F♯)

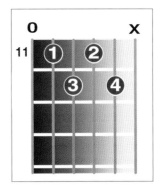

E9   E Dominant 9th
1st (E), 3rd (G♯), 5th (B),
♭7th (D), 9th (F♯)

E Advanced Chords

E5 **E 5th (power chord)**
1st (E), 5th (B)

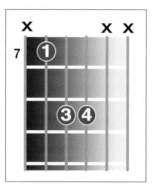

E5 **E 5th (power chord)**
1st (E), 5th (B)

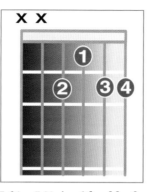

E 6/9 **E Major 6th add 9th**
1st (E), 3rd (G#), 5th (B),
6th (C#), 9th (F#)

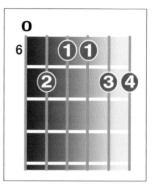

E 6/9 **E Major 6th add 9th**
1st (E), 3rd (G#), 5th (B),
6th (C#), 9th (F#)

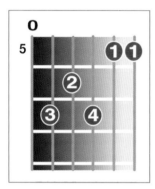

E11 **E Dominant 11th**
1st (E), 3rd (G#), 5th (B),
♭7th (D), 9th (F#), 11th (A)

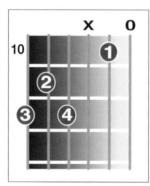

E11 **E Dominant 11th**
1st (E), 3rd (G#), 5th (B),
♭7th (D), 9th (F#), 11th (A)

E13 **E Dominant 13th**
1st (E), 3rd (G#), 5th (B),
♭7th (D), 9th (F#), 13th (C#)

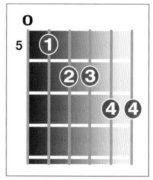

E13 **E Dominant 13th**
1st (E), 3rd (G#), 5th (B),
♭7th (D), 9th (F#), 13th (C#)

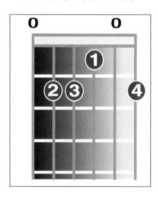

Eadd9 **E Major add 9th**
1st (E), 3rd (G#), 5th (B), 9th (F#)

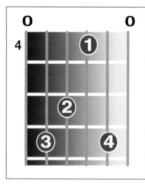

Eadd9 **E Major add 9th**
1st (E), 3rd (G#), 5th (B), 9th (F#)

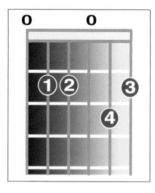

Em9 **E Minor 9th**
1st (E), ♭3rd (G), 5th (B),
♭7th (D), 9th (F#)

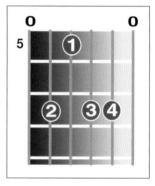

Em9 **E Minor 9th**
1st (E), ♭3rd (G), 5th (B),
♭7th (D), 9th (F#)

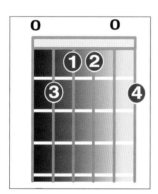

Emaj9 **E Major 9th**
1st (E), 3rd (G#), 5th (B),
7th (D#), 9th (F#)

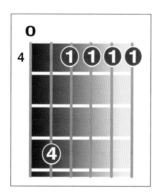

Emaj9 **E Major 9th**
1st (E), 3rd (G#), 5th (B),
7th (D#), 9th (F#)

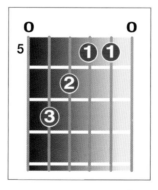

E+ **E Augmented**
1st (E), 3rd (G#), #5th (B#)

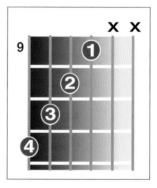

E+ **E Augmented**
1st (E), 3rd (G#), #5th (B#)

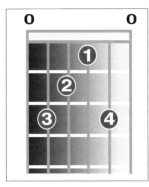

E7♯5 **E Dominant 7th ♯5**
1st (E), 3rd (G♯),
♯5th (B♯), ♭7th (D)

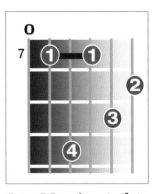

E7♯5 **E Dominant 7th ♯5**
1st (E), 3rd (G♯),
♯5th (B♯), ♭7th (D)

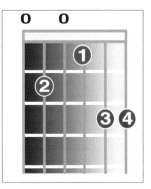

E7♯9 **E Dominant 7th ♯9**
1st (E), 3rd (G♯), 5th (B),
♭7th (D), ♯9th (Fx)

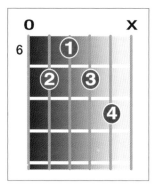

E7♯9 **E Dominant 7th ♯9**
1st (E), 3rd (G♯), 5th (B),
♭7th (D), ♯9th (Fx)

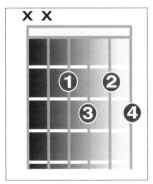

E○7 **E Diminished 7th**
1st (E), ♭3rd (G),
♭5th (B♭), ♭♭7th (D♭)

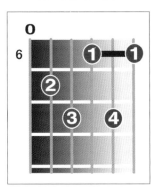

E○7 **E Diminished 7th**
1st (E), ♭3rd (G),
♭5th (B♭), ♭♭7th (D♭)

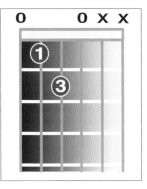

E○ **E Diminished triad**
1st (E), ♭3rd (G), ♭5th (B♭)

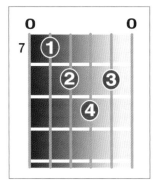

E○ **E Diminished triad**
1st (E), ♭3rd (G), ♭5th (B♭)

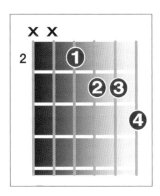

E7♭5 **E Dominant 7th ♭5**
1st (E), 3rd (G♯),
♭5th (B♭), ♭7th (D)

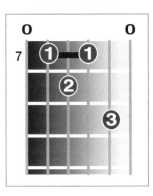

E7♭5 **E Dominant 7th ♭5**
1st (E), 3rd (G♯),
♭5th (B♭), ♭7th (D)

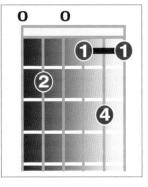

E7♭9 **E Dominant 7th ♭9**
1st (E), 3rd (G♯), 5th (B),
♭7th (D), ♭9th (F)

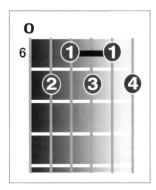

E7♭9 **E Dominant 7th ♭9**
1st (E), 3rd (G♯), 5th (B),
♭7th (D), ♭9th (F)

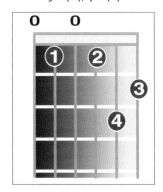

E9♭5 **E Dominant 9th ♭5**
1st (E), 3rd (G♯), ♭5th (B♭),
♭7th (D), 9th (F♯)

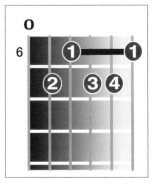

E9♭5 **E Dominant 9th ♭5**
1st (E), 3rd (G♯), ♭5th (B♭),
♭7th (D), 9th (F♯)

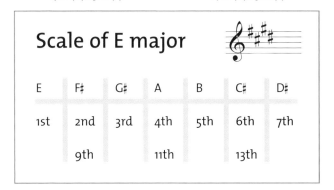

Scale of E major

E	F♯	G♯	A	B	C♯	D♯
1st	2nd	3rd	4th	5th	6th	7th
	9th		11th		13th	

F Main Chords

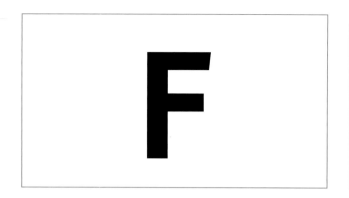

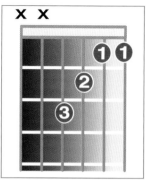

F   F Major
1st (F), 3rd (A), 5th (C)

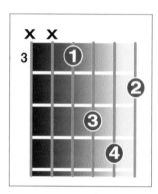

F   F Major
1st (F), 3rd (A), 5th (C)

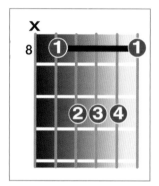

F   F Major
1st (F), 3rd (A), 5th (C)

Fm   F Minor
1st (F), ♭3rd (A♭), 5th (C)

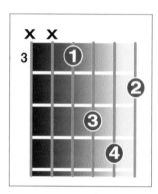

Fm   F Minor
1st (F), ♭3rd (A♭), 5th (C)

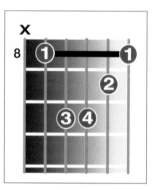

Fm   F Minor
1st (F), ♭3rd (A♭), 5th (C)

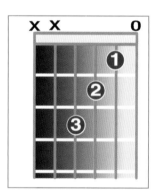

Fmaj7   F Major 7th
1st (F), 3rd (A), 5th (C), 7th (E)

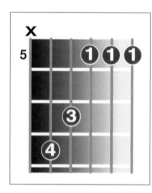

Fmaj7   F Major 7th
1st (F), 3rd (A), 5th (C), 7th (E)

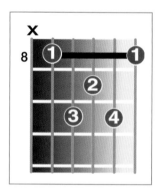

Fmaj7   F Major 7th
1st (F), 3rd (A), 5th (C), 7th (E)

Fm7   F Minor 7th
1st (F), ♭3rd (A♭),
5th (C), ♭7th (E♭)

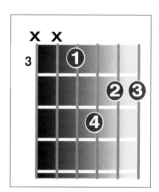

Fm7   F Minor 7th
1st (F), ♭3rd (A♭),
5th (C), ♭7th (E♭)

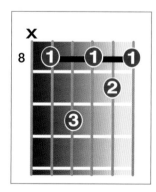

Fm7   F Minor 7th
1st (F), ♭3rd (A♭),
5th (C), ♭7th (E♭)

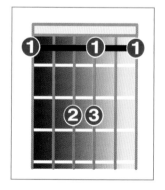

Fsus4   F Suspended 4th
1st (F), 4th (B♭), 5th (C)

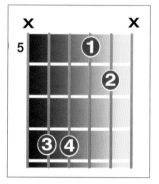

Fsus4   F Suspended 4th
1st (F), 4th (B♭), 5th (C)

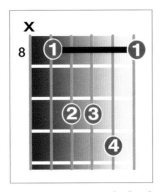

Fsus4 F Suspended 4th
1st (F), 4th (B♭), 5th (C)

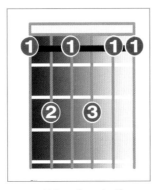

F7sus4 F Dominant 7th sus4
1st (F), 4th (B♭), 5th (C), ♭7th (E♭)

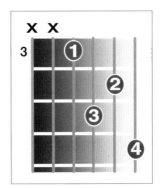

F7sus4 F Dominant 7th sus4
1st (F), 4th (B♭), 5th (C), ♭7th (E♭)

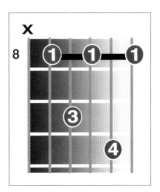

F7sus4 F Dominant 7th sus4
1st (F), 4th (B♭), 5th (C), ♭7th (E♭)

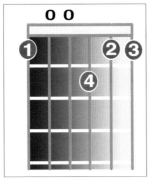

F6 F Major 6th
1st (F), 3rd (A), 5th (C), 6th (D)

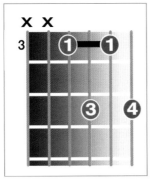

F6 F Major 6th
1st (F), 3rd (A), 5th (C), 6th (D)

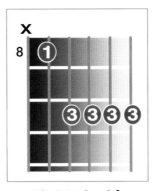

F6 F Major 6th
1st (F), 3rd (A), 5th (C), 6th (D)

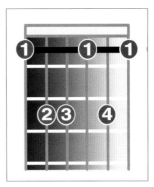

Fm6 F Minor 6th
1st (F), ♭3rd (A♭),
5th (C), 6th (D)

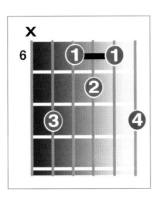

Fm6 F Minor 6th
1st (F), ♭3rd (A♭),
5th (C), 6th (D)

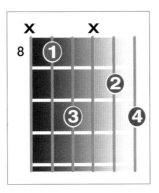

Fm6 F Minor 6th
1st (F), ♭3rd (A♭),
5th (C), 6th (D)

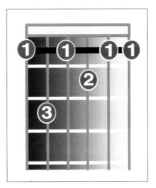

F7 F Dominant 7th
1st (F), 3rd (A), 5th (C), ♭7th (E♭)

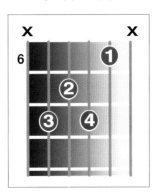

F7 F Dominant 7th
1st (F), 3rd (A), 5th (C), ♭7th (E♭)

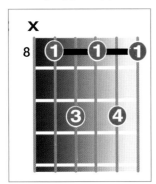

F7 F Dominant 7th
1st (F), 3rd (A), 5th (C), ♭7th (E♭)

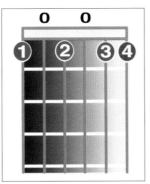

F9 F Dominant 9th
1st (F), 3rd (A), 5th (C),
♭7th (E♭), 9th (G)

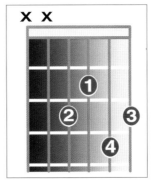

F9 F Dominant 9th
1st (F), 3rd (A), 5th (C),
♭7th (E♭), 9th (G)

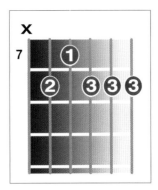

F9 F Dominant 9th
1st (F), 3rd (A), 5th (C),
♭7th (E♭), 9th (G)

F Advanced Chords

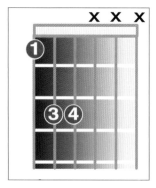

F5   F 5th (power chord)
1st (F), 5th (C)

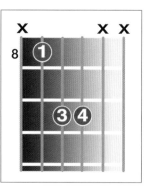

F5   F 5th (power chord)
1st (F), 5th (C)

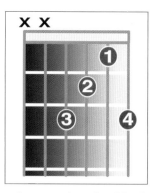

F 6/9   F Major 6th add 9th
1st (F), 3rd (A), 5th (C),
6th (D), 9th (G)

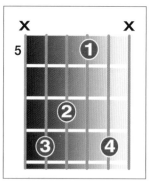

F 6/9   F Major 6th add 9th
1st (F), 3rd (A), 5th (C),
6th (D), 9th (G)

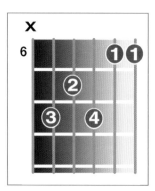

F11   F Dominant 11th
1st (F), 3rd (A), 5th (C),
♭7th (E♭), 9th (G), 11th (B♭)

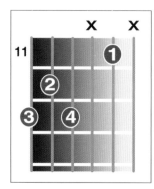

F11   F Dominant 11th
1st (F), 3rd (A), 5th (C),
♭7th (E♭), 9th (G), 11th (B♭)

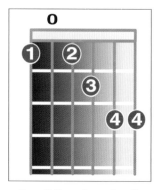

F13   F Dominant 13th
1st (F), 3rd (A), 5th (C),
♭7th (E♭), 9th (G), 13th (D)

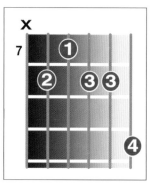

F13   F Dominant 13th
1st (F), 3rd (A), 5th (C),
♭7th (E♭), 9th (G), 13th (D)

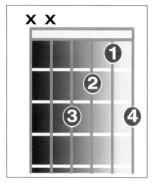

Fadd9   F Major add 9th
1st (F), 3rd (A), 5th (C), 9th (G)

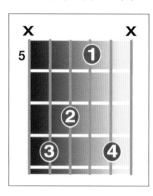

Fadd9   F Major add 9th
1st (F), 3rd (A), 5th (C), 9th (G)

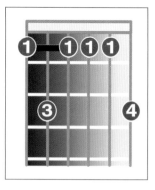

Fm9   F Minor 9th
1st (F), ♭3rd (A♭), 5th (C),
♭7th (E♭), 9th (G)

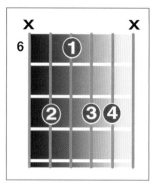

Fm9   F Minor 9th
1st (F), ♭3rd (A♭), 5th (C),
♭7th (E♭), 9th (G)

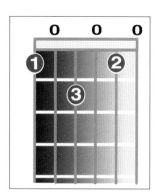

Fmaj9   F Major 9th
1st (F), 3rd (A), 5th (C),
7th (E), 9th (G)

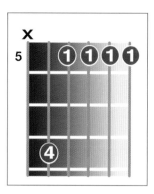

Fmaj9   F Major 9th
1st (F), 3rd (A), 5th (C),
7th (E), 9th (G)

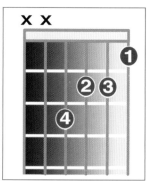

F+   F Augmented
1st (F), 3rd (A), #5th (C#)

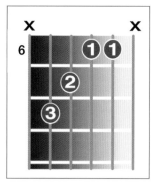

F+   F Augmented
1st (F), 3rd (A), #5th (C#)

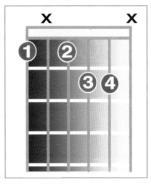

F7#5 **F Dominant 7th ♯5**
1st (F), 3rd (A), ♯5th (C♯), ♭7th (E♭)

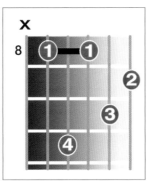

F7#5 **F Dominant 7th ♯5**
1st (F), 3rd (A), ♯5th (C♯), ♭7th (E♭)

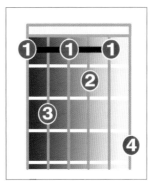

F7♯9 **F Dominant 7th ♯9**
1st (F), 3rd (A), 5th (C), ♭7th (E♭), ♯9th (G♯)

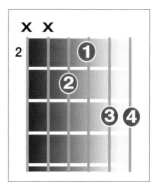

F7♯9 **F Dominant 7th ♯9**
1st (F), 3rd (A), 5th (C), ♭7th (E♭), ♯9th (G♯)

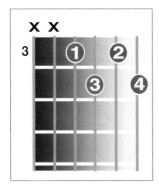

F○7 **F Diminished 7th**
1st (F), ♭3rd (A♭), ♭5th (C♭), ♭♭7th (E♭♭)

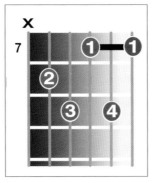

F○7 **F Diminished 7th**
1st (F), ♭3rd (A♭), ♭5th (C♭), ♭♭7th (E♭♭)

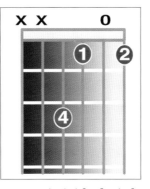

F○ **F Diminished triad**
1st (F), ♭3rd (A♭), ♭5th (C♭)

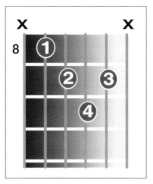

F○ **F Diminished triad**
1st (F), ♭3rd (A♭), ♭5th (C♭)

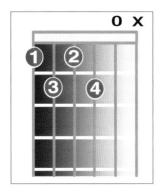

F7♭5 **F Dominant 7th ♭5**
1st (F), 3rd (A), ♭5th (C♭), ♭7th (E♭)

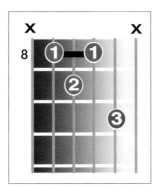

F7♭5 **F Dominant 7th ♭5**
1st (F), 3rd (A), ♭5th (C♭), ♭7th (E♭)

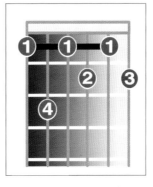

F7♭9 **F Dominant 7th ♭9**
1st (F), 3rd (A), 5th (C), ♭7th (E♭), ♭9th (G♭)

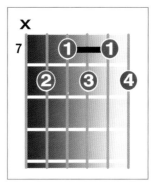

F7♭9 **F Dominant 7th ♭9**
1st (F), 3rd (A), 5th (C), ♭7th (E♭), ♭9th (G♭)

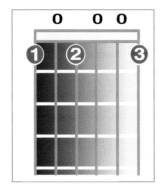

F9♭5 **F Dominant 9th ♭5th**
1st (F), 3rd (A), ♭5th (C♭), ♭7th (E♭), 9th (G)

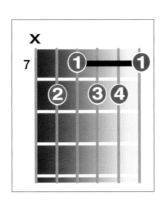

F9♭5 **F Dominant 9th ♭5th**
1st (F), 3rd (A), ♭5th (C♭), ♭7th (E♭), 9th (G)

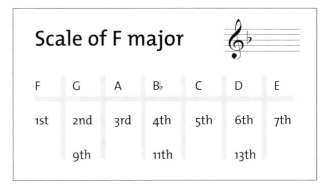

Scale of F major

F	G	A	B♭	C	D	E
1st	2nd	3rd	4th	5th	6th	7th
	9th		11th		13th	

F#/G♭ Main Chords

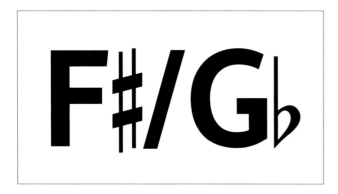

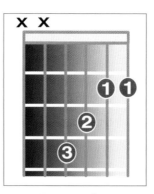

F# F# Major
1st (F#), 3rd (A#), 5th (C#)

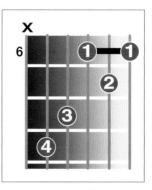

F# F# Major
1st (F#), 3rd (A#), 5th (C#)

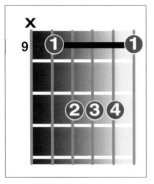

F# F# Major
1st (F#), 3rd (A#), 5th (C#)

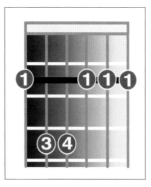

F#m F# Minor
1st (F#), ♭3rd (A), 5th (C#)

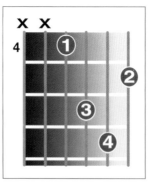

F#m F# Minor
1st (F#), ♭3rd (A), 5th (C#)

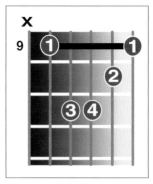

F#m F# Minor
1st (F#), ♭3rd (A), 5th (C#)

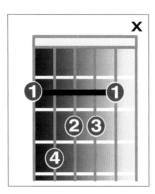

F#maj7 F# Major 7th
1st (F#), 3rd (A#),
5th (C#), 7th (E#)

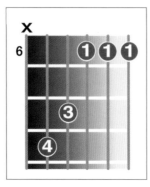

F#maj7 F# Major 7th
1st (F#), 3rd (A#),
5th (C#), 7th (E#)

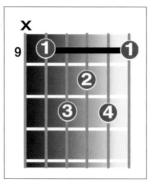

F#maj7 F# Major 7th
1st (F#), 3rd (A#),
5th (C#), 7th (E#)

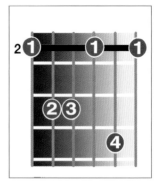

F#m7 F# Minor 7th
1st (F#), ♭3rd (A),
5th (C#), ♭7th (E)

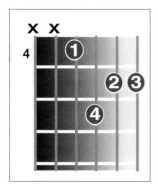

F#m7 F# Minor 7th
1st (F#), ♭3rd (A),
5th (C#), ♭7th (E)

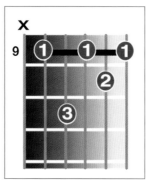

F#m7 F# Minor 7th
1st (F#), ♭3rd (A),
5th (C#), ♭7th (E)

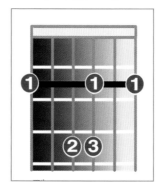

F#sus4 F# Suspended 4th
1st (F#), 4th (B), 5th (C#)

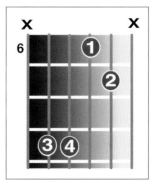

F#sus4 F# Suspended 4th
1st (F#), 4th (B), 5th (C#)

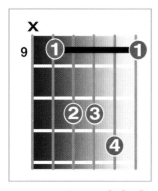

F♯sus4 F♯ Suspended 4th
1st (F♯), 4th (B), 5th (C♯)

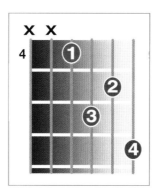

F♯7sus4 F♯ Dominant 7th sus4
1st (F♯), 4th (B), 5th (C♯), ♭7th (E)

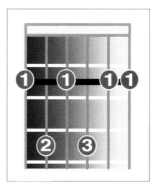

F♯7sus4 F♯ Dominant 7th sus4
1st (F♯), 4th (B), 5th (C♯), ♭7th (E)

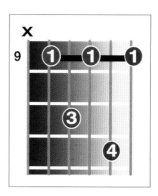

F♯7sus4 F♯ Dominant 7th sus4
1st (F♯), 4th (B), 5th (C♯), ♭7th (E)

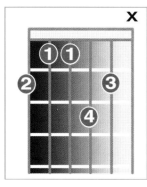

F♯6 F♯ Major 6th
1st (F♯), 3rd (A♯),
5th (C♯), 6th (D♯)

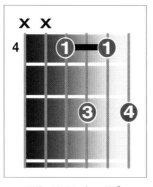

F♯6 F♯ Major 6th
1st (F♯), 3rd (A♯),
5th (C♯), 6th (D♯)

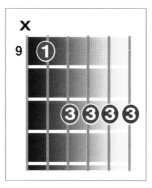

F♯6 F♯ Major 6th
1st (F♯), 3rd (A♯),
5th (C♯), 6th (D♯)

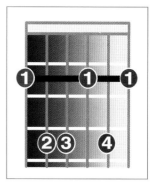

F♯m6 F♯ Minor 6th
1st (F♯), ♭3rd (A), 5th (C♯), 6th (D♯)

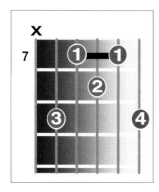

F♯m6 F♯ Minor 6th
1st (F♯), ♭3rd (A), 5th (C♯), 6th (D♯)

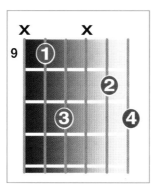

F♯m6 F♯ Minor 6th
1st (F♯), ♭3rd (A), 5th (C♯), 6th (D♯)

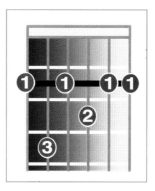

F♯7 F♯ Dominant 7th
1st (F♯), 3rd (A♯),
5th (C♯), ♭7th (E)

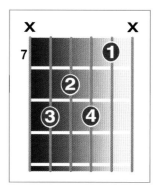

F♯7 F♯ Dominant 7th
1st (F♯), 3rd (A♯),
5th (C♯), ♭7th (E)

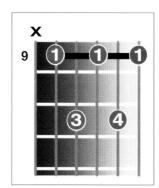

F♯7 F♯ Dominant 7th
1st (F♯), 3rd (A♯),
5th (C♯), ♭7th (E)

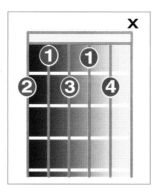

F♯9 F♯ Dominant 9th
1st (F♯), 3rd (A♯), 5th (C♯),
♭7th (E), 9th (G♯)

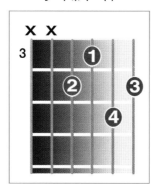

F♯9 F♯ Dominant 9th
1st (F♯), 3rd (A♯), 5th (C♯),
♭7th (E), 9th (G♯)

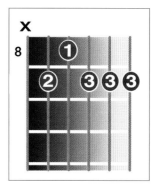

F♯9 F♯ Dominant 9th
1st (F♯), 3rd (A♯), 5th (C♯),
♭7th (E), 9th (G♯)

F♯/G♭ Advanced Chords

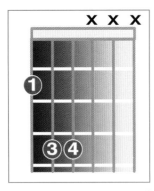

F♯5 F♯ 5th (power chord)
1st (F♯), 5th (C♯)

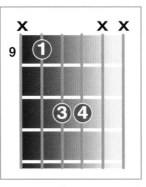

F♯5 F♯ 5th (power chord)
1st (F♯), 5th (C♯)

F♯ 6/9 F♯ Major 6th add 9th
1st (F♯), 3rd (A♯), 5th (C♯),
6th (D♯), 9th (G♯)

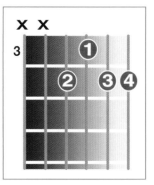

F♯ 6/9 F♯ Major 6th add 9th
1st (F♯), 3rd (A♯), 5th (C♯),
6th (D♯), 9th (G♯)

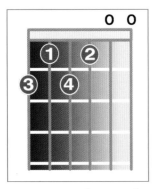

F♯11 F♯ Dominant 11th
1st (F♯), 3rd (A♯), 5th (C♯),
♭7th (E), 9th (G♯), 11th (B)

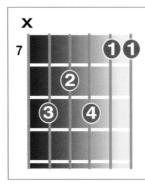

F♯11 F♯ Dominant 11th
1st (F♯), 3rd (A♯), 5th (C♯),
♭7th (E), 9th (G♯), 11th (B)

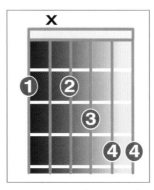

F♯13 F♯ Dominant 13th
1st (F♯), 3rd (A♯), 5th (C♯),
♭7th (E), 9th (G♯), 13th (D♯)

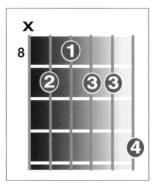

F♯13 F♯ Dominant 13th
1st (F♯), 3rd (A♯), 5th (C♯),
♭7th (E), 9th (G♯), 13th (D♯)

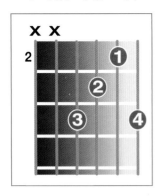

F♯add9 F♯ Major add 9th
1st (F♯), 3rd (A♯), 5th (C♯), 9th (G♯)

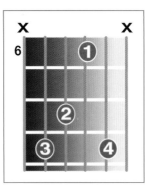

F♯add9 F♯ Major add 9th
1st (F♯), 3rd (A♯), 5th (C♯), 9th (G♯)

F♯m9 F♯ Minor 9th
1st (F♯), ♭3rd (A), 5th (C♯),
♭7th (E), 9th (G♯)

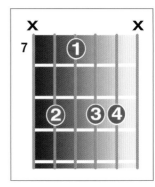

F♯m9 F♯ Minor 9th
1st (F♯), ♭3rd (A), 5th (C♯),
♭7th (E), 9th (G♯)

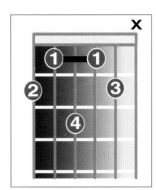

F♯maj9 F♯ Major 9th
1st (F♯), 3rd (A♯), 5th (C♯),
7th (E♯), 9th (G♯)

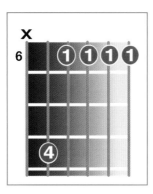

F♯maj9 F♯ Major 9th
1st (F♯), 3rd (A♯), 5th (C♯),
7th (E♯), 9th (G♯)

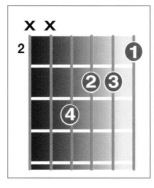

F♯+ F♯ Augmented
1st (F♯), 3rd (A♯), ♯5th (Cx)

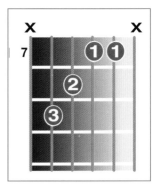

F♯+ F♯ Augmented
1st (F♯), 3rd (A♯), ♯5th (Cx)

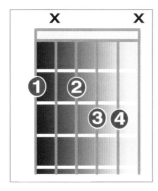

F♯7♯5 **F♯ Dominant 7th ♯5**
1st (F♯), 3rd (A♯), ♯5th (Cx), ♭7th (E)

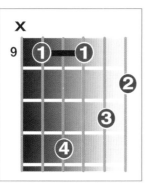

F♯7♯5 **F♯ Dominant 7th ♯5**
1st (F♯), 3rd (A♯), ♯5th (Cx), ♭7th (E)

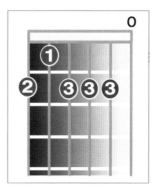

F♯7♯9 **F♯ Dominant 7th ♯9**
1st (F♯), 3rd (A♯), 5th (C♯),
♭7th (E), ♯9th (Gx)

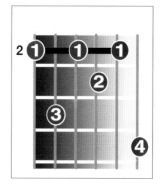

F♯7♯9 **F♯ Dominant 7th ♯9**
1st (F♯), 3rd (A♯), 5th (C♯),
♭7th (E), ♯9th (Gx)

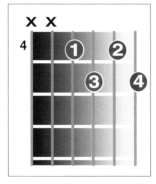

F♯o7 **F♯ Diminished 7th**
1st (F♯), ♭3rd (A), ♭5th (C), ♭♭7th (E♭)

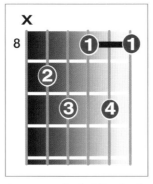

F♯o7 **F♯ Diminished 7th**
1st (F♯), ♭3rd (A), ♭5th (C), ♭♭7th (E♭)

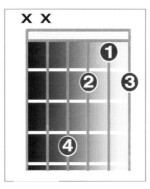

F♯o **F♯ Diminished triad**
1st (F♯), ♭3rd (A), ♭5th (C)

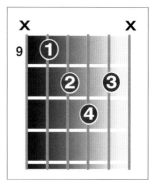

F♯o **F♯ Diminished triad**
1st (F♯), ♭3rd (A), ♭5th (C)

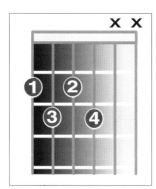

F♯7♭5 **F♯ Dominant 7th ♭5**
1st (F♯), 3rd (A♯), ♭5th (C), ♭7th (E)

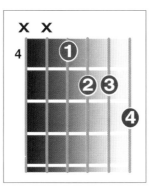

F♯7♭5 **F♯ Dominant 7th ♭5**
1st (F♯), 3rd (A♯), ♭5th (C), ♭7th (E)

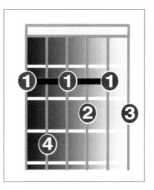

F♯7♭9 **F♯ Dominant 7th ♭9**
1st (F♯), 3rd (A♯), 5th (C♯),
♭7th (E), ♭9th (G)

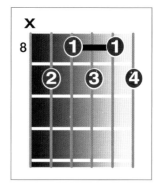

F♯7♭9 **F♯ Dominant 7th ♭9**
1st (F♯), 3rd (A♯), 5th (C♯),
♭7th (E), ♭9th (G)

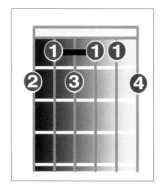

F♯9♭5 **F♯ Dominant 9th ♭5th**
1st (F♯), 3rd (A♯), ♭5th (C),
♭7th (E), 9th (G♯)

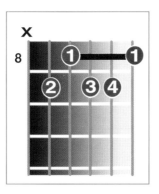

F♯9♭5 **F♯ Dominant 9th ♭5th**
1st (F♯), 3rd (A♯), ♭5th (C),
♭7th (E), 9th (G♯)

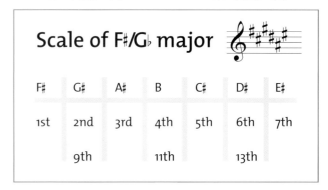

Scale of F♯/G♭ major

F♯	G♯	A♯	B	C♯	D♯	E♯
1st	2nd	3rd	4th	5th	6th	7th
	9th		11th		13th	

G Main Chords

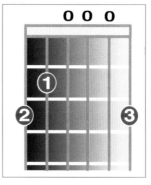

G   G Major
1st (G), 3rd (B), 5th (D)

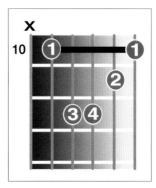

G   G Major
1st (G), 3rd (B), 5th (D)

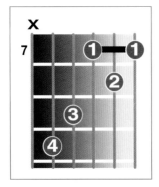

G   G Major
1st (G), 3rd (B), 5th (D)

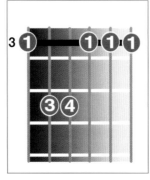

Gm   G Minor
1st (G), ♭3rd (B♭), 5th (D)

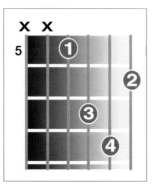

Gm   G Minor
1st (G), ♭3rd (B♭), 5th (D)

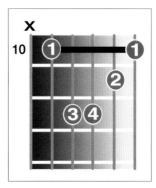

Gm   G Minor
1st (G), ♭3rd (B♭), 5th (D)

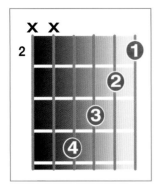

Gmaj7   G Major 7th
1st (G), 3rd (B), 5th (D), 7th (F♯)

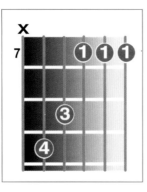

Gmaj7   G Major 7th
1st (G), 3rd (B), 5th (D), 7th (F♯)

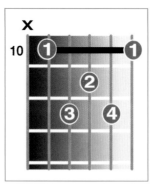

Gmaj7   G Major 7th
1st (G), 3rd (B), 5th (D), 7th (F♯)

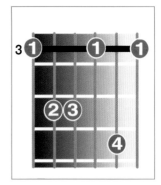

Gm7   G Minor 7th
1st (G), ♭3rd (B♭),
5th (D), ♭7th (F)

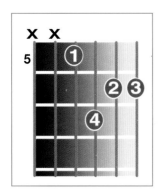

Gm7   G Minor 7th
1st (G), ♭3rd (B♭),
5th (D), ♭7th (F)

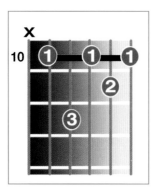

Gm7   G Minor 7th
1st (G), ♭3rd (B♭),
5th (D), ♭7th (F)

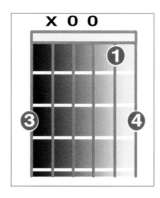

Gsus4   G Suspended 4th
1st (G), 4th (C), 5th (D)

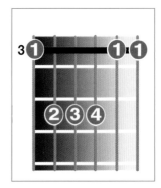

Gsus4   G Suspended 4th
1st (G), 4th (C), 5th (D)

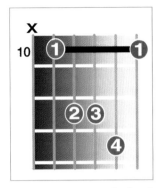

Gsus4 G Suspended 4th
1st (G), 4th (C), 5th (D)

G7sus4 G Dominant 7th sus4
1st (G), 4th (C), 5th (D), ♭7th (F)

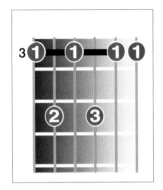

G7sus4 G Dominant 7th sus4
1st (G), 4th (C), 5th (D), ♭7th (F)

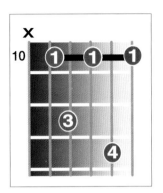

G7sus4 G Dominant 7th sus4
1st (G), 4th (C), 5th (D), ♭7th (F)

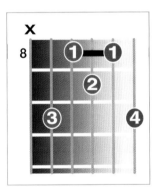

G6 G Major 6th
1st (G), 3rd (B), 5th (D), 6th (E)

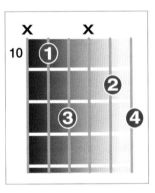

G6 G Major 6th
1st (G), 3rd (B), 5th (D), 6th (E)

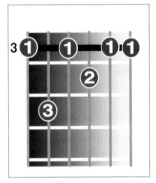

G6 G Major 6th
1st (G), 3rd (B), 5th (D), 6th (E)

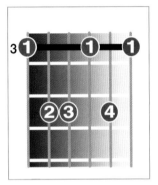

Gm6 G Minor 6th
1st (G), ♭3rd (B♭),
5th (D), 6th (E)

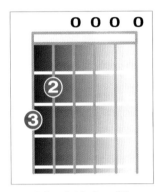

Gm6 G Minor 6th
1st (G), ♭3rd (B♭),
5th (D), 6th (E)

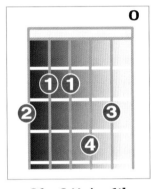

Gm6 G Minor 6th
1st (G), ♭3rd (B♭),
5th (D), 6th (E)

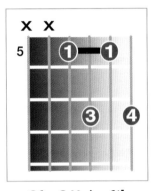

G7 G Dominant 7th
1st (G), 3rd (B), 5th (D), ♭7th (F)

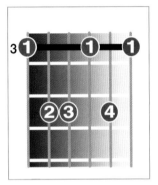

G7 G Dominant 7th
1st (G), 3rd (B), 5th (D), ♭7th (F)

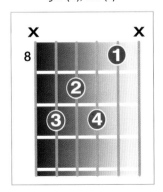

G7 G Dominant 7th
1st (G), 3rd (B), 5th (D), ♭7th (F)

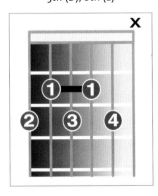

G9 G Dominant 9th
1st (G), 3rd (B), 5th (D),
♭7th (F), 9th (A)

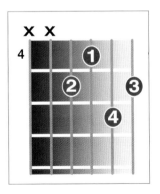

G9 G Dominant 9th
1st (G), 3rd (B), 5th (D),
♭7th (F), 9th (A)

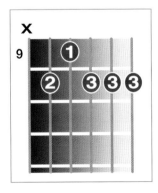

G9 G Dominant 9th
1st (G), 3rd (B), 5th (D),
♭7th (F), 9th (A)

G Advanced Chords

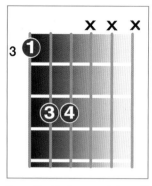

G5 G 5th (power chord)
1st (G), 5th (D)

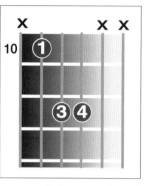

G5 G 5th (power chord)
1st (G), 5th (D)

G 6/9 G Major 6th add 9th
1st (G), 3rd (B), 5th (D),
6th (E), 9th (A)

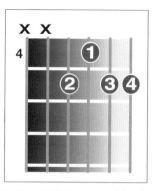

G 6/9 G Major 6th add 9th
1st (G), 3rd (B), 5th (D),
6th (E), 9th (A)

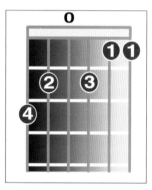

G11 G Dominant 11th
1st (G), 3rd (B), 5th (D),
♭7th (F), 9th (A), 11th (C)

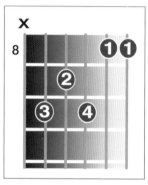

G11 G Dominant 11th
1st (G), 3rd (B), 5th (D),
♭7th (F), 9th (A), 11th (C)

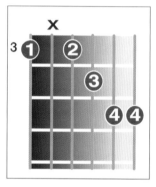

G13 G Dominant 13th
1st (G), 3rd (B), 5th (D),
♭7th (F), 9th (A), 13th (E)

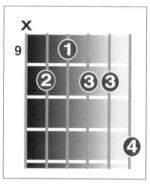

G13 G Dominant 13th
1st (G), 3rd (B), 5th (D),
♭7th (F), 9th (A), 13th (E)

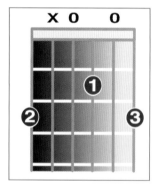

Gadd9 G Major add 9th
1st (G), 3rd (B), 5th (D), 9th (A)

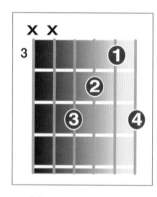

Gadd9 G Major add 9th
1st (G), 3rd (B), 5th (D), 9th (A)

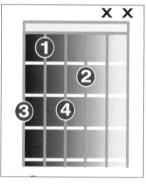

Gm9 G Minor 9th
1st (G), ♭3rd (B♭), 5th (D),
♭7th (F), 9th (A)

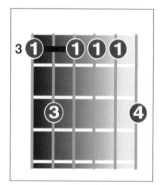

Gm9 G Minor 9th
1st (G), ♭3rd (B♭), 5th (D),
♭7th (F), 9th (A)

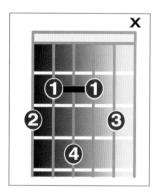

Gmaj9 G Major 9th
1st (G), 3rd (B), 5th (D),
7th (F♯), 9th (A)

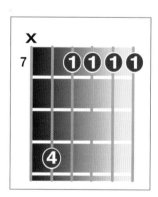

Gmaj9 G Major 9th
1st (G), 3rd (B), 5th (D),
7th (F♯), 9th (A)

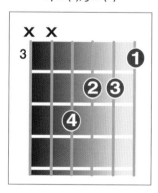

G+ G Augmented
1st (G), 3rd (B), ♯5th (D♯)

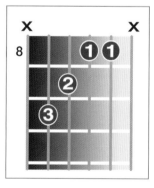

G+ G Augmented
1st (G), 3rd (B), ♯5th (D♯)

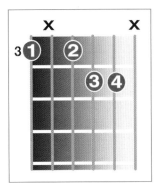

G7♯5 G Dominant 7th ♯5
1st (G), 3rd (B), ♯5th (D♯), ♭7th (F)

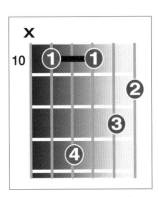

G7♯5 G Dominant 7th ♯5
1st (G), 3rd (B), ♯5th (D♯), ♭7th (F)

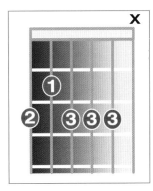

G7♯9 G Dominant 7th ♯9
1st (G), 3rd (B), 5th (D),
♭7th (F), ♯9th (A♯)

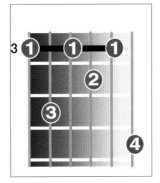

G7♯9 G Dominant 7th ♯9
1st (G), 3rd (B), 5th (D),
♭7th (F), ♯9th (A♯)

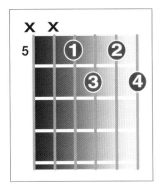

Go7 G Diminished 7th
1st (G), ♭3rd (B♭), ♭5th (D♭), ♭♭7th (F♭)

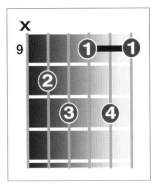

Go7 G Diminished 7th
1st (G), ♭3rd (B♭), ♭5th (D♭), ♭♭7th (F♭)

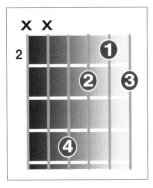

Go G Diminished triad
1st (G), ♭3rd (B♭), ♭5th (D♭)

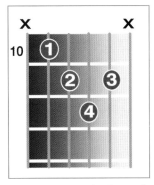

Go G Diminished triad
1st (G), ♭3rd (B♭), ♭5th (D♭)

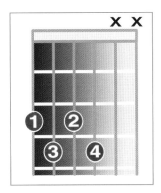

G7♭5 G Dominant 7th ♭5
1st (G), 3rd (B), ♭5th (D♭), ♭7th (F)

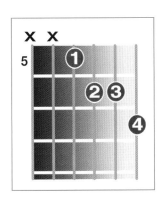

G7♭5 G Dominant 7th ♭5
1st (G), 3rd (B), ♭5th (D♭), ♭7th (F)

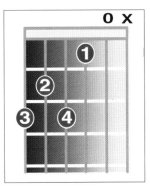

G7♭9 G Dominant 7th ♭9
1st (G), 3rd (B), 5th (D),
♭7th (F), ♭9th (A♭)

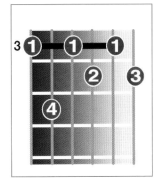

G7♭9 G Dominant 7th ♭9
1st (G), 3rd (B), 5th (D),
♭7th (F), ♭9th (A♭)

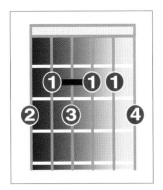

G9♭5 G Dominant 9th ♭5th
1st (G), 3rd (B), ♭5th (D♭),
♭7th (F), 9th (A)

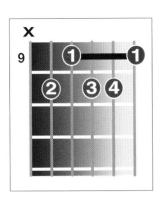

G9♭5 G Dominant 9th ♭5th
1st (G), 3rd (B), ♭5th (D♭),
♭7th (F), 9th (A)

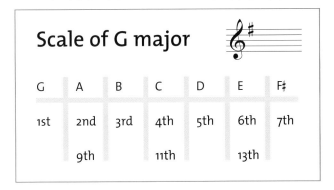

Scale of G major

G	A	B	C	D	E	F♯
1st	2nd	3rd	4th	5th	6th	7th
	9th		11th		13th	

A♭/G♯ Main Chords

A♭ A♭ Major
1st (A♭), 3rd (C), 5th (E♭)

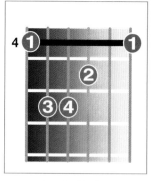

A♭ A♭ Major
1st (A♭), 3rd (C), 5th (E♭)

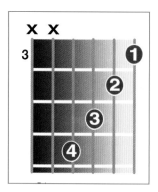

A♭ A♭ Major
1st (A♭), 3rd (C), 5th (E♭)

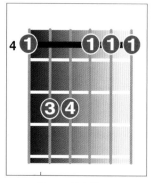

A♭m A♭ Minor
1st (A♭), ♭3rd (C♭), 5th (E♭)

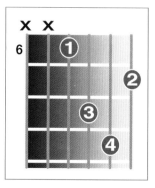

A♭m A♭ Minor
1st (A♭), ♭3rd (C♭), 5th (E♭)

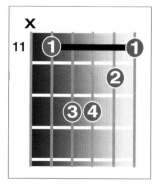

A♭m A♭ Minor
1st (A♭), ♭3rd (C♭), 5th (E♭)

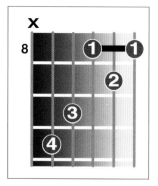

A♭maj7 A♭ Major 7th
1st (A♭), 3rd (C),
5th (E♭), 7th (G)

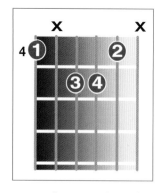

A♭maj7 A♭ Major 7th
1st (A♭), 3rd (C),
5th (E♭), 7th (G)

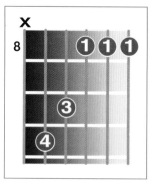

A♭maj7 A♭ Major 7th
1st (A♭), 3rd (C),
5th (E♭), 7th (G)

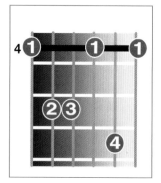

A♭m7 A♭ Minor 7th
1st (A♭), ♭3rd (C♭),
5th (E♭), ♭7th (G♭)

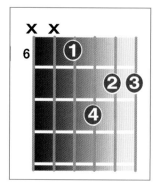

A♭m7 A♭ Minor 7th
1st (A♭), ♭3rd (C♭),
5th (E♭), ♭7th (G♭)

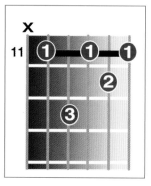

A♭m7 A♭ Minor 7th
1st (A♭), ♭3rd (C♭),
5th (E♭), ♭7th (G♭)

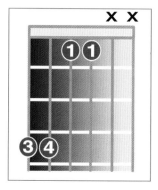

A♭sus4 A♭ Suspended 4th
1st (A♭), 4th (D♭), 5th (E♭)

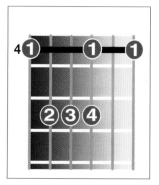

A♭sus4 A♭ Suspended 4th
1st (A♭), 4th (D♭), 5th (E♭)

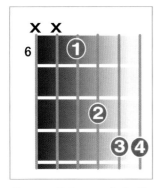

A♭sus4 A♭ Suspended 4th
1st (A♭), 4th (D♭), 5th (E♭)

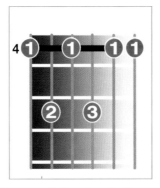

A♭7sus4 A♭ Dominant 7th sus4
1st (A♭), 4th (D♭), 5th (E♭), ♭7th (G♭)

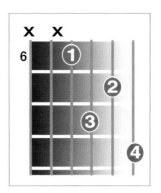

A♭7sus4 A♭ Dominant 7th sus4
1st (A♭), 4th (D♭), 5th (E♭), ♭7th (G♭)

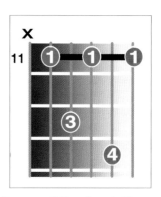

A♭7sus4 A♭ Dominant 7th sus4
1st (A♭), 4th (D♭), 5th (E♭), ♭7th (G♭)

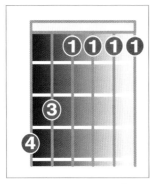

A♭6 A♭ Major 6th
1st (A♭), 3rd (C), 5th (E♭), 6th (F)

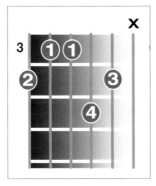

A♭6 A♭ Major 6th
1st (A♭), 3rd (C), 5th (E♭), 6th (F)

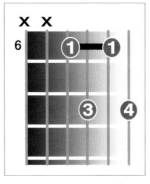

A♭6 A♭ Major 6th
1st (A♭), 3rd (C), 5th (E♭), 6th (F)

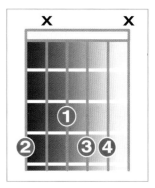

A♭m6 A♭ Minor 6th
1st (A♭), ♭3rd (C♭), 5th (E♭), 6th (F)

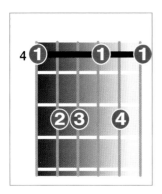

A♭m6 A♭ Minor 6th
1st (A♭), ♭3rd (C♭), 5th (E♭), 6th (F)

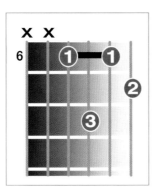

A♭m6 A♭ Minor 6th
1st (A♭), ♭3rd (C♭), 5th (E♭), 6th (F)

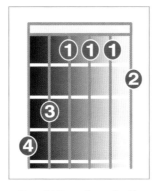

A♭7 A♭ Dominant 7th
1st (A♭), 3rd (C), 5th (E♭), ♭7th (G♭)

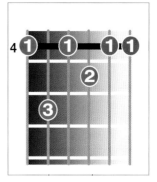

A♭7 A♭ Dominant 7th
1st (A♭), 3rd (C), 5th (E♭), ♭7th (G♭)

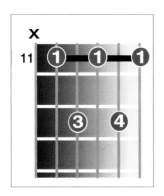

A♭7 A♭ Dominant 7th
1st (A♭), 3rd (C), 5th (E♭), ♭7th (G♭)

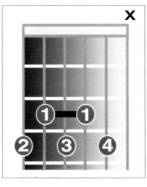

A♭9 A♭ Dominant 9th
1st (A♭), 3rd (C), 5th (E♭),
♭7th (G♭), 9th (B♭)

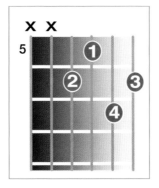

A♭9 A♭ Dominant 9th
1st (A♭), 3rd (C), 5th (E♭),
♭7th (G♭), 9th (B♭)

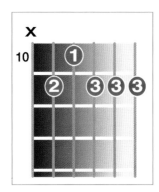

A♭9 A♭ Dominant 9th
1st (A♭), 3rd (C), 5th (E♭),
♭7th (G♭), 9th (B♭)

A♭/G♯ Advanced Chords

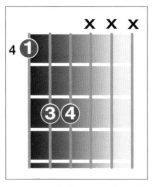

A♭5 A♭ 5th (power chord)
1st (A♭), 5th (E♭)

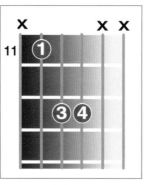

A♭5 A♭ 5th (power chord)
1st (A♭), 5th (E♭)

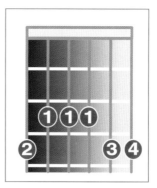

A♭6/9 A♭ Major 6th add 9th
1st (A♭), 3rd (C), 5th (E♭),
6th (F), 9th (B♭)

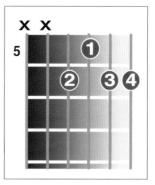

A♭ 6/9 A♭ Major 6th add 9th
1st (A♭), 3rd (C), 5th (E♭),
6th (F), 9th (B♭)

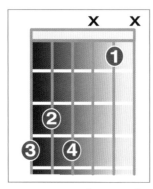

A♭11 A♭ Dominant 11th
1st (A♭), 3rd (C), 5th (E♭),
♭7th (G♭), 9th (B♭), 11th (D♭)

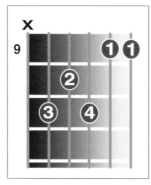

A♭11 A♭ Dominant 11th
1st (A♭), 3rd (C), 5th (E♭),
♭7th (G♭), 9th (B♭), 11th (D♭)

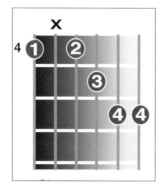

A♭13 A♭ Dominant 13th
1st (A♭), 3rd (C), 5th (E♭),
♭7th (G♭), 9th (B♭), 13th (F)

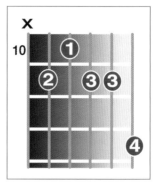

A♭13 A♭ Dominant 13th
1st (A♭), 3rd (C), 5th (E♭),
♭7th (G♭), 9th (B♭), 13th (F)

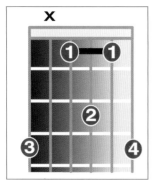

A♭add9 A♭ Major add 9th
1st (A♭), 3rd (C), 5th (E♭), 9th (B♭)

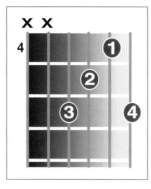

A♭add9 A♭ Major add 9th
1st (A♭), 3rd (C), 5th (E♭), 9th (B♭)

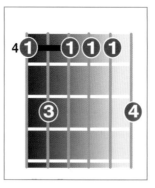

A♭m9 A♭ Minor 9th
1st (A♭), ♭3rd (C♭), 5th (E♭),
♭7th (G♭), 9th (B♭)

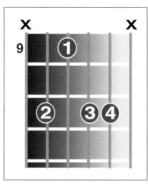

A♭m9 A♭ Minor 9th
1st (A♭), ♭3rd (C♭), 5th (E♭),
♭7th (G♭), 9th (B♭)

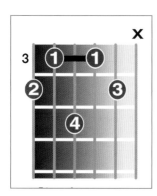

A♭maj9 A♭ Major 9th
1st (A♭), 3rd (C), 5th (E♭),
7th (G), 9th (B♭)

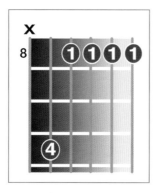

A♭maj9 A♭ Major 9th
1st (A♭), 3rd (C), 5th (E♭),
7th (G), 9th (B♭)

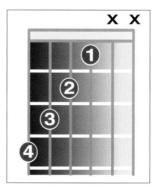

A♭+ A♭ Augmented
1st (A♭), 3rd (C), ♯5th (E)

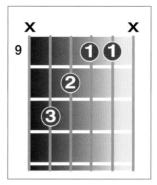

A♭+ A♭ Augmented
1st (A♭), 3rd (C), ♯5th (E)

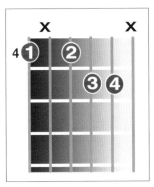

A♭7♯5 A♭ Dominant 7th ♯5
1st (A♭), 3rd (C), ♯5th (E), ♭7th (G♭)

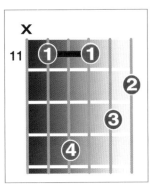

A♭7♯5 A♭ Dominant 7th ♯5
1st (A♭), 3rd (C), ♯5th (E), ♭7th (G♭)

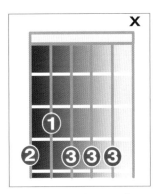

A♭7♯9 A♭ Dominant 7th ♯9
1st (A♭), 3rd (C), 5th (E♭),
♭7th (G♭), ♯9th (B)

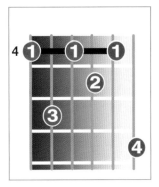

A♭7♯9 A♭ Dominant 7th ♯9
1st (A♭), 3rd (C), 5th (E♭),
♭7th (G♭), ♯9th (B)

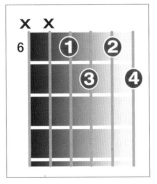

A♭○7 A♭ Diminished 7th
1st (A♭), ♭3rd (C♭), ♭5th (E♭♭),
♭♭7th (G♭♭)

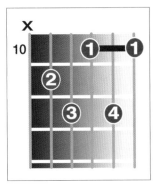

A♭○7 A♭ Diminished 7th
1st (A♭), ♭3rd (C♭), ♭5th (E♭♭),
♭♭7th (G♭♭)

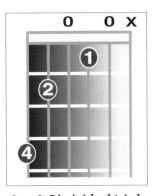

A♭○ A♭ Diminished triad
1st (A♭), ♭3rd (C♭), ♭5th (E♭♭)

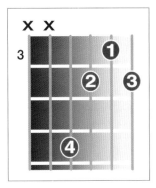

A♭○ A♭ Diminished triad
1st (A♭), ♭3rd (C♭), ♭5th (E♭♭)

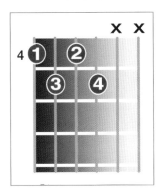

A♭7♭5 A♭ Dominant 7th ♭5
1st (A♭), 3rd (C), ♭5th (E♭♭), ♭7th (G♭)

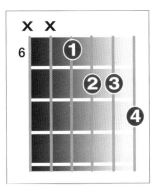

A♭7♭5 A♭ Dominant 7th ♭5
1st (A♭), 3rd (C), ♭5th (E♭♭), ♭7th (G♭)

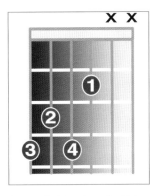

A♭7♭9 A♭ Dominant 7th ♭9
1st (A♭), 3rd (C), 5th (E♭),
♭7th (G♭), ♭9th (B♭♭)

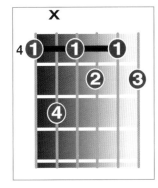

A♭7♭9 A♭ Dominant 7th ♭9
1st (A♭), 3rd (C), 5th (E♭),
♭7th (G♭), ♭9th (B♭♭)

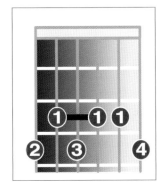

A♭9♭5 A♭ Dominant 9th ♭5
1st (A♭), 3rd (C), ♭5th (E♭♭),
♭7th (G♭), 9th (B♭)

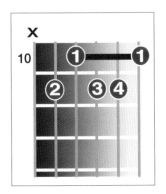

A♭9♭5 A♭ Dominant 9th ♭5
1st (A♭), 3rd (C), ♭5th (E♭♭),
♭7th (G♭), 9th (B♭)

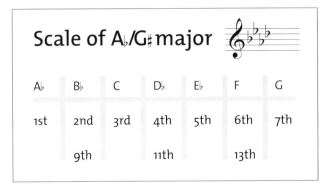

Scale of A♭/G♯ major

A♭	B♭	C	D♭	E♭	F	G
1st	2nd	3rd	4th	5th	6th	7th
	9th		11th		13th	

GLOSSARY

Action
The 'action' of a guitar refers to the height of the strings from the fingerboard and determines how much pressure you have to put on the strings in order to play them.

Active electronics
Active electronics is a battery powered circuitry that boosts a guitar signal to make it easier to drive an amplifier into distortion and can change the tone of the guitar.

Archtop
An archtop guitar is an instrument with an arched (curved) top and back. Carved from solid pieces of wood, they are louder than a standard classical guitar.

Arpeggio
An arpeggio is the sounding of the notes of a chord in succession rather than all simultaneously. These can be played individually while holding a chord down or by picking out the notes separately on the fingerboard.

Barre chord
A barre chord is a chord where one of a guitarist's fretting fingers (usually the first finger) is held down across many or all of the strings in addition to other fingers holding down separate notes.

Bend
A common lead guitar techniques is string bending, where a player plays a note on a string and pushes it up towards the next string while still holding the note down.

Bottleneck
A technique where a player moves a glass or metal bar up and down the guitar neck while playing to produce sliding pitches.

Box-shape
Most guitarists normally learn scales as box-shapes, which show the finger positions for notes in a particular region of the fingerboard.

Bridge
This part of the guitar, along with the saddle, transmits energy from the string vibrations to the body of a guitar and spreads the mechanical tension of the strings. A fixed bridge is glued to the top of the soundboard with the strings anchored to it, while a floating bridge is held in place by the tension in the strings that pass over it.

Classical guitar
A large acoustic guitar with a wide neck, over which metal-wound silk bass strings and gut treble strings are usually strung. It was the first type of guitar to feature struts – pieces of wood attached to the inside of the body to improve volume and tonal response – and is always played fingerstyle.

Comping
'Comping' is a jazz term for accompanying. It usually means playing rhythm chords while a vocalist is singing or a lead performer is playing a solo.

Crown
The crown is the top of a fret on the guitar fingerboard. Crowns vary in width and curvature, and these differences influence the tone of a vibrating string.

Cutaway
This is a rounded area cut out of a guitar's body next to the neck so that a player can comfortably reach further up the neck.

Dot marker
Most guitars have these markers along the neck to help players navigate the fingerboard. They are usually behind the 3rd, 5th, 7th, 9th, 12th, 15th, 17th, 19th and 21st frets.

Double-stop
A two-note chord, melody or phrase.

Electro-acoustic
An electro-acoustic guitar is an acoustic or semi-acoustic guitar fitted with a 'piezo-electric' transducer (usually under the bridge saddle) and an on-board pre-amplifier. When plugged into a suitable amp, this produces a crisp acoustic sound with plenty of sustain and little feedback.

EQ
EQ is short for equalisation, a term describing the sound spectrum or parts of the sound spectrum of an audio signal. All audible sounds are pitched somewhere between 20Hz (the lowest) and 20KHz (the highest). An equaliser is a tone control that uses capacitors or other devices to cut or boost frequencies within this range.

F-hole
F-holes are ornamental sound holes found on a number of acoustic and electric guitars.

Fingerstyle
Fingerstyle classical and flamenco players articulate their notes with the separate fingers and thumb of their plucking hand. The thumb plays the bass notes, usually with downstrokes on the bottom three strings, while the fingers play the other strings.

Flamenco
A popular folk music style from Andalucia in southern Spain.

Flatpicking
Flatpicking is a style where all notes, scalar and chordal, are articulated with a plectrum.

Footswitch
A footswitch is a device that allows you to change guitar sounds during a live performance without having to stop playing.

Fret
Frets are metal strips placed across the radius of a guitar's fingerboard to mark out notes a semitone apart. They make it easy for a guitarist to find precise notes in scales and chords.

Glissando
A glissando is a slide in which every note under the left hand finger is articulated. This is different from a basic slide, in which only the first and last notes played by the left hand finger can be clearly heard.

Guitar, 12-string
These guitars have 12 strings arranged into pairs (courses) so that a 6-string player can easily handle them. Six of the strings are tuned identically to those on a 6-string instrument, while the other six are tuned as follows; the lowest four are usually tuned an octave above the conventional E, A, D and G strings, while the other two are tuned the same as the conventional B and E strings.

Guitar, 7-string
The seven string guitar is like a standard six string instrument with an additional low string, usually tuned down to a low A.

Hammer-on
A hammer-on is a common lead guitar technique where you play a note behind a fret on the fingerboard and then hammer one of your other fingers down behind another fret higher up on the same string.

Headstock
The headstock is a wooden structure attached to the end of a guitar's neck that the machine heads or tuning pegs are mounted on. It is also usually the part of the guitar that carries the manufacturer's name and logo, plus any other significant details of the guitar model.

Humbucking pickups
Humbucking pickups have two coils, which are wired in such a way that any electrical hum produced by one is cancelled out by the other. The result is a 'fatter' sound with less background noise. Humbuckers were originally launched by Gibson in 1955 and soon became a standard feature on many of their guitars.

Intonation
The intonation of a guitar is correct when the notes behind every fret of the fingerboard all have the right pitch when the guitar is in tune. To check the intonation of your guitar, tune it up accurately and then listen to each note on each string. If any notes on any string are out of tune, you should be able to make intonation adjustments on the bridge screw that controls the vibrating length of that string.

Lick
A lick is a small musical motif such as a phrase or riff that can be incorporated into a lead guitar solo. All good solo players have a vocabulary of licks that they use in their lead lines.

Luthier
A luthier is a guitar maker. Originally the term was only used to describe lute and classical guitar makers but now it is generally considered to apply to builders of all kinds of guitars and fretted instruments.

Nut
The nut is a structure at the headstock end of the fingerboard that the strings pass over before they reach the machine heads or pegs. The strings lean on the nut and all string vibrations occur between here and the guitar's bridge.

Palm-muting
You can mute a guitar's strings by placing your right hand lightly across them. This is very useful if you're playing at high volume and don't want the strings to ring out unnecessarily. It can also be used to add more colour and texture to a rhythm or solo.

Pickup selector
A switch that allows a guitar player to choose between different pickups.

Pre-amp
Many amplifiers and DI boxes contain a pre-amplifier, a device that can be used to generate extra signal gain. Such devices are often used when acoustic instruments are amplified and when electric players need a bit more edge in their tone.

Pre-bend
A pre-bend is when you bend a note before you actually play it. In this situation you play the string from the top of the bend and then pull it back into its original position.

Pull-off
In many ways, a pull-off can be seen as the reverse of a hammer-on. In this case, a note is played and then the finger playing that note is pulled off the string to sound a lower note that is either an open string or one fretted by another finger.

Rake
A rake is an interesting effect a guitarist can produce by rubbing one of their fingers or hands along one or several of the guitar strings. A harsher raking effect can be created by performing it with a hard object such as a plectrum.

Rasgueado
Rasgueado (also spelt Rascuedo) is an instantly recognisable flamenco technique where the fingers of the right hand (or left hand if the player is left-handed) individually strum across the strings in rapid succession.

Riff
A riff is a short series of chords or notes that can be repeated to form a catchy sequence.

Saddle
The saddle is the place on a guitar's bridge for supporting the strings. The distance between it and the nut determines the scale length (length of vibrating open string) of a guitar.

Scratchplate
A scratchplate is a plastic plate that is fixed to the lower front part of a guitar's body (underneath the soundhole on an acoustic steel-string instrument) to protect the body from wear and tear caused by the player's plectrums or finger picks.

Semi-solid
During the late 1950s, Gibson introduced a range of semi-acoustic guitars that had increased sustain and didn't suffer from the feedback problems that traditional 'electric-acoustic' models produced. These guitars, including the ES-355, ES-345, and the now famous ES-335, had thin, hollow bodies with f-holes to let the sound out.

Semitone
The smallest interval between two notes on a fretted guitar is called a semitone (S). Notes on either side of a fret are separated by a semitone. An interval of two semitones is called a tone (T).

Slide
This effect is produced when you play one note on the guitar and, while still holding the note down, slide up or down the guitar neck to another note. In a true slide, the only two notes you can hear clearly are the first and last notes, at the beginning and end of the slide.

Solid-body
A solid-body guitar is a guitar with a body that has no cavities other than those used for inserting pickups and other electrical components. Solid-body electric guitar prototypes were developed during the 1920s and 1930s when amplified acoustic guitars gave musicians too much feedback.

Soundhole
The soundhole is the hole in the front of the guitar body through which sound projects from the soundchamber. Most acoustic guitar soundholes are round, although some are oval, D-shaped or violin-like f-holes.

Sweep-picking
Sweep picking is an advanced technique in which a guitarist plays notes across the neck with economic pick movements. In some ways it is similar to the way a violinist will sustain a note with the bow by bowing in both directions at a consistent speed. This technique can be used to play ultra-fast arpeggios.

Sympathetic strings
Sitars and some specialist lutes and guitars have sympathetic strings which are not played but sound together with strings that are. The sympathetic strings are tuned to particular notes and when those notes are played on the instrument, the corresponding strings start to vibrate and thus 'sing in sympathy'.

Thumbpick
Thumbpicks are often used by fingerstyle players who want to play the guitar forcefully without risk of damaging their thumbnails. A thumbpick fits over the end of the thumb with the pick protruding to strike the strings.

Time signature
A time signature is a sign placed after the clef at the beginning of a piece of music to indicate its meter.

Tremolando
Tremolando is a classical and flamenco guitar technique in which the first, second and third fingers of the picking hand play a continuous, repeating pattern on one note.

Tremolo arm
A tremolo arm (a.k.a. 'whammy bar') is a mechanical arm attached to the bridge of an electric guitar that can alter the pitch of the strings; as the arm is depressed, the pitch of a note played drops, and when the arm is let go, the altered pitch returns back to normal.

Triad
Triads are basic, three-note chords that are also the building blocks of most other chords. There are four basic triads: a major triad is the first, third and fifth notes of the diatonic major scale (C, E and G in the key of C); a minor triad is the first third and fifth notes of the natural minor scale (C, E flat and G in the key of C); an augmented triad is a major triad with a sharpened fifth note (C, E and G# in the key of C); and a diminished triad is a minor triad with a flattened fifth note (C, E flat and G flat in the key of C).

Truss rod
The truss rod is a metal bar used for reinforcing and adjusting a steel-strung guitar's neck. It can be adjusted to keep the neck straight if the tension in it changes when different gauge strings are used.

Vibrato
Vibrato is a fret hand technique in which a played note is moved rapidly to produce a fluctuation in pitch that gives more richness to the tone. Vibrato can be applied vertically (across the neck) or horizontally (along the neck).

Violining
Violining is an effect in which you use a guitar's volume control (or a volume pedal) to fade notes or chords in from nothing to get a nice, smooth effect.

PICTURE CREDITS

Arbiter Group Plc Fender Musical Instruments Inc 104; 136 (l); 140

Boss 124; 129 (t); 131 (b); 132 (t); 134

Rusty Cutchin 131 (t); 135 (t)

DOD 121 (t)

Dorling Kindersley Ltd 136 (r); 162 (t); 179 (b)

Foundry Arts 9; 10; 11; 16; 82; 92; 101; 102; 107; 110; 111; 113 (b); 115 (t); 117; 125 (b); 135 (b); 142; 143; 144; 145; 146; 147; 148; 149; 150; 151; 152; 153; 154; 155; 156; 157; 158; 160; 161; 162 (b); 163; 164; 165; 166 (t); 169; 171; 173 (b); 174 (t); 179 (t); 183; 186; 191; 199;

Ibanez 121 (b)

Line 6 137; 159 (r)

London Features International 118

C. F. Martin & Co. Inc., Nazareth, PA USA 138

Marshall Amplification plc 195

Parker Guitars 159 (l)

Redferns
Richie Aaron 201; Paul Bergen 28; 126; Glen Baker 127 (t); Dick Barnatt 88; 196; Carey Blander 108; Fin Costello 181; Pete Cronin 192 (b); DeltaHaze Corporation 22; 166 (b); Patrick Ford 33; GEMS 170; William Gottleib 60; Beth Gwinn 114; Mick Hutson 56; Max Jones 188; Robert Knight 40; 113 (t); Gerard Mankowitz 192 (t); Steve Morley 129 (b); Odile Noel 27 (t); Michael Ochs Archive 25; 41; 116; 123; 128; 130; 176; 184; PALM/RSCH 172; Dave Peabody 187; David Redfern 21; 32; 73; 167; 173 (t); 178; 189; Ebet Roberts 26; 106; 115 (b); 177; 197; John Rodgers 120; Lorne Rusnick 133; Donna Santisi 57; Max Scheler 132 (b); Jim Sharpe 125 (t); Jon Super 24; Gai Terrell 185; Richard Upper 72; Robert Vinight 76; Bob Willoughby 50; Graham Wiltshire 62

Roland Corporation 27 (b)

TC Electronics 119

Topham Picturepoint 112; 122; 180; Arena PAL 174 (b); Roger Viollet 182

William Worsley 200

CONTRIBUTOR BIOGRAPHIES

Michael Leonard (General Editor)
Michael Leonard began playing guitar at the age of 12, inspired by his elder brother's budget-priced but very fine Yamaha acoustic. He's worked in the music press since 1990, and has edited *The Guitar Magazine*, *Guitar Techniques* and – currently – Europe's longest-established musicians' magazine, *Guitarist*. As a freelance writer, he's contributed to *Q*, *Mojo*, *Blender* and many others. He lives with his wife and two children in Bath, England.

Rusty Cutchin (Consultant Editor)
Rusty Cutchin has been a musician, recording engineer, producer and journalist for over 25 years. His articles have appeared in *Cashbox, Billboard, Hits, Musician, Country Fever, International Musician* and *Recording World*. Songwriting and production work for Atlantic Records and Motown led him to a studio career during which he worked on recordings by artists including Mariah Carey and Yoko Ono, as well as on countless jazz, dance and hip-hop records. At the same he built a pro-quality home studio, before returning full-circle to journalism, becoming editor-in-chief of *Home Recording* and technical editor of *GuitarOne*. He is currently associate editor of *Electronic Musician*, the leading US magazine for the home-studio musician.

Cliff Douse (Musical Styles; Glossary)
Cliff Douse is a music author, editor and composer based in the UK. His first book, *Scales & Modes for Guitar*, was published in 1990 with an endorsement from the legendary rock guitarist, Pete Townshend, and he has since written a number of other books and countless articles for some of the UK's foremost music and computer magazines. Cliff also recently edited *Guitar Techniques* magazine and the *Guitarist Icons* series for Future Publishing in England.

Richard Riley (Maintenance)
Richard Riley is a guitar player and writer. He has recorded and performed with a wide range of artists and is a long-time contributor to many of the UK's leading music technology publications. As an artist and musician he is regularly seen in the mp3.com charts.

Michael Ross (Using Effects)
Michael Ross is a freelance guitarist/ producer/ writer/editor living in New York. He is the author of *Getting Great Guitar Sounds* (Hal Leonard). He is the gear editor for *Guitar One* magazine, and a contributor to amazon.com, *What Guitar, No Depression*, puremusic.com and others. He would like to remind guitarists that it is 90% in the fingers.

Tony Skinner (The Basics; Playing Rhythm Guitar; Playing Lead Guitar; Chords and Tunings; Essential Techniques)
Tony Skinner is widely respected as one of the UK's premier music educators. He is the director of the Registry of Guitar Tutors – the world's foremost organization for guitar education. He is also the principal guitar examiner for London College of Music Exams and has compiled examination syllabi in electric, bass and classical guitar playing, as well as popular music theory, rock/pop band and popular music vocals. He has written and edited over 50 music-education books and is the editor of *Guitar Tutor* magazine and a columnist for *Total Guitar* magazine.

INDEX

Page numbers in *italics* indicate illustrations;
those in **bold** indicate major references

Abercrombie, John 131
AC/DC 192
accidentals 43
Alabama 177
alegrias 182
Allman, Duane 73, 170, *170*
alternating bass 18
ambience **122–3**, 126–7, 130
amplifiers 110–12, 114, 116–17, 131, 137, 158,
 171, 191, 195, 200–1
 acoustic 187
 amp modelling boxes 191, 195
 in folk music 187
 plug-ins and simulators 171, *171*
Anderson, Brett 198
animal sounds 117
Animals, the 199
Arnold, Eddy 177
arpeggios 73, **94–6**, 107, 129, 186, 199
 extending 97, 101
artificial harmonics 101
Asian Dub Foundation 185
Autry, Gene 176, *176*

backing tracks 24
backwards guitar effects 129
Badly Drawn Boy 24
Baez, Joan 185, *185*
Beach Boys 130
Beatles, the 198
Beck, Jeff 40, *40*, 73, 105, 113, *113*, 117, 126
Belew, Adrian *114*
Bettencourt, Nuno 106
black metal music 193
Black Sabbath 77, 192, 196
Blackmore, Ritchie 40, 47, 89–90, 196
Blink 77
bluegrass music 176, 187
blues music 48, 73, **166–72**, 176, 178
 acoustic blues 168
 call and response 166, 170
 electric blues 168–9
 scales 51
 techniques 102–3
blues-rock music 167
Bluesbreakers 196
Blur 198
Bo Diddley 24
Bon Jovi 198
bottlenecks *see* slides
Bream, Julian 173, *173*
bridges 154–5
Brit Rock bands 45
British blues music 167
Britpop 198
Brooks, Garth 177
Broonzy, Big Bill 167–8
Buck, Peter 24, 56, *56*, 198
Burrell, Kenny 189
Burton, James 179
Butler, Bernard 198
Butler, Geezer 192

cables 110
cajun music 176
capos 183, *183*
Carlton, Larry 132, 189

Carter Family, the 176
Carthy, Martin 185
Cash, Johnny 177
cello effects 117, 132
Chacon, Antonio 180
Chicago blues music 167
chicken picking *def* 179
chords **12–15, 20–1, 56–69, 76–7**, 105, 108, 170,
 198, **202–51**
 altered chords 67, 96–7, 190
 augmented chords 63, 77
chord charts 25, 30, **32–5**
Chord Dictionary **202–51**
chord riffs 73, **80–1**
chord sequences 14–15
chord shapes 73, 87, 178
chord symbols 12
 embellishing 68–9
 extending and altering 18, *66–7*, **66–7**, 81, 97, 190
 inversions 18, 69
 jazz chords 188–9
 major chords 12–13, 15, 20–3, 56–7, 60–1, 69,
 78–9, 94–5, 194, 198
 fingering *13*, 15, *20*, 20–1, 60–1, 78–9
 symbols 12
 minor chords 13–15, 21–3, 56–7, 62–3, **63**,
 66–7, 67, 69, 79, 94–5, 194, 198
 fingering *13*, 14, *21*, *21*, 62–3, 78–9
 symbols 12
 power chords 194, 199, *199*
 progressions 22–3, 41, 169, 190–1
 fingering 25
 sequences **14–15**
 slash chords *def* 69
 sliding 87
 substitution 69, 190
 suspended (sus) chords 63, 65
 fingering 65
 varying and substituting 56–7, **65–6, 68–9**
 barre chords 78–9, 198
 diads 63, 179
diminished chords 63, 67, 77
 diminished 7th 67
 half-diminished 53
 dominant 7th chords 67, 69, 167
 fifth chords (power chords) **76–7**, 81, 194
 fingering 65, *65*, 76–7, 195
 sixth chords 64, *64*, 96
 fingering 64, 96
 seventh chords 64–5, *65*, 67, 69, 96, 167
 fingering 64–5, 96
 ninth chords *66*, 66–7
 eleventh chords 67, *67*
 thirteenth chords 67, *67*
 see also arpeggios, fingering, patterns
choruses and chorus pedals 115, **118–19**, *119*,
 120–1, 121, 134, 191
Christian, Charlie 116, *116*, 188
circuit breakers 111
Clapton, Eric 40, 90, 167–8, 192, 196
Clash, the 197, *197*
classical music **172–5**, 182, 193
 picking 174–5
Cline, Patsy 177
Cobain, Kurt 198
coda 35
Collins, Albert 72, 168, 171
colour and tone 48, *57*, 95, 102, 104–5, 124, 133,
 135, 164, 171, 191, 195, 201
compressors 107, 110, **114–15**, 134

computers 137, 159
Cooder, Ry *62*, 73
Corn Cob Trio 184
country and western music 176
country music 45, 73, **176–9**
 chicken picking 115
 techniques 102–3
country rock music 49, 176
Cray, Robert 167, 171
Cream 196
crossover music 187

Damned, the 197
Davies, Dave 73, *73*
Davies, Gary 166
Davis, Miles 189
de Lucia, Paco 181, *181*
death metal music 193
Deep Purple 196–7
Def Leppard 192
delay 20, 119, 122–3, **124–9**, 131–3
 analogue 124, 131
 digital 125, 127, 131
 tape 123–4
Di Franco, Ani 187
Di Meola, Al 181, 187, 189
diads *see under* chords
Diaz, Alirio 173
DiFranco, Ani 185
Dire Straits 133, *133*
distortion 107, 115, **116–17**, 201, *def* 114
 distortion pedals 134, 195
dive bomb effect 105
Dixieland music 176
Dobro guitars 137
dotted notes 31
double-stops 179
drum machines 24, 27, *27*
drums 29, 128, *128*
dubbing 118–19
Dylan, Bob 185, *185*

echo effects 130, 177
 slap-back echos 123, *123*
Eddy, Duane 104, 131
Edge, The 113, *113*, 124, *125*, 128
effects 111, 134–5
 see also backwards guitar effects, cello effects,
 echo effects, flanging, loop, overdrive,
 sequencers, wah-wah effects
ethnic music 184–5

fandagos 182
Farlow, Tal 188
farruca 182
feedback 111, 119, 121, 129
Fender, Leo 137
 see also under guitars
fifth chords *see under* chords
fingering **202–51**
 minimum movement principle 10, 74–5
 sliding 25
 see also under chords
fingerpicking **18–19**, 177, *181*, 182, 186
 see also flatpicking, hands, strumming, tapping
Fisk, Eliot 173
flamenco music **180–3**
 fingering 182–3
 scales 52–3
flanging and flanging pedals **120–1**, *121*, 134

flatpicking *186*, 186–7
foldback 111
folk music 182, **184–7**
    American folk 176
Ford, Robben *126*, 167–8
Free 45
fretboxes 12, 42
frets 74, 77, 79, 100–1, 107, 138–9, 156–7, 194
    cleaning and replacing **144–5**
fretbuzz 103, 144, *144*, 153
Fripp, Robert 125, 129, *129*
Frisell, Bill 129, 131, 189
Fuller, Blind Boy 166
fusion music 47, 49
    see also jazz-rock
fuzz 117, *def* 116
    pedals 134

Gallagher, Noel 24, *33*, 45
Garrish, Sonny 177
garrotin 182
Gatton, Danny 45, 177
Gilmour, Dave 72, 90, 113, 126
glissando 86
golpe 182
Gough, Damon *24*
Grappelli, Stephane 188
Greco, José 181
Green, Peter 72, 89, 167
grunge music 77, 193, 198–9
guajiras 182
guitars
    acoustic guitars 115, 136–7, 171, 181, 186–7
        construction of *138*, **138–9**
        pickups 163
        and strings 147, **148–9**, *153*, 154–5
    bass guitar 72
    classical guitars 147
    doubling 118
    electric guitars 90, 104, 107, **136–7**, 167, 188, 191, 195–6, 200
        construction of *140*, **140–1**
        electric country 179
        grounding 165
        maintaining
            tools 160–1
        pickups **162–3**, 164–5
        setting the bridge 154–5
        string height 155
        strings *153*
        and strings **150–1**
        technology **158–65**
    flamenco guitars 183, *183*
    lead guitar playing and techniques 24, **40–1**, 48, 72–3, 95, 168, 200
        techniques 96, 108–9
    maintenance **136–65, 142–3**
    rhythm guitars 16, 24, 26–7, 62, 72–3, 168
    12-string 118
    BC Rich Warlock 195
    Dobro Style O *136*
    ESP JH2 195
    Fender 160
        Broadcaster 137
        Stratocaster 117, 136, *136*, 137, 150, 165, 171
        Telecaster 136–7, 150, 165, 171, 179, *179*
    Gibson 160, 195
        ES-175 191
        ES-355 171
    Jackson Kelly 195
    Les Paul 117, 150, 165
    Line 6 Variax 137, *137*, 159
    Parker Fly Mojo *159*

PRS 150, 195
    Variax 500 *159*
    Washburn Dime 195, *195*
Guns N' Roses 198
Guthrie, Woody *184*, 184–5
Guy, Buddy 40, *41*, 72, 89, *167*, 168

Hall, Jim 189
hammer-ons 72, 84–5, 152, 175, 179
Hammett, Kirk 193
hand positions **10–11**
    fretting hand 10, *10*, 21, 38, 86
    picking hand 10–11, *11*, 18, 168, 183, 189, 195, 199
    see also fingering, fingerpicking, picking, strumming, thumbs
hard rock music 167, 199
harmonics 73, **100–1**
    fingering 100–1
harmony bends 179
Harrison, George 132, *132*
Hawaiian music 176–7
Hayes, Isaac 132
Healy, Fran 24
heavy metal music 53, 77, 167, 192–5, 197–8
Henderson, Scott 189
Hendrix, Jimi 85, 90, *112*, 113, 117, 121, 132, 147, 192, 196, 201
hillbilly music 176
Holdsworth, Allan 189
Honky tonk music 177
Hooker, John Lee 167
House, Son 166, 168
Howlin' Wolf 167
humbuckers *see under* pickups

improvisation 41, 53, 96, 108–9, 129, 190–1
Indie rock music 197–8
intervals **58–9**, 109
    see also chords, scales, octaves
Iommi, Tony 192, 196
Iron Maiden 77, 192, *192*

James, Elmore 170
Jansch, Bert 185
jazz music 47, 49, 152, **188–91**
    chords 190
    comping 191
    scales 190
        jazz melodic minor scale 53
    solos 188
jazz-rock (fusion) music 47, 189, 191
Jefferson, Blind Lemon 166, *166*
Jennings, Waylon *177*
Johnson, Robert 22, 166, *166*
Jordan, Stanley 189
Judas Priest 77, 192
Judds, the 177

Kessel, Barney *21*, 56, 188
keys 22–3, 41, *def* 22
    changing 183, 190
key signatures 43
King, B. B. *28*, 40, 72, *72*, 90, 167–8, 171
King, Freddie 168
King, Kerry 193
Kinks, the 73, *73*
Knopfler, Mark *133*
Kossoff, Paul 72, 89

Lang, Eddie 188, *188*
Latin music 182, 189
Leadbelly 168

Led Zeppelin 192, 196–7, 199
Lee, Albert 177
Legoya, Alexandre 173
Lennon, John 24
Levellers, the 185
licks 107, 186
    fingering 54
ligado technique 175
looping 129
Lover, Seth 137
Lynyrd Skynyrd 177

Mahavishnu Orchestra 189
Maines, Lloyd 177
Malmsteen, Yngwie 89, 193
Marr, Johnny *57*, 197
Martin, Juan *17*
Martyn, John 185
Marvin, Hank 73, 104
Marx, Chico 188
McLaughlin, John 181, 189
McTell, Ralph 185
Metallica 77, *192*, 193
Metheny, Pat *50*, 56, 131, 135, 189
metronomes 24, 27, *27*
MIDI 135
mixing 111–12
modes **50–3**, 195
monitors 111, *127*
Monroe, Bill 176
Montgomery, Wes 189
Montoya, Carlos 180
Montoya, Ramon 180
Moore, Christy 185
Moore, Gary 46, 72, 89
Morrissey 197
Morse, Steve 177, 187
Motorhead 192

Nashville music 177
natural harmonics 100–1
necks 139, **156–7**
Nelson, Willie 177, *177*
new country music 49
new wave rock music 197
Nirvana 77, 198
noise 110
notation 18, 25, **42–3**, 89, 175
    note values 30–1
    rhythm notation **30–1**
    see also tablature, key signatures under keys, time signatures
nu-metal music 193
NWOBHM music 192

Oasis 45, 198
octaves 73, **98–9**, 100–1
Oldfield, Mike 197
Osbourne, Ozzy 192
overdrive effects 201, *def* 116

Page, Jimmy 40, *40*, *118*, 192, 196
Parkening, Christopher 173
Pass, Joe 189, *189*
patterns 18–19, 124, 126–9
Patton, Charley 166
Paul, Les 123
Pearl 77
pedal-steel effects 132–3
pedalboards and bags 134
pedals 112–13, 129, 134–5, 179, 191, 195, *200*, 201
    Fuzz Face 113
    Octavia 113

Uni-Vibe 113
see also delay, distortion, volume, wah-wah
Peterson, Oscar 188–9
phase shifters **120–1**, *121*
phrasing 108–9
picking 11, 18–19, 168
    alternate picking 92–3
    in classical guitar music 174–5
    sweep-picking 195
picking hand *see under* hand positions
pickups 107, 117, 158, *158*, 159, **162–3**, 163, 165
    humbuckers 117, 162–3, *163*, 195
    PAF 137
pinched harmonics 101
Pink Floyd 113
pitch, changing **54–5**, 105, 119
Plant, Robert 192
plectrums (picks) 10–11, 159, 168, 186, 195, 199
    and harmonics 101
    technique **92–3**
Police, the 121
pop music 37, 117, 177, 196
    techniques 18
potentiometers 158
power chords *see* fifth chords *under* chords
practice and rehearsal tips 16–17, 54, 76–7, 93
    listening to other bands 26–7, 111
    listening to your own band 24–5, 27, 41, 128,
        128, 170
    and scales 54–5
    and string bends 90–1
Presley, Elvis *123*
psychedelia music 117
pull-offs 72, 84–5, 107, 152, 179
punk rock music 197–8

Queen 197, *201*

Radiohead 198
rasqueado 182
recording sessions 36
Reeves, Jim 177
Reinhardt, Django *60*, 188
Renbourn, John 185
repetition 41, 109, 126, 128, 130
rests 31, 41, 80
reverb effects **130–1**
Rhodes, Randy 106
rhumbas 182
rhythm **24–5**, 82, 108–9, 115, 118, 124, 127, *182*,
    183, 186, 194–5
rhythm charts **36–7**
rhythmic variety 41, 108–9
riffs 73, 192, 196–7, *199*
    changing fingering 54–5
riff chords 73, **80–1**
    techniques 95
rock music 37, 45, 73, 76, 104, 152, **196–201**
    fusion with country music 177
    techniques 18, 85, 102–3
    see also Brit rock, grunge music, Indie rock
        music, new wave music, punk rock music,
        stadium rock music
rockabilly music 123
rodeña 182
Rodgers, Jimmie 176
Rodgers, Nile *26*
Rogers, Roy 176
Rolling Stones, the 45, *196*
Ronson, Mick 73
Roth, David Lee 192

Sabicas 181
safety precautions 111, 161, 165

Samson 192
Santana, Carlos *32*, 40, 46
Satriani, Joe 106, *108*, 193
scales 40–1, 108, 186
    blues scale 48, 51, 157, 167
    changing fingering 54–5
    chromatic scales 48, 190
    country scales 49
    diminished scales 49, 190
    major scales **44–5**, 50, 55, 64, 200
    minor scales **46–7**, 200
        harmonic minor 46–7, 52–3, 190
        jazz melodic minor 47
        melodic minor 47, 190
        pentatonic 46–7, 48, 157
    pentatonic scales 45, 178, 195
    transposition 44–5
    whole-tone scales 49, 190
    see also modes
Scofield, John 135, 189
Segovia, Andrés *172*, 172–3
selector switches 164
sequencer effects 129
sequencers 191
Sex Pistols 197
Shadows, the 104
Simon, Paul 185
Skaggs, Ricky 177, 187
Slayer 193
slides (bottlenecks) and sliding 25, 73, 86–7, **102–3**,
    109, 169–70, 179
Slipknot 77
slurs **84–5**, 109
Small Faces 120
Smith, Johnny 188
Smiths, the 197–8
soleares 182
solos **108–9**, 111, 169–70, 188, 196, 200–1
Springsteen, Bruce 197
staccato 11, 83
stadium rock music 197
stagecraft 110–11
Stipe, Michael 198
string bends 72, **90–1**, 109, 167, 169, *169*
    harmony bend 179
string damping 73, **82–3**
    fretting-hand damping 83
strumming-hand damping 82–3
strings 136, **146–7**, 183, 186
    controlling volume between 115
    damping 107
    fitting **148–51**
    height **150–6**, *153*, 183
    maintaining 142, *143*
    muting 83, 98–9, 183
    omitting 13, 38, 77, 81
    tuning 110, 151
    varying between 99
    see also tuning
strumming 16–17, 21, 33, 77, 80–1, 98, 105, 183,
    186, 186–7, 194, 198–9
    open vamp strum 75
    patterns 38–9
    with plectrum *186*, 186–7
Suede 198
Summers, Andy *115*, 121, 124, 128
Supergrass 45
sustain 107, 115, *def* 114
swamp music 117
sweep 120–1, 195
synthesizers
    emulating 133

tanquillos 182
tapes 123
    echoes 124
tapped harmonics 101
tapping **106–7**
Taylor, Martin 189
tempo 36–7
Terry, Sonny 166
theatre and function bands 37
Thorogood, George 73
thrash music 193, 195
thumbs 18, 21, 38, 79, 183, 189
ties 31
time signatures 25, **28–9**, 32
timing **26–7**
Townshend, Pete 24, *25*, 136
transducers 131
Travis 24, 45
Travis, Merle 177
Travis, Randy 177
tremolo 175, 182
    arms 73, **104–5**, 133
    pedals 134
triads *see* chords
trills 85
triplets 31, 93
truss-rods 156–7
tuning **8–9**, *9*, 110, 118, 151, 155, 170
    altered 70–1, 103
    alternative tunings 57
    D tunings 103
    D Modal tuning 70–1
        dropped 70
        open 71
    G tuning 103
    open E tuning 71
    slack key tuning 71
tuning forks and machines 8, 110, 134, 148

U2 113, *113*

Vai, Steve 73, 85, 105, 135, 193
Van Halen, Eddie 106, *106*, 117, 121, 126, 192
Vaughan, Stevie Ray 121, 147, 167–8, 171
vibrato 72, **88–9**, 91, 103, 109, 169
    across-the-string 167
    horizontal 88–9
    wrist 89
    see also tremolo arms *under* tremolo
violin effects 132
violining *def* 179
volume and dynamics 36, 73, 111, 115, 130, 158,
    179, 187–8
    pedals 110, 132, 179

wah-wah effects 201
    and pedals 113, 133–4
Walker, T-Bone 167
Ward, Bill 192
Waters, Muddy 73, 167
Watson, Doc 177
Weller, Paul 24, 73
whammy bars *see* tremolo arms
Williams, Hank 177
Williams, John 173
Wills, Bob 176
wrist flexibility 16, 38, 89

Yardbirds 192
Young, Angus 73, 192

zydeco (cajun music) 176